CONSOLIDATING PEACE IN AFRICA

ALSO BY THE AUTHOR

African Development in the 21st Century: Adebayo Adedeji's Theories and Contributions (co-edited with Amos Sawyer and Afeikhena Jerome), 2015

CONSOLIDATING PEACE IN AFRICA

*The Role of the United Nations
Peacebuilding Commission*

Ejeviome Eloho Otobo

Published by

AMV Publishing Services
P.O. Box 661
Princeton, NJ 08542-0661
Tel: 609-785-5135 Fax: 609-7164770
emails: publisher@amvpublishingservices.com &
customerservice@amvpublishingservices.com
worldwide web: www.amvpublishingservices.com

Consolidating Peace in Africa
The Role of the United Nations Peacebuilding Commission
Copyright © 2015 Ejeviome Eloho Otobo

All rights reserved. No part of this publication may be reproduced, stored in a retrieval system, or transmitted in any form or by any means, electronic, mechanical, photocopying, recording or otherwise without the written permission of the Publisher.

Book Design: AMVPS Origination & Design Division
Cover Design: Dapo Ojo-Ade

Library of Congress Control Number: 2015900435

Paperback Edition ISBN: 978-0-9894917-5-4
e-Book Edition ISBN: 978-0-9894917-6-1

Dedicated to my Wife:
ESTHER ARUORIWO OTOBO

CONTENTS

List of Tables and Boxes	*viii*
List of Acronyms and Abbreviations	*ix*
About the Author	*xii*
Acknowledgements	*xiii*
Introduction	1
Chapter 1: The New Peacebuilding Architecture: An Institutional Innovation of the United Nations	9
Chapter 2: A United Nations Architecture to Build Peace in Postconflict Situations	35
Chapter 3: The United Nations Peacebuilding Architecture: African Countries as Early Beneficiaries	43
Chapter 4: Leading the Peacebuilding Commission: An Institutional History in the Making	57
Chapter 5: Facts, Fictions, and Frustrations with the Functioning of the Peacebuilding Commission	81
Chapter 6: Reflections on Three Important Questions Concerning the Performance of the Peacebuilding Commission	115
Chapter 7: The Centrality and Challenges of Institution Building in Peacebuilding	159
Epilogue	197
Bibliography	207
About the Book	217
Index	219

List of Tables and Boxes

Table 1. Peacebuilding Priorities Identified in
the Strategic Framework   37

Table 2. Peacebuilding Fund (PBF) Key Figures:
Allocations and Projects Approved as of 15 May 2009   38

Table 3. Peacebuilding Priorities Identified in the Strategic
Framework for the First Four Countries   53

Table 4. PBF Key Figures: Allocations and Projects
Approved as of 22 December 2009   55

Table 5. List of PBC Chairpersons and Vice-Chairs
2006-2012   75
Table 6. Number of PBC Meetings, 2006-2012   76

Table 7. Comparative Timeline for Completing Instruments
of Engagement — Strategic Framework/Statement of Mutual
Commitments   77

Table 8. PBF Country Summary of PRF and IRF
Allocations as at 31 December 2014   109

Table 9. Details of PBC Engagement with Countries
on the Agenda   148

Table 10. Basic Political, Economic, and Social Facts on
Countries on PBC Agenda   152

Table 11. List of Conferences on Afghanistan   153

Table 12. Functions of the State   176

Box 1. Key Elements of Engagement with the PBC   45

Box 2. Improved Synergy between the PBC and the PBF   70

LIST OF ACRONYMS AND ABBREVIATIONS

AfDB	African Development Bank
AMIB	African Mission in Burundi
APC	All Peoples Congress
APRD	Popular Army for the Restoration of Democracy
ARC	Advocacy, Resource Mobilisation and (fostering) Coherence
AU	African Union
BINUB	United Nations Integrated Office in Burundi
BINUCA	United Nations Integrated Peacebuilding Office in Central African Republic
BUNB	United Nations Office in Burundi
BONUCA	United Nations Political Office in the Central African Republic
CAFOD	Catholic Aid Agency for England and Wales
CEMAC	Economic and Monetary Community of Central Africa
CNDD	National Council for Defence of Democracy
CSC	Country Specific Configuration of the Peacebuilding Commission
CSM	Country Specific Meeting of the Peacebuilding Commission
CPJP	Convention of Patriots for Justice and Peace
CPSK	Koro Salute Patriotic Convention
DDR	Disarmament, Demobilisation, and Reintegration
DPA	Department of Political Affairs
DPKO	Department of Peacekeeping Operations
ECA	Economic Commission for Africa
ECOMOG	Economic Community of West African States Ceasefire and Monitoring and Observer Group
ECOMIB	ECOWAS Mission in Guinea-Bissau
ECOMIL	ECOWAS Mission in Liberia
ECOWAS	Economic Community of West African States
ECCAS	Economic Community of Central African States
ECOSOC	Economic and Social Council

ERSG	Executive Representative of the Secretary-General
FDD	Forces for the Defence of Democracy
FNL	National Liberation Front
FOMUC	Multinational Force in Central Africa
FPDC	Democratic and Popular Forces of the Central African Republic
GDP	Gross Domestic Product
IFI	International Financial Institutions
IMF	International Monetary Fund
INCAF	International Network on Conflict and Fragility
IPI	International Peace Institute
IPBS	Integrated Peacebuilding Strategy
IRF	Immediate Response Facility of the Peacebuilding Fund
JSC	Joint Steering Committee
JVMM	Joint Verification and Monitoring Mechanism
LURD	Liberians United for Reconciliation and Democracy
KNK	National Convergence Kwa Na Kwa
MICOPAX	The Mission for the Consolidation of Peace in Central Africa Republic
MISCA	African Union Africa-led International Support Mission in Central African Republic
MINURCA	United Nations Mission in Central Africa
MISAB	Inter-African Mission to Monitor the Implementation of the Bangui Accords
MISSANG	Angolan Technical Military Cooperation Mission
NPLF	National Patriotic Front of Liberia
OC	Organisational Committee of the Peacebuilding Commission
OECD	Organisation for Economic Cooperation and Development
ONUB	United Nations Operations in Burundi
PAIGC	African Party for the Independence of Guinea and Cape Verde
Palipehutu	FNL Party for the Liberation of the Hutu People
PBC	Peacebuilding Commission

PBA	Peacebuilding Architecture
PBF	Peacebuilding Fund
PBSO	Peacebuilding Support Office
PCF	Peacebuilding Cooperation Framework
PCNA	Post Conflict Needs Assessment
PSC	Peace and Security Council of the African Union
PRF	Peacebuilding Recovery Facility of the Peacebuilding Fund
PRS	Social Renovation Party
PRSP	Poverty Reduction Strategy Paper
RUF	Revolutionary United Front
SF	Strategic Framework for Peacebuilding
SG	Secretary-General
SLPP	Sierra Leone Peoples Party
SMC	Statement of Mutual Commitments
SRSG	Special Representative of the Secretary-General
SSR	Security Sector Reforms
UK	United Kingdom of Great Britain and Northern Ireland
UFDR	Union of Democratic and Republican Forces
UN	United Nations
UNAMSIL	United Nations Assistance Mission in Sierra Leone
UNDP	United Nations Development Programme
UN Habitat	United Nations Human Settlements Programme
UNMIL	United Nations Mission in Liberia
UNOGBIS	United Nations Peacebuilding Support Office in Guinea-Bissau
UNIOGBIS	United Nations Integrated Peacebuilding Support Office
UNIOSIL	United Nations Integrated Office in Sierra Leone
UNIPSIL	United Nations Integrated Peacebuilding Office in Sierra Leone
UNICEF	United Nations Children's Fund
WGLL	Working Group on Lessons Learnt of the Peacebuilding Commission
WHO	World Health Organisation

ABOUT THE AUTHOR

Ejeviome Eloho Otobo is currently a Non-Resident Senior Expert in Peacebuilding and Global Economic Policy at the Global Governance Institute, Brussels, Belgium. Previously, he was director and deputy head of the UN Peacebuilding Support Office (PBSO) at the United Nations Headquarters, New York, where he also acted as Assistant Secretary-General from February-August 2009. Before joining PBSO, he served in various departments of the United Nations, including the Office of the Special Adviser on Africa; UN Department of Economic and Social Affairs; and the UN Economic Commission for Africa in Addis Ababa, Ethiopia. He joined the United Nations after a distinguished career in the diplomatic service of the Federal Republic of Nigeria. During the course of his diplomatic career, he served on the Policy Planning Staff of the Ministry of Foreign Affairs, represented Nigeria in several countries, and participated in various bilateral political and multilateral economic negotiations. In recognition of his contribution to Nigeria's diplomacy and foreign policy, he was appointed ambassador-in-situ. He is widely published and has written on a wide range of issues, including peacebuilding, public service reforms, institutional development, governance, regulatory policy and management, and international trade. He recently co-edited *African Development in the 21st Century: Adebayo Adedeji's Theories and Contributions* (2015). Otobo obtained his undergraduate education at the University of Lagos, Nigeria, and did graduate studies at the Harvard Kennedy School of Government, Harvard University, Cambridge, Massachusetts, USA.

ACKNOWLEDGEMENTS

This book brings together the papers that I wrote mainly on the United Nations Peacebuilding Commission during and immediately after my tenure as Director and Deputy Head of the UN Peacebuilding Support Office (PBSO). The papers have been transmuted to chapters in this book.

I have accumulated many debts of gratitude in the course of preparing these papers. My first expression of gratitude goes to my colleagues at PBSO who played several roles in the course of writing these papers. There are those who helped in researching for or providing specific pieces of information in their areas of work. More importantly, they also served as a sounding board of ideas on various issues in course of writing some of the papers. Included in this category are the following former and current staff members of PBSO: Dominic Bartsch, Patrice Chiwota, Paolo Fontana, Enkhtungalag Ganbold, Philip Helminger, Vincent Kayijuka, Bautista Logioco, Ihab Awad Moustafa, Christine Muhigana, Parvina Nadjibulla, Jian Pak, Aboubacar Saibou, Stefania Piffanelli, Tammi Sharpe, and Alessandra Trabattoni.

Other colleagues at the PBSO, Henk Jan Brinkman and Brian James Williams, provided written comments on some of the chapters at different times. Lucy Apia, my staff assistant at PBSO, compiled some the tables that appear in the book.

During my time at PBSO, I served under three assistant secretaries-general and heads of PBSO: Carolyn McAskie, Jane Holl Lute, and Judy Cheng-Hopkins, in that order. I was hired by the first of these to the position of Director and Deputy Head of PBSO. They were all very supportive of my efforts to write and publish on the work of what we now refer to as the new institutional arrangements for UN peacebuilding architecture. And they all had the opportunity, during their tenures to review and approve my papers for publication, as required by United Nations rules and regulations, for the serving staff. Indeed, one of them, in the course of reviewing one of my papers, remarked that I was well-placed to tell the story of the historical evolution and performance of the nascent institutional arrangements, sometimes referred to as the UN new peacebuilding architecture. It was a challenge to which I have endeavoured to rise up to.

Outside of the PBSO, I have also benefited greatly from the insights and comments of Adedeji Ebo, as well as from research support by Obinna Okamgba while he was studying at Harvard University.

My special appreciation goes to Daniel Omoweh, who strongly encouraged me to publish in one volume all that I have written on peacebuilding during and after my tenure as Director and Deputy Head of PBSO.

I would like to thank my children, Ufuoma Otobo, Aghogho Elo Otobo, Oheri Otobo and Ejiro Otobo, who provided support in numerous ways. In the back and forth leading to the publication of the book, one technical problem arose: how to convert the footnotes at the bottom of every page to notes at the end of each chapter. The credit for resolving this issue goes to Oheri who handled the problem with dexterity and calm. My sincere appreciation also goes to Ejiro who assisted in the compilation of the index.

I would like to especially thank my wife, Esther Aruoriwo Otobo, for her understanding and for encouraging me to bring this book to completion. She has been a true pillar of support not only as regards this book but also in many areas of my professional development and endeavours. She is a "patient peace-builder" where peacebuilding matters most — in the family. For these reasons, this book is dedicated to her.

Ejeviome Eloho Otobo
March, 2015

Introduction

The United Nations has a long and impressive history of involvement in peacebuilding in Africa. Some of the roots of that effort are traceable to United Nations role in supporting the process of decolonization in the region. Other roots lie in the peacebuilding work usually associated with peacekeeping missions in African countries, where they operate. Yet others are directly linked to its contemporary work in postconflict peacebuilding in the various countries emerging from conflict.

The decision by the world leaders, at their 2005 Summit, to establish the new institutional arrangements for peacebuilding gave fresh impetus to UN's postconflict peacebuilding work. That decision stemmed from international recognition that, despite decades of efforts by the United Nations and the broader international community, many postconflict countries were repeatedly relapsing into violent conflict. The decision also responded to the reality, couched in the observation of the then Secretary-General that there was a "gaping hole in the United Nations institutional machinery: no part of the United Nations system effectively addresses the challenge of helping countries with the transition from war lasting to peace." The Peacebuilding Commission (PBC), generally regarded as the institutional linchpin of the new institutional arrangements created to advance the cause of peacebuilding, was inaugurated in 2006. The other components of the new institutional arrangements include the Peacebuilding Fund and Peacebuilding Support Office. The focus of this book is on the PBC.

The Commission's key tasks include advising postconflict countries on the development of integrated strategies for postconflict peacebuilding and recovery; helping to marshal resources and ensuring predictable financing for immediate postconflict activities and sustained financial investment over the medium to longer-term; and ensuring sustained attention by the international community to post-conflict recovery. All six countries currently on the agenda of the Commission are in Africa.

Institutions evolve over time and do not mature overnight. The PBC is no exception. This book presents a collection of essays that delves into various aspects of the PBC since the body was inaugurated in 2006. In a real and important sense, this book represents both a historical record and an analytical work on the evolution of the Peacebuilding Commission.

As a historical account, it provides an overview of the evolution of the structure and functioning of the PBC as well as the challenges that it encountered in its formative years and up to the period leading to the 2015 Review. The chapters in the book were written at different times and each of them gives a sense of the performance of the PBC at different stages of its evolution. Each chapter, therefore, represents a fragment of a bigger picture that unfolds gradually.

As an analytical effort, the book offers rich insights into the expectations of the Commission, assesses its performance in fulfilling those expectations, and offers proposals on how the performance of the Commission could be improved. The author joined the Peacebuilding Support Office (PBSO) as the first Director and Deputy Head of PBSO in December 2006 — six months after the PBC was inaugurated — and served in that position until his retirement at the end of October 2013.

Organisation of the Book

The seven main chapters in the book are presented roughly in a chronological order, which enables the reader to appreciate the ebb and flow of the perception of PBC's performance at various times. The exceptions to the chronological order are chapters 1 and 2. This is because, although chapter 1 was first written in 2008 and subsequently updated, the release of the book in which that chapter was first published occurred only in 2010, after chapter 2 was published in October 2009 by a journal of the World Bank. Chapter 5 was written soon after the author retired from the United Nations at the end of October 2013; it has since been updated. Chapters 6 and 7 are being published here for the first time and were written one year after the author retired from the United Nations. Those last two chapters capture the author's reflections on the issues addressed. There is an inevitable overlap in the content of some of the chapters in terms of basic facts about the evolution of the work of the PBC; but the orientation and focus of each chapter is very different.

Chapter 1 is predicated on the premise that in order to understand the role the Commission is playing in Africa, we must first understand the mandate entrusted to the Commission in its founding resolutions. Writing this chapter began on the second anniversary of the Commission in 2008. The chapter provides a description of the design and functions assigned to each of the three components of the new institutional additions to the UN peacebuilding architecture (the Peacebuilding Commission, the Peacebuilding Support Office, and the Peacebuilding Fund). This is followed by a brief discussion of the selection process and characteristics of the first two countries placed on the agenda of the Commission in 2006: Burundi and Sierra Leone. The chapter delves into the nature and scope of the engagement of the Peacebuilding Commission with those two countries. In addition, it offers a glimpse of the challenges initially faced by the Commission in those two countries.

Chapter 2 gives a brief overview of the work of the Commission on its third anniversary in 2009. By then, two additional countries had been placed on the agenda, bringing to four the number of countries on the Commission's agenda. The chapter explains the Commission's methodology in putting its mandate into practice in these countries: by bringing together in a single forum all major stakeholders relevant for each country's peacebuilding process, by helping to develop an integrated peacebuilding approach between interventions meant to restore peace and security and those aimed at reconstruction and development in these countries; by sustaining international political and financial support to these countries well beyond the evaporation of the "CNN effect." Since the chapter was written for and published by a World Bank journal, the chapter made the case for enhanced collaboration and strategic partnership between the PBC and IFIs. It notes that from the inception of the Commission, it was agreed that the World Bank, the International Monetary Fund, and other institutional donors should participate in all PBC meetings. The chapter argues that the PBC provides the best platform for the World Bank to engage with other stakeholders in determining critical peacebuilding priorities, sequencing, and coordination of peacebuilding efforts.

Chapter 3 was published in 2010, the year of the first quintennial review of the Commission, when attention was focussed assessing its performance. The chapter notes that postconflict peacebuilding is a painstaking, complex, and multidimensional process; and that the results of peacebuilding must be measured in decades not years. Even so, a preliminary assessment of the incremental added value of the peacebuilding architecture could be made as the Commission entered its fourth year since its inauguration. The assessment in the chapter was organised around three main questions: Has the engagement aided peace consolidation? Have the countries received increased financial support as a consequence of engagement with the Commission? Do the countries on the agenda of the Commission find the experience helpful to their peacebuilding efforts? These questions were seen at as crucial tests of PBC's relevance.

Chapter 4 provides a detailed institutional history of the Commission, with a focus on the Organisational Committee. The paper was presented in March 2013 at a meeting organised by the Global Governance Institute in Brussels. The chapter represents the first attempt to examine the main highlights of the Commission's work under successive Chairs of the PBC, reflecting their individual priorities and contributions since the PBC's inauguration in June 2006. Hitherto, this remained an essentially unexplored issue in the growing literature on the PBC. The chapter examines the first six years (2006-2012) of the PBC and its approach is to highlight three main contributions of each chair during his or her tenure. The chapter is predicated on the belief that the growth of any new intergovernmental institution critically depends on the creative adjustments made by the successive leadership, as the institution evolves. Such adjustments are necessarily incremental, borne out of persistent experimentation. This assessment draws on the insights of those who were and have been present since the establishment of the PBC, on the annual reports of the PBC and other related documents, and on conversations with the successive Chairpersons themselves.

Chapter 5 notes that every new institution grapples with the challenge of fulfilling expectations. Performance expectations arise — or are cast — not only in relation to the stated objectives of institutions but also from the presumptions of what various stakeholders think a particular institution ought to do. Where such stakeholders are very diverse, as in the case of PBC, it begs the question of whose views should be regarded as the most valid in assessing its performance: the country on the agenda, members of PBC, the UN mission/country team, or independent experts? There is a strong link between the goal of achieving an institution's full potential and the expectations about improvement in institutional performance. This chapter has been offered as a contribution to separating out the facts from the fictions in the experience of PBC and, by so doing, shed light on practical results, possible challenges, and potential constraints in peacebuilding. It concludes by highlighting some key issues in the future of PBC.

Chapter 6 represents an effort to reflect on the role of PBC in postconflict peacebuilding in Africa, following the author's retirement from the PBSO. The chapter examines three issues that have often been overlooked in many of the reviews or assessments of the functioning and effectiveness of the PBC: Why have some countries on the PBC agenda done relatively better than others? Was the PBC willed enough means to achieve the desired ends? And has the position and the authority of the PBC among the constellation of UN bodies and processes affected its effectiveness? Most assessments of PBC tend to take for granted the last two of these three issues, in particular. That no longer seems a reasonable assumption. In examining these questions, it helps to remember that there is no single lever to be pulled by national authorities or their partners to engender postconflict peacebuilding. Peacebuilding success depends on a composite of measures, including the commitment of the national authorities, the individual country context, careful targeting of interventions, and the scale and scope of international support. It is the positive interactions among these factors that create a positive dynamic for peacebuilding. The concluding section of this chapter examines the issue of the sudden outbreak of Ebola in three of the countries on the agenda and notes that Ebola illustrates how an entirely unexpected event can intrude into and set back peacebuilding efforts in countries emerging from conflict. It is a rude reminder that the PBC will sometimes be confronted with and will be required to respond to a range of crises — from political crisis to natural or man-made disasters — in the countries on the agenda. The author offers some thoughts on how the PBC should respond in such situations.

Unlike the other six chapters, chapter 7 does not focus exclusively on the Commission. Instead, it examines one of the issues that featured prominently in the Commission's mandate: institution building. The chapter makes the argument that institution building is the most critical task in peacebuilding. It notes that effective institutions are the main vehicles for facilitating and sustaining the transition of countries from conflict to durable peace and notes that, in a real and important sense, institution building is the ultimate peace dividend. In fragile countries or countries emerging from conflict, virtually every activity aimed at laying the foundation or creating the conditions for a durable peace ineluctably entails institution building. Yet, institution building efforts are marked by several challenges. These include the challenge of timing the commencement of the institution building effort; the challenge of setting priorities for institution building; the challenge of linking institution building to nationbuilding and state building; the challenge of promoting partnership in support of institution building; and the challenge of financing institution building. The role of the PBC in coordination is examined in the context of the challenge of promoting partnership for institution building and in that regard the Commission faces many challenges in fulfilling the coordination role entrusted to it in the founding resolution.

Overall, the chapter concludes that tackling each of the five main challenges in institution building will require a combination of factors: notably national ownership and leadership; political commitment; strengthened partnership, reflected mostly in improved coordination among all key international partners; careful and proper sequencing of priorities; and long-term financial commitment. Progress in institution building will critically depend on how post-conflict countries are able to marshal all these elements to bear on that effort.

The Epilogue notes that the 2015 Review represents an important opportunity to grapple with many of the policy and institutional challenges that have impeded the performance of the PBC. It outlines some of those challenges and suggests what should be done about them. It concludes that smart reforms are needed to strengthen the PBC: these will combine serious improvements in operational or working methods with some major policy and institutional changes.

Chapter 1

The New Peacebuilding Architecture: An Institutional Innovation of the United Nations*

Filling an Institutional Gap

The decision to create new peacebuilding architecture was one of the key outcomes of the World Summit held at the United Nations Headquarters in September 2005.[1] The prelude to that decision started with the report of the High-level Panel on Threats, Challenges and Change[2] which recommended the establishment of a peacebuilding commission within the United Nations. In the Secretary-General's In Larger Freedom report, that recommendation was slightly modified.[3] The Secretary-General eliminated the High-level Panel proposal to give the PBC an early warning or monitoring function in conflict situations.[4]

As a follow-up the to the World Summit, the General Assembly and the Security Council concurrently adopted identical

---

* Source: Originally published in Peter Danchin and Horst Fischer, eds. *United Nations Reform and the New Collective Security* (Cambridge: Cambridge University Press, 2010) p. 212-34.

resolutions in December 2005[5] establishing the Peacebuilding Commission (PBC), the Peacebuilding Support Office (PBSO), and the Peacebuilding Fund (PBF). This new peacebuilding architecture is an important institutional innovation in the history of the United Nations. It builds on longstanding efforts by the United Nations, dating back to the 1992 report by the Secretary-General entitled "An Agenda for Peace"[6], to develop a coherent approach linking conflict prevention, peacemaking and peacekeeping to postconflict peacebuilding and development.

While "An Agenda for Peace" made an important conceptual contribution to the debate on peacebuilding, the report of the Panel on United Nations Peace Operations (the Brahimi Report)[7] provided additional impetus for the peacebuilding effort by highlighting its importance. The report also proposed the creation of a focal point for peacebuilding within the United Nations Secretariat, a reform that ultimately did not materialise. Meanwhile, the instances of relapse into conflict,[8] especially in countries having United Nations peacekeeping operations, pointed to the need to intensify efforts in countries emerging from conflict to sustain their transition from war to postconflict recovery and development.

The creation of the new peacebuilding architecture thus reflected international recognition that, despite decades of efforts, the United Nations and the broader international community have not succeeded in addressing post-conflict peacebuilding, in particular ensuring that countries do not relapse into conflict. Indeed, the Secretary-General observed that there had been a "gaping hole in the United Nations institutional machinery: no part of the United Nations system effectively addresses the challenge of helping countries with the transition from war lasting to peace."[9] The establishment of the new peacebuilding architecture is meant to close that gap.

This chapter was written on the second anniversary of the establishment of the various components of the new peacebuilding architecture. The Peacebuilding Commission was inaugurated in June 2006, the Peacebuilding Support Office was established in June 2006, and the Peacebuilding Fund was launched in October 2006. This is a short period in the life of any institution, but long enough to make preliminary assessments of its performance. In this chapter, I argue that in spite of some challenges here and there, the new peacebuilding architecture is off to an encouraging start[10] and, more crucially, it is adding value in incremental steps to international peacebuilding efforts and has much potential value added over the longterm.

This chapter provides a description of the design and functions assigned to each of the three components of the peacebuilding architecture (the Peacebuilding Commission, the Peacebuilding Support Office, and the Peacebuilding Fund). This is followed by a brief discussion of the selection process and characteristics of the Peacebuilding Commission's recent efforts in Burundi and Sierra Leone, including an examination of the nature and scope of the engagement of the Peacebuilding Commission with those two countries. In addition, I present an analysis of the challenges facing the peacebuilding architecture; highlight its present and potential added value, and present conclusions explaining how the new architecture responds to some crucial tests of relevance.

The Peacebuilding Commission

The Peacebuilding Commission (PBC) is an intergovernmental advisory body. Its mandated functions include: bringing together all relevant actors to marshal resources; supporting the development of integrated strategies in order to lay the foundation for sustainable development; focusing on reconstruction and institution-building efforts necessary for recovery from conflict; providing recommendations and information to improve the coordination of all relevant actors within and outside the United Nations; developing best practices and helping to ensure predictable financing for early recovery activities; and extending the period of attention paid by the international community to post-conflict countries.[11]

The Peacebuilding Commission consists of thirty-one Member States drawn from five categories of countries. Seven come from the General Assembly, seven from the Security Council, seven from the Economic and Social Council, five from among the highest troop-contributing countries to United Nations peacekeeping operations, and five from the highest financial contributors to the

United Nations.[12] Mark Malloch-Brown has noted that the last two criteria were designed to reflect "global good citizenship."[13]

The Peacebuilding Commission conducts its work in three configurations:[14] the Organisational Committee; the country-specific configurations or meetings; and the working group on lessons learnt. The Organisational Committee serves as the forum for discussions on strategy and procedural issues. The country-specific meetings serve as the forum for deliberations and decisions on engagement with the countries under consideration. The working group on lessons learnt provides a vehicle for review of experiences from other postconflict situations and their potential application to countries currently under consideration.

The Peacebuilding Support Office

The Peacebuilding Support Office (PBSO) is headed by the Assistant Secretary-General for Peacebuilding Support, who performs her duties under the direction and authority of the Secretary-General.

The main functions of the PBSO are to support the work of the PBC in developing peacebuilding strategies for countries under its consideration, to develop and document best practices and lessons learnt in postconflict peacebuilding, and to help gather and analyse information on financial resources available for peacebuilding. An important aspect of the work of the PBSO is to bring together the entities of the UN in order to improve the coherence and coordination of its peacebuilding activities. The practical expressions of this role are reflected in the two groups convened by the PBSO: the Senior Policy Group on Peacebuilding which consists of assistant secretaries-general/directors from several departments and offices, and the Peacebuilding Contact Group at the working level. These mechanisms, together with its participation in various inter-departmental and inter-agency processes, enable the PBSO to undertake discussions on strategic peacebuilding priorities and options for the purpose of developing integrated peacebuilding strategies.

The Peacebuilding Fund

The Peacebuilding Fund (PBF), as stated in its terms of reference,[15] aims to address the immediate needs of countries emerging from conflict. The scope of the activities of the fund will include:

(a) Activities in support of the implementation of peace agreements;
(b) Activities in support of efforts by countries to build and strengthen capacities that promote coexistence and the peaceful resolution of conflict;
(c) Establishment or re-establishment of essential administrative services and related human and technical capacities;
(d) Critical interventions designed to respond to imminent threats to the peacebuilding process." [16]

The Fund was designed to provide catalytic funding to reinforce financial assistance by other agencies and donors and to address critical financial gaps and to support interventions directly related to immediate peacebuilding efforts.

The Fund had exceeded the initial target of $250 million, having received a total contribution $269.2 million as of June 2008. Financial assistance from the Fund was initially organised around three windows: countries under the Peacebuilding Commission's consideration are supported from the first window; countries that the Secretary-General determines might be on the verge of lapsing or relapsing into conflict benefit from support from the second window; and countries that require access to immediate funding in order to respond to unforeseen threats to the peace process receive assistance from the (third) emergency window, although the financial outlay for such purposes cannot exceed $1 million per project. The name and number of recipient countries from the three windows, as of 15 May 2009 are provided in the last section of chapter 2.

PBC: The Selection Process and the Characteristics of the Countries under Consideration

The General Assembly and Security Council resolutions establishing the PBC stipulated that countries shall be referred for the consideration by the PBC on the request of the Security Council or the Secretary-General. Burundi and Sierra Leone, the first two countries to be placed on the PBC agenda as well as

Guinea-Bissau and Central African Republic, were referred by the Security Council. In addition, the General Assembly, the Economic and Social Council, or the concerned member state can request for referral. These entities can only do so in situations where a country is on the verge of lapsing or relapsing into conflict. In each case, the concerned member state must give explicit consent to the referral to the PBC.

Burundi and Sierra Leone underwent similar processes before reaching peace. In both cases the conflicts were brought to an end after lengthy negotiations between government and the rebel factions which led to a peace agreement. The Burundi peace negotiations culminated in The Arusha Peace and Reconciliation Agreement of 2000[17] and the Sierra Leone peace negotiations led to the Lome Agreement in 1999.

Both countries received regional or subregional intervention missions that were taken over by United Nations peacekeeping operations. The peacekeeping operations were in turn withdrawn and replaced by the UN Integrated Offices. In Burundi, the United Nations Operations in Burundi (ONUB) replaced the African Mission in Burundi (AMIB) in June 2004. Then, ONUB was in turn replaced by the Integrated Office in Burundi (BINUB) on 1 January 2007. In Sierra Leone, the Economic Community of West African States Ceasefire and Monitoring Group (ECOMOG), which intervened in March 1998, were replaced by the UN Assistance Mission in Sierra Leone (UNAMSIL) in November 1999. UNAMSIL was replaced by the UN Integrated Office in Sierra Leone (UNIOSIL) on 1 January 2006. The updates on evolution of UN presence in these two countries are detailed in chapter 6.

There are a number of economic similarities between Burundi and Sierra Leone: Both are among the poorest countries in the world, having a low Human Development Index (HDI) ranking, both depend on primary commodities for a substantial share of their exports, and both are fairly reliant on official development assistance (ODA).[18] These structural vulnerabilities have several important implications. First, research indicates that poor countries typically face a high risk of reverting to conflict within five years of the ending of a prior conflict.[19] Second, according to Paul Collier, the "three economic characteristics that make a country prone to civil war are low income, slow growth and dependence upon primary commodity exports."[20] Third, these trends underline the need for the PBC to pay particular attention and to help these two countries avoid a relapse into conflict.

Nature and Scope of the PBC's Engagement with Burundi and Sierra Leone on its Agenda

To understand the performance of the PBC in the first two years, it is useful to explain its engagement with the first two countries under its consideration: Burundi and Sierra Leone. This is because engagement with these two countries was as of 2008 more advanced than the other two countries on the PBC's agenda: Guinea-Bissau and the Central African Republic. It should be noted that the nature and scope of PBC's engagement varies from country to country. This is because the underlying causes of conflict, the conditions under which each country emerged from war, and the stage of postconflict recovery are different and require individualised treatment. The PBC's engagement with Burundi and Sierra Leone had initially focused on supporting the development of integrated peacebuilding strategies, bringing together various actors in support of peacebuilding efforts, and offering assistance and encouragement to the governments to sustain the peacebuilding efforts.

Supporting the Development of the Integrated Peacebuilding Strategy

The Integrated Peacebuilding Strategy (IPBS) is the PBC's instrument of engagement with countries under its consideration. The process of developing an integrated peacebuilding strategy for both countries entailed intensive interaction between the PBC in New York, on the one hand, and the two governments, the UN country team, donors, and domestic civil society organisations, on the other. The process included a series of inter-related steps beginning with a discussion of the peacebuilding needs based on the presentations by senior government leaders from the two countries to the country-specific meetings of the PBC in New York in October 2006. This led to an endorsement of the peacebuilding priorities for the two countries, followed by a series of thematic discussions on these priorities in the country-specific meetings.

As part of the preparatory process for developing the Strategic Framework, delegations from the PBC visited Burundi in April 2007 and Sierra Leone in March 2007. These visits were carried out to exchange views on priorities, to identify gaps in peacebuilding, to set a framework for enhanced dialogue with the governments and provide a platform for advocacy and interaction with partners.

The instrument, developed in cooperation with the national government is called the Strategic Framework for Peacebuilding in Burundi. The articulation of the Strategic Framework took place against the background of a series of policy frameworks already articulated by the government, in collaboration with its partners, to guide the process of its national reconciliation and postconflict recovery and development. These frameworks comprised the government's emergency programme, the poverty-reduction strategy, and the UN common action plan and joint roadmap, and the various peace agreements.

Recognising that peacebuilding encompasses political, security, and development issues, the Strategic Framework for Peacebuilding in Burundi,[21] adopted by its government of Burundi and the PBC on 20 June 2007, identified the following selected peacebuilding priorities: "promotion of good governance; supporting the Comprehensive Ceasefire Agreement between the government of Burundi and the National Liberation Forces (FNL); security sector reforms; justice sector reforms; promotion of human rights and action to combat impunity; ensuring land reforms and socio-economic recovery; mobilisation and coordination of international assistance; sub regional dimension; and a gender dimension."[22]

The strategic framework also defined the mutual commitments (referred to as mutual engagements) between the PBC and Burundi. The PBC commitments included providing sustained attention to, and support for, the mobilisation of resources to Burundi in support of its peacebuilding priorities, advocating within the international community for support to the peacebuilding process, and promoting the subregional dimension of peacebuilding by assisting the advancement of Burundi's integration into the African Great Lakes region.

Following the adoption of the strategic framework, the PBC and the government of Burundi developed a Monitoring and Tracking Mechanism that outlined institutional mechanisms as well as procedures for tracking progress in the implementation of the Strategic Framework and detailed the relevant benchmarks. Crucially, the institutional mechanism for monitoring at the country level used the existing institutional arrangement for monitoring the country's poverty reduction strategy developed by the government.

The integrated peacebuilding strategy for Sierra Leone called the Peacebuilding Cooperation Framework was adopted on 12 December 2007.[23] Developing the framework had slowed down in the prelude to the presidential and parliamentary elections in August and September 2007 but resumed immediately thereafter. The development of the Cooperation Framework was built on a series of policy frameworks that had been articulated by the government to guide the postconflict recovery and development process. The main peacebuilding priorities reflected in the Peacebuilding Cooperation Framework included "youth employment and empowerment, justice and security sector reform, consolidation of democracy and good governance, capacity building, and subregional dimensions of peacebuilding."[24]

In addition to making specific commitments to the main peacebuilding priorities, the PBC undertook to support implementation of the Cooperation Framework within the context of the governing bodies of international institutions. It advocated for a sustained partnership and an enhanced dialogue between the government of Sierra Leone and its international partners. This included efforts to increase the number of international partners supporting peace consolidation efforts in Sierra Leone. Furthermore, the PBC supported the development of a Sierra Leone National Aid Policy to ensure effective and timely implementation of aid effectiveness policies and good practices such as the Paris Declaration. More significantly, the PBC also committed to galvanizing attention and sustained levels of financial resources and technical assistance to support implementation of the framework.[25]

The first biannual reviews of the Strategic Framework for Peacebuilding in Burundi and the Peacebuilding Cooperation Framework for Sierra Leone were conducted in June 2008.[26] The biannual reviews comprised six monthly assessments of progress in the implementation of the peacebuilding priorities and commitments jointly agreed to by the PBC and the government of the two countries as well as other stakeholders. These reviews are an important part of the PBC sustained attention to the countries on its agenda and they offer an opportunity for course correction, depending on developments in the country.

Bringing Various Actors Together in Support of National Peacebuilding Efforts

The process of articulating the Strategic Framework for Peacebuilding in Burundi was as important as the outcome itself. One of the strengths of the PBC is its ability to bring various actors together and involving them in various facets of its work. This approach was used to good effect in the development of the Burundi Strategic Framework, where it convened the government, donors, the UN country team, and a wide variety of civil society organisations — including private sector organisations, women's associations, religious groups, and traditional associations. In so doing, the PBC not only fulfilled the task entrusted to it in its founding resolutions but also built national and international consensus around key peacebuilding priorities. The significance of bringing the civil society organisations into this process is discussed below in the section entitled "Present and Potential Added Value."

As in Burundi, the effort to develop a Cooperation Framework for Sierra Leone benefited from increased dialogue between the government and other stakeholders, in particular the donors, the civil society organisations and the UN country team. Such collaboration, especially with the development partners, was critical in making progress on a range of programmes. As the report of the Chairman of the Country Specific Meeting (CSM) mission to Sierra Leone in October 2007 noted, "The Peacebuilding

Commission should play a pivotal role in strengthening dialogue between the Government and its international partners as well as broadening the donor base in Sierra Leone. A critical element for broadening the donor base and attracting non-traditional partners will be the development of government led sector-wide strategies and master plans in areas such as energy, physical infrastructure, water supply, and health and the private sector and flexible funding mechanisms and structures."[27]

Offering Assistance and Encouragement to Governments to Sustain the Peacebuilding Effort

The engagement of the PBC extends beyond the development of the Strategic Framework and bringing the actors together in support of that effort. The PBC also offered a helping hand to the governments in situations of real or potential crisis. The visit of the Chairman of the Burundi Country Specific Meeting to Bujumbura (the capital of Burundi) in early September 2007 provided a striking illustration of this kind of engagement. The visit was aimed at and enabled the Chairman to dialogue with the relevant stakeholders, in particular the government, opposition parties, and donors. The Chairman urged them to overcome the budgetary impasse, to break the parliamentary deadlock, and to end the withdrawal of FNL from the Joint Verification and Monitoring Mechanism that had been established to monitor the Comprehensive Framework Agreement of 2006. Following the visit, the PBC issued a statement outlining a set of specific recommendations to all stakeholders.[28]

The need to improve energy supply in Sierra Leone was well recognised, and the new government declared energy as an utmost priority. In its report on the October 2007 mission to Sierra Leone, the Chair of the country specific meeting on Sierra Leone recommended that "the Peacebuilding Commission should support the government's effort by galvanizing additional resources and commitments for an immediate response and holistic medium-term energy sector."[29] In response, the CSM for Sierra Leone held a meeting on 13 November 2007 to examine how various actors can support the government's effort to increase energy supply. An efficient and reliable energy supply was seen as critical to reviving the economy of Sierra Leone, in particular its agricultural, industrial, and commercial production.

The Challenges

The new peacebuilding architecture faced a range of challenges. In its first annual report, the PBC identified a few:

> The main challenge facing the Commission is to maximize its impact on the ground to make the United Nations peacebuilding architecture an effective instrument of international collaboration in support of countries emerging from conflict. The Commission's future work will need to focus on ensuring that peacebuilding processes remain on track and that challenges and gaps are addressed in a timely manner by all relevant stakeholders...others will include further development of the Commission's working methods and monitoring mechanisms for the IPBS; enhancing operational relationships with other intergovernmental bodies and regional and sub regional organisations; and improving interaction with the field based on lessons learnt during its first year of operations.[30]

Getting the process right is fundamental to the functioning and effectiveness of the new peacebuilding architecture, in particular the PBC. More significantly, the PBC's emphasis on its need "to maximize its impact on the ground" reflected an awareness that its operational success will be judged by whether its work enables war-torn countries to achieve durable peace and to avoid relapse into conflict.

Yet there were other challenges. One of these relates to the sequencing of financial allocation from the Peacebuilding Fund (PBF) and the development of the integrated peacebuilding strategy (IPBS). Burundi and Sierra Leone received funding from the PBF before the development of the Strategic Peacebuilding Framework for Burundi or the Sierra Leone Peacebuilding Cooperation Framework. In its report in March 2007, the PBC mission to Sierra Leone noted that "many stakeholders in the country remain primarily focused on the disbursement of the US$35 million allocated to Sierra Leone by the PBF."[31] This raised the question of whether the development of an IPBS should precede the allocation of resources from the PBF. The short term catalytic nature of the PBF, however, required that financial allocation be made as soon as possible to the countries. The IPBS should serve as the framework for more substantive long-term funding for peacebuilding.

This was linked to another challenge: the PBC's ability to marshal resources to fund peacebuilding. It had been noted that "we must not confuse the peacebuilding fund (with a target of US$ 250 million) with funding for peacebuilding. If peacekeeping can draw on up to US$6-$8 billion to fund its operations through assessed budgets, how can we ensure that the PBC can develop the capacity to generate sufficient assured resources for peace building?"[32] The actual figure for the proposed budget for peacekeeping for 2008-2009 is US$7.3 billion.[33] The potential for individual PBC members to contribute to that effort is discussed in the next section.

Although there is wide recognition that peacebuilding efforts span the entire conflict cycle, from conflict prevention to peacemaking, peacekeeping, and postconflict peacebuilding, there is an expectation that the PBC should help in smoothing the transition from peacekeeping to postconflict peacebuilding. It had been observed that "one of the main challenges for the Peacebuilding Commission will be to find ways of drawing down the current caseload of UN peace operations without precipitating a relapse to conflict. If it were able to do so in even just one or two cases initially, it would make an important contribution."[34] The PBC, however, should focus on postconflict situations that can benefit from peacebuilding.

The Present and Potential Added Value

There is a considerable diversity of perspectives concerning the areas where the new peacebuilding architecture, in particular the PBC, can or should bring added value to its work. It is possible to make a distinction between its present and potential added value. We begin by examining some of the added value thus far.

Ensuring predictable financing for peacebuilding efforts is one area where the PBC has made a good start. The involvement of PBC in the donors' roundtable through the Chairman of the country-specific configuration on Burundi was a contributory factor for the successful partners' Round Table held in Bujumbura at the end of May 2007. That meeting was co-sponsored by the Netherlands and Norway (the latter in its capacity as Chair of the Burundi configuration of the Peacebuilding Commission). Norway played a key role in mobilising the international community for active participation in the Round Table, through bilateral efforts and by linking it to the work of the Peacebuilding Commission. In this regard, it was noted that "the US$655.6 million in funds pledged from international donors to Burundi in May would probably have been much lower if it had not been for the Commission, in particular the influence of Norway's Ambassador to the United Nations, John Lovald, who chairs the Commission's Burundi Committee."[35]

The PBC has also added value by assisting the countries under its consideration in efforts to *stay the course* and to better manage political crises. In both Burundi and Sierra Leone, the PBC had contributed to helping the countries stay the course at critical political turning points. In early September 2007, the Chair of the Burundi configuration of the Peacebuilding Commission undertook a fact-finding mission, which resulted in the adoption of "Conclusions and Recommendations."[36] The recommendations inspired a concerted approach by the international community to respond to three critical issues faced by the country, namely, a deadlock in parliament that prevented the passage of legislative measures, the withdrawal of PALIPEHUTU-FNL from the Joint Verification and Monitoring Mechanism (JVMM), and serious economic governance problems that led to a delay in concluding a review by the International Monetary Fund (IMF). The completion of the IMF review was partly due to the effort of the Chair of the Burundi CSM, which opened the way for resumption of negotiations between the IMF and the government of Burundi.

In Sierra Leone, a striking illustration of the commitment to galvanise international attention in support of the Sierra Leone Peacebuilding Cooperation Framework was provided by the convening of the High-level Stakeholders Consultation on Sierra Leone in New York on 19 May 2008. That meeting brought together senior representatives of member states, the United Nations, the private sector, and the civil society. During that meeting several participating international organisations and member states "expressed commitments to continue or increase their support to Sierra Leone in line with the Peacebuilding Cooperation Framework."[37]

A specific example of the capacity of PBC to galvanise international attention on a particular peacebuilding priority was provided by the focus that Sierra Leone CSM has turned on energy. The inclusion of energy among the peacebuilding priorities for Sierra Leone enabled the government to attract assistance from a range of bilateral and multilateral partners for the rehabilitation of the power sector, including strengthening management capacity for the energy sector.

Moreover, the PBC held three meetings on the 2007 Sierra Leone presidential and parliamentary elections, bringing together the government, the UN country team, donors, and civil society organisations. This was in response to the Security Council's request to the Chairman of the country-specific configuration on Sierra Leone to track progress on the main peacebuilding issues, including the presidential and parliamentary elections held in August, 2007. The PBC adopted a Chair's Declaration on the Presidential and Parliamentary Elections in which "members of the Commission advised of the need for all stakeholders to make every effort to ensure that the elections were conducted in a peaceful and orderly manner, in accordance with international standards for democratic elections."[38] As the Security Council Report has noted, "the PBC's focus on Sierra Leone seems to have underlined to all parties the importance of agreeing to accept the outcome of the 11 August 2007 election. It may therefore have helped those involved in preparing for the election, in both the government and the UN, to be more alert to potential disruptions before and after the election."[39]

In Burundi, the engagement of the PBC created an environment at the country level for improved government-civil society dialogue. The work at the country level, both on the development of projects of the PBF and on the Strategic Framework for Peacebuilding in Burundi, provided an important opportunity to bring the government and civil society organisations into dialogue. The National Steering Committee (Comite de Pilotage) brought together government representatives, the UN, donors and civil society organisations. The involvement of civil society organisations in such a process was ground breaking and was a result of the process established by the PBC.

The value of the PBF rests mainly in its unique capacity to fill critical funding gaps for peacebuilding. It channels resources for focused and time-limited activities deemed critical to the peace process, where funding is traditionally insufficient but contributes directly to peace consolidation, and where funding for priorities in sectors that are usually difficult to finance. Sierra Leone provides an illustration on how PBF resources proved critical in support of the national elections of 2007. The PBF provided readily available financing to the National Electoral Commission and the Sierra Leone Police, enabling them to manage the elections. In certain emergency situations, such funding can provide immediate support to address an imminent threat to peace consolidation or to reinforce the peace process.

The PBF has also added value in its unique catalytic role. In the preparation and implementation phases, the Fund not only kick starts critical peacebuilding interventions — for instance, to foster inclusive dialogue in Burundi or Côte d'Ivoire — it also attracts additional external resources from bilateral or multilateral sources. Several donors, thanks in part to the knowledge and cooperation built through the steering committees of the respective countries, pursued and deepened certain initiatives launched in cooperation with the Fund. This catalytic impact was also visible within currently existing projects, such as in Burundi, where a $1.5 million project to support reinforcement of mechanisms to fight corruption involved two government entities, the Ministry of Good Governance and the General Inspection and Local Administration, in addition to the Integrated Office in Burundi (BINUB) and the UN Development Programme. Finally, by linking up and coordinating with other funding windows of UN agencies, the international finance institutions and nongovernmental organisations, the Fund helps to ensure that longer-term funding mechanisms will be able to take over after the initial catalytic impact of the PBF runs its course.

There are myriad ways in which the PBC might potentially add value over time. One potential added value resides "in improving coordination between all national and international actors involved in peacebuilding and postconflict reconstruction, helping to maintain a coalition of interests around a country in a postconflict situation, contributing to bridging the "relief to development gap" and generally improving the sequencing of various phases of peacebuilding efforts."[40]

Building consensus around strategic peacebuilding frameworks in postconflict countries is yet another way that the PBC can have added value. Burundi and Sierra Leone developed various policy frameworks before their respective engagements with the PBC, because they were further down the road to postconflict recovery and development than the typical immediate postconflict country would be. Even so, the PBC has developed peacebuilding frameworks and built consensus among the various stakeholders around the Strategic Framework for Peacebuilding in Burundi and the Sierra Leone Peacebuilding Cooperation Framework. Indeed, the strategic frameworks have proven useful in bringing together the political, security, and development dimensions into a single framework to support the transition from stabilisation phase to long-term development. Thus, these frameworks have demonstrated considerable potential to serve as essential guides to keep the countries on track for sustainable peace. The opportunities to use such frameworks as guides to international action will be potentially greater in countries immediately emerging from conflict. Though these umbrella peacebuilding frameworks may not replace existing structures, they can reinforce complex policy frameworks to support postconflict recovery, reconciliation, and development. Examples include postconflict needs assessment and poverty reduction strategy papers.

Marshalling resources is another area where PBC has great potential. Its influence within the constellation of UN intergovernmental bodies will depend among other things on "its potential to generate additional resources for a conflict-affected state whose perceived importance on the international agenda has receded."[41] The composition of the PBC gives it considerable advantage over other options as to resource mobilisation for postconflict countries, and particularly for those under its consideration.

To appreciate the potential added value in this regard, one need look no further than the volume of Official Development Assistance (ODA) provided by the Development Assistance Committee (DAC) members on the PBC. The ten members of the PBC that belong to DAC provided a total of $77.76 billion (75 per cent) of the $103.65 billion in ODA given by DAC in 2007.[42] When that amount is added to the resources that non-DAC and other developing member states of the PBC give in aid annually, the enormous financial power that resides within the PBC becomes evident. Among its members in the first two years were Brazil, Russia, India and China,[43] as well as OPEC members Angola and Nigeria.

It would be wrong to conclude from this, however, that a significant redirection of ODA resources to peacebuilding could occur from PBC members in a short period of time. Foreign policy considerations reinforced by domestic politics influence the amount, destination, and sectors to which donor countries allocate ODA. Still, in the long run, and provided that there is commitment among the membership of the PBC to support postconflict countries, there is considerable scope for PBC members to offer financial resources and technical expertise to help countries under the consideration of the Commission.

The assessments of the first year of the performance of the PBC made by two groups of NGOs and of eighteen-months performance by a government-commissioned study provide us with a fitting conclusion to this section. The first group, Action Aid, CAFOD and CARE International have noted that "[t]he PBC's impact has been largely positive and well received, but important challenges remain."[44] The Security Council Report — another nongovernmental organisation — has noted that "the PBC has made considerable contributions in its first year, not only in terms of its own systems and processes but also in marshalling international resources and focusing attention on two countries that needed assistance in their transition from peacekeeping to development…this will be a long process, but an important and valuable beginning has been made."[45] For its part, an independent analysis commissioned by the Permanent Mission of Denmark to the United Nations concluded that "the PBC is work in progress, but one that so far has proved the potential for its contribution. Continued focus on its performance by all stakeholders will be necessary if it is to (a) consolidate its positive impact on cases undertaken to date, and to (b) extend its reach to new cases."[46]

An Encouraging Start

So much hope has been raised by the creation of the new peacebuilding architecture, in particular the PBC, that there has been impatience for quick results. It is important to emphasise that the new peacebuilding architecture is in its infancy and much "learning by doing" is to be expected. It is not surprising, for example, that the PBC, the linchpin of the new peacebuilding architecture, spent a good part of its first year addressing what the Chairman of the PBC has called "critical organisational and methodological issues."[47] Still, there are some crucial tests of relevance to which the new peacebuilding architecture can be subjected, even at this stage in its life cycle. This test is based on some questions.

Do the first two countries on the PBC agenda find the experience helpful to their peacebuilding efforts? As the first two countries to be referred to the PBC, Burundi and Sierra Leone form the proving ground for the work of the new peacebuilding architecture. The Permanent Representative of Burundi to the United Nations has said that "[by] selecting Burundi as the first beneficiary of its work, the Commission [has] demonstrated its commitment to building lasting peace and relaunching Burundi's national economy."[48] And the then newly elected President of Sierra Leone stated in his inaugural address that the government of Sierra Leone "will continue to work with the United Nations in peacebuilding and will take full advantage of the opportunities provided by the newly established United Nations Peacebuilding Commission."[49] These are early encouraging affirmations that there is value in engagement with the PBC.

Are more countries seeking to be considered by the PBC? If countries emerging from conflict consider engagement with the

PBC useful, requests to be placed on the agenda of the PBC will increase. The President of Timor-Leste, in his address to the Sixty-Second session of the UN General Assembly expressed the hope that "as the situation [in his county] progresses the Peacebuilding Commission will consider placing Timor-Leste on its agenda as a follow-up to the United Nations Mission in Timor-Leste (UNMIT)."[50] The government of Timor-Leste did not make the request to be placed on PBC agenda. However, Guinea-Bissau became the third country to be placed on PBC's agenda on 19 December, 2007 and Central African Republic became the fourth country to be placed on the agenda of the PBC on 12 June 2008.

Is the PBF responding to the peacebuilding efforts of countries in need? The PBF has also begun to respond to peacebuilding needs beyond Burundi and Sierra Leone, the first two countries on the agenda of the PBC. These first two countries together with Guinea-Bissau have been declared eligible for and have benefited from funding from the First window of the PBF in 2008. Since then, the PBF has responded to funding requests from other countries from the second and third (emergency) windows. Moreover, during the same time, Liberia and Central Africa Republic have received funding under the second window, while Nepal and Cote d'Ivoire have been declared eligible for these funds. The countries which received support from the emergency window of the PBF at this stage were Burundi, the Central African Republic, Cote d'Ivoire, Guinea-Conakry, Haiti, Kenya, and Liberia.

Dag Hammarskjöld, the second Secretary General of the United Nations, once remarked that "The United Nations was created not to lead mankind to heaven, but to save mankind from hell". He could just as well have been speaking of the new peacebuilding architecture and its role in postconflict situations. The PBC was not designed to provide early warning for impending conflicts nor to dissuade countries from resorting to war; but rather, it was designed to ensure that the countries under its watch achieve sustainable peace and do not relapse into conflict. Postconflict peacebuilding is a complex and painstaking process, with the results not showing up in the short run. It is analogous to a marathon rather than to a sprint. Nonetheless, the work of the

PBC during its first two years provides reason for hope and offers an encouraging start.

Notes to Chapter 1 - *The New Peacebuilding Architecture: An Institutional Innovation of the United Nations*

1. 2005 World Summit Outcome UN Doc. A/60/1 of 15 September 2005.
2. The report of the panel was published under the title A More Secure World: Our Shared Responsibility, UN Doc A/59/565 of 2 December 2004, para. 85.
3. In Larger Freedom: Towards Development, Security and Human Rights for All, A/59/2005 21 March 2005, para. 31-3.
4. Ibid., para. 115.
5. See United Nations General Assembly Resolution, UN Doc. A/RES/60/180 of 20 December 2005; and Security Council Resolution, UN Doc. S/1645 of 20 December 2005.
6. Security Council Summit Meeting, 21 January 1992, An Agenda for Peace: Preventive Diplomacy, Peacemaking and Peacebuilding, UN Doc. A/47/277-S/2411of 17 June 1992.
7. Report of the Panel on United Nations Peace Operations,(also called Brahimi Report), UN Doc. A/55/305-S/2000/809, 21 August 2000.
8. For a very interesting discussion on portraits of such relapses, see Carolyn McAskie 'The International Peacebuilding Challenge: Can New Players and New Approaches bring New Results', lecture delivered at Simon Fraser University School for International Studies, Vancouver, British Columbia, Canada, 19 October 2007.
9. In Larger Freedom, para 114.
10. This assessment finds echoes in two recent reports by two reputable NGO groups, See ActionAid, CAFOD, and CARE International, 'Consolidating The Peace?: Views from Sierra Leone and Burundi on the United Nations Peacebuilding Commission', June 2007. Available at:<http://www.actionaid.org/assets/pdf/peace_consolidating_the_final.pdf>; see also Security Council Report 'Special Research Report No.2: Peacebuilding Commission', 5 October 2007. Available at: <http://www.securitycouncilreport.org/atf/cf/%7B65BFCF9B-

6D27-4E9C-8CD3-CF6E4FF96FF9%7D/Research%20Report_PBC%20 5%20Oct%2007.pdf>. (Note: The Security Council Report is the name of a non-governmental organisation, not a report of the UN Security Council.)

11. See United Nations General Assembly Resolution, UN Doc. A/RES/60/180 of 20 December 2005, operative para. 2, and Security Council Resolution, UN Doc. S/1645/2005 of 20 December 2005.

12. The founding 31 members were China, France, Russian Federation, United Kingdom, United States plus Belgium and South Africa from the Security Council; Angola, Brazil, Czech Republic, Guinea-Bissau, Luxembourg, Indonesia and Sri Lanka from the Economic and Social Council; Burundi, Chile, Egypt, El Salvador, Fiji, Georgia, and Jamaica from the General Assembly; Germany, Italy, Japan, The Netherlands, and Norway from the category of major UN financial contributors; and Bangladesh, Ghana, India, Nigeria and Pakistan from the category of major troop contributing countries.

13. Mark Malloch-Brown, 'Holmes Lecture: Can the UN Be Reformed?' annual meeting of the Academic Council on UN System (ACUNS) of 7 June 2007, page 7.

14. The word *configuration* is synonymous with *committee* and is also used interchangeably with meeting. Thus in the parlance of the PBC, there is country specific configuration or country-specific meeting.

15. The Terms of Reference are annexed to Arrangements for establishing the Peacebuilding Fund, report of the Secretary-General, UN Doc. A/60/984 of 22 August 2006.

16. Ibid., page 4.

17. Note that the Forces for Defence of Democracy (FDD), the National Liberation Forces (FNL), armed factions of the National Council for Defence of Democracy (CNDD), and the Party for the Liberation of the Hutu People (Palipehutu) did not sign the Arusha Accords. But CNDD-FDD signed the cease-fire and power-sharing agreements with the government in 2003; and the Palipehutu-FNL signed a comprehensive ceasefire agreement with the Government in 2006.

18. See the annex at the end of chapter 6 for an updated summary of the basic political, economic and social facts on all six countries on agenda of PBC.

19. The figures on the chances of reversal is rounded up to 50 percent in many reports and speeches, but the actual figure is 44 percent. However, a recent study has indicated that the authors of the original figures revised it down to 20 percent four years after the first study. The original study was by Paul Collier et. Al., Breaking the Conflict Trap:

Civil War and Development Policy – A World Bank Policy Research Report (jointly published by the World Bank and Oxford University Press, 2003), p. 83; For the reference relating to the revision, see Astri Surhrke and Ingrid Samset, 'What's in a Figure? Estimating Recurrence of Civil War', International Peacekeeping vol. 14, no. 2, 195-203, 2007.

20. Paul Collier, The Bottom Billion: Why the Poorest Countries Are Failing and What Can Be Done About It (New York: Oxford University Press, 2007), p.32.

21. See Strategic Framework for Peacebuilding in Burundi, UN Doc. PBC/1/BDI/4 of 30 July 2007.

22. Ibid., page 7-12

23. See Sierra Leone Peacebuilding Cooperation Framework, UN Doc. PBC/2/SLE/1 of 3 December 2007.

24. Ibid., page 4-8

25. Ibid., page 10-11.

26. The key findings can be found in Recommendations of the Biannual Review of the implementation of the Strategic Framework for Peacebuilding in Burundi, PBC/2/BDI/L.2 of 19 June 2008 and Conclusions and Recommendations of the Biannual Review of the Implementation of the Sierra Leone Peacebuilding Cooperation Framework PBC/2/SLE/2 of 19 June 2008.

27. See Report of the Mission of the Chairman of the Peacebuilding Commission in Sierra Leone configuration to Sierra Leone, 8-15 October 2007, page. 2-3.

28. See Conclusions and Recommendations of the Peacebuilding Commission following the report of the Chair of the Burundi configuration in Identical Letters, dated 20 September 2007, from the Chairman of the Burundi configuration of the Peacebuilding Commission to the President of the Security Council, the President of the General Assembly, and the President of the Economic and Social Council, UN Doc. PBC/2/BDI/2 of 21 September 2007.

29. Report of the Mission of the Chairman of the Peacebuilding Commission in Sierra Leone Configuration to Sierra Leone,8-15 October 2007, para. 9.

30. See Report of the Peacebuilding Commission on its first session, UN Doc. A/62/137-S/2007/458 of 25 July 2007, page 2.

31. See Report of Peacebuilding Commission mission to Sierra Leone from 19-25 March 2007, UN Doc. PBC/1/SLE/2 of 23 April 2007, page 2.

32. McAskie, 'The International Peacebuilding Challenge', page 16.

33. See 'UN Peacekeeping in the line of Fire', *Financial Times*, 17-18 May 2008, page 5.

34. Salman Ahmed, Paul Keating, and Ugo Salinas 'Shaping the future of UN Peace Operations: Is There a Doctrine in This House?', Cambridge Review of International Affairs Vol.20, No.1 (March 2007), page 11-28.
35. Security Council Report, October 2007, page 8.
36. See Conclusions and Recommendations of the Peacebuilding Commission following the report of the Chair of the Burundi configuration in identical letters to the General Assembly and Security Council dated 20 September 2007.
37. See Chairs' Summary Statement on Peacebuilding Commission High-level Stakeholders Consultation on Sierra Leone on 19 May 2008.
38. See Chair's Declaration adopted by the Peacebuilding Commission Country-specific Meeting on Sierra Leone on the Upcoming Presidential and Parliamentary elections in Sierra Leone, UN Doc. PBC/1/SLE/4 of 22 June 2007.
39. See Security Council Report, October 2007, para. 8-9.
40. See, for example, David Atwood and Fred Tanner, 'The UN Peacebuilding Commission and International Geneva', Disarmament Forum (UNIDIR) 2 (2007), 29.
41. See Richard Ponzio, 'The United Nations Peacebuilding Commission: Origins and Initial Practice', Disarmament Forum (UNIDIR) 2 (2007), 8. Available at http://www.unidir.org/pdf/articles/pdf-art2627.pdf
42. This is based on preliminary ODA data for 2007. See OECD: Table 1 on Net Official Development Assistance in 2007--Preliminary data for 2007; released on 4 April 2008 Available at http://www.oecd.org/dataoecd/27/55/40381862.pdf. The ten members in the order of volume of their net ODA are the United States (US$21.75 bn), Germany (US$12.26 bn), France (US$9.94 bn), The United Kingdom (US$9.92 bn), Japan (US$7.69 bn), The Netherlands (US$6.21bn), Italy (US$3.92 bn), Norway (US$3.72 bn), Belgium (1.95 bn) and Luxembourg (US$0.365 bn).
43. These four countries are the original named the BRICs. The concept of BRIC was developed and popularized by Goldman Sachs in 'Dreaming of the BRICs: The Path to 2050', Global Economic Paper No 99 (2003). According to Jim O'Niell, who was the lead author of the 2003 Goldman Sachs report, BRICs, which are emerging donors, now account for 15-16 per cent of the global output; see Jim O'Niell 'Dwindling US Trade Deficit Could Shape World Trade' Financial Times, 26 September 2007, p. 28. [South Africa joined the BRIC group in 2011 at a meeting of the group in Hainan Island, China]
44. ActionAid, 'Consolidating The Peace?', page 2.

45. Special Research Report No.2, of the Security Council Report (the NGO) on the Peacebuilding Commission, page 11.
46. See Taking Stock, Looking Forward: A Strategic Review of the Peacebuilding Commission — An Independent Analysis by the NYU Center on International Cooperation and the International Peace Institute, April 2008.
47. See Statement by Ambassador Yukio Takasu, Chairman of the Peacebuilding Commission, at the Debate at Security Council on the First Report of the Peacebuilding Commission, 17 October 2007, page 1.
48. See United Nations General Assembly Doc. GA/10635, statement by Mr. Joseph Ntakirutimana, Ambassador of Burundi to the United Nations of 10 October 2007, p. 3. Available at: <http://www.un.org/News/Press/docs/2007/ga10635.doc.htm>.
49. See Presidential Address delivered by His Excellency Mr. Ernst Bai Koroma, President of Sierra Leone and Commander-in-Chief of the Armed Forces of the Republic of Sierra Leone on the occasion of the State Opening of the Third Parliament, Freetown, 5 October 2007, page 15.
50. See Address by H.E. Dr. Jose Ramos-Horta, President of the Democratic Republic of Timor-Leste to the 62nd session of the United Nations General Assembly, 27 September 2007.

Chapter 2

A United Nations Architecture to Build Peace in Post-Conflict Situations*

Over the last decade, the international community has learnt that the countries most likely to lapse into conflict are those that have been there before. Studies have shown that about half of all countries that emerge from violent conflict relapse into violence within ten years. Recognising that much more effort has to be devoted to consolidating the peace after it has been won, leaders at the 2005 World Summit created the institutional arrangements of the UN Peacebuilding Architecture.

Peacebuilding Architecture Overview

The UN Peacebuilding Architecture (PBA) is the latest in a series of efforts to reform the way the UN supports conflict-affected countries, in particular those at the postconflict end of the spectrum. It consists of three components: the Peacebuilding Commission, the Peacebuilding Fund, and the Peacebuilding Support Office.

---

* Source: Originally published in World Bank Institute, Development Outreach, October 2009.

The Peacebuilding Commission (PBC) — the institutional lynchpin of the architecture — is an inter-governmental advisory body to the Security Council and the General Assembly mandated to:

- Bring together all relevant actors and advise on integrated strategies for post-conflict peacebuilding and recovery;
- Help to marshal resources and ensure predictable financing for immediate post-conflict activities and sustained financial investment over the medium to longer term;
- Extend the period of attention by the international community to postconflict recovery;
- Develop and disseminate best practices in support of countries emerging from conflict.

As of mid-2009, the PBC had four countries on its agenda: Burundi, Sierra Leone, Guinea-Bissau, and the Central African Republic. There are five ways in which the Commission has put into practice its mandate in these countries.

First, the PBC has brought together in a single forum all major stakeholders relevant for each country's peacebuilding process: the UN, international financial institutions, countries contributing troops, major donor countries, neighbouring countries, regional organisations and institutions, and the permanent members of the UN Security Council.

Second, the Commission has articulated an integrated peacebuilding approach between interventions meant to restore peace and security and those aimed at reconstruction and development in these countries.

Third, the PBC is sustaining international political and financial support to these countries well beyond the evaporation of the "CNN effect".

Fourth, the PBC has sought to ensure that all stakeholders engaged with these countries collaborate around an agreed upon integrated strategy, or a "roadmap" for peace consolidation, developed jointly by national authorities and the Commission. Table 1 shows the key peacebuilding challenges and priorities identified in the strategic frameworks agreed upon by the PBC and the first four countries on its agenda. Finally, through its Working Group on Lessons Learnt, the Commission has sought to capture and disseminate good practices from the experiences of post-conflict countries for broader application to countries on the agenda of the PBC and in similar situations.

Table 1: Peacebuilding Priorities Identified in the Strategic Framework

Country	Priorities and Challenges
Burundi (2007*)	Promotion of good governance; comprehensive Ceasefire Agreement between the Government of Burundi and PALIPEHUTU-FNL; security sector reform; justice, promotion of human rights and action to combat impunity; the land issue and socioeconomic recovery; mobilisation and coordination of international assistance; subregional dimension; and gender dimension.
Sierra Leone (2007*)	Youth employment and empowerment; justice and security sector reform; consolidation of democracy and good governance; capacitybuilding; energy sector; and subregional dimensions of peacebuilding.
Guinea-Bissau (2008*)	Elections and institutionbuilding for the National Electoral Commission; measures to jump-start the economy and rehabilitate infrastructure, in particular the energy sector; security sector reform; strengthening of the justice sector, consolidating the rule of law and fighting against drug trafficking; public administration reform and modernisation; and social questions critical for peacebuilding.
Central African Republic (2009*)	Reform of the security sector and disarmament, demobilisation and reintegration; governance— rule of law; and development poles.

*Year that the Strategic Framework was adopted between the PBC and the Country.

Source: Peacebuilding Support Office

The second component of the architecture, the Peacebuilding Fund (PBF), is under the authority of the UN Secretary-General and is administered by the Peacebuilding Support Office. The PBF combines the scope of a global fund with the country-specific focus of a multidonor trust fund. It is designed to quickly release resources needed to launch peacebuilding activities in countries emerging from conflict and to bridge funding gaps in pertinent areas. As of May 2009, a total sum of $312.7m had been pledged to the PBF against an initial target of US$250m. By then, allotments have been made to twelve countries. Table 2 provides a summary on the key aspects of the Fund.

Table 2: PBF Key Figures: Peacebuilding Fund Allocations and Projects Approved as of 15 May, 2009

Window	Country	Allocation (US$)	Projects Approved No.	Projects Approved US$
PBF WINDOW I	Burundi	$35,000,000	17	$32,836,315
	Central African Republic	$10,000,000	12	$10,000,000
	Guinea-Bissau	$6,000,000	4	$5,686,889
	Sierra Leone	$35,000,000	14	$32,669,828
	Total PBF Window I	$86,000,000	47	$81,193,032

PBF WINDOW II	Comoros	$9,000,000	-	-
	Cote d'Ivoire	$5,000,000	2	$5,000,000
	Guinea-Conakry	$6,000,000	-	-
	Liberia	$15,000,000	20	$14,287,394
	Nepal	$10,000,000	-	-
	Total PBF Window II	**$45,000,000**	**22**	**$19,287,394**
PBF WINDOW III EMERGENCY PROJECTS	Projects Funded in Burundi Central African Republic Côte d'Ivoire Guinea Haiti; Liberia and Kenya	$6,353,903	0	$7,353,903
	Total PBF III Window Emergency	**$6,353,903**	**8**	**$7,353,903**
Total - PBF WINDOWS I, II, & III		$137,353,903	77*	$107,834,329

*Note: These projects cover a wide range of areas such as supporting national peace dialogues, promoting community reconciliation, strengthening rule of law, rehabilitating military barracks and prisons, disarmament, demobilisation and reintegration, providing seed capital for entrepreneurs and addressing youth unemployment.

Source: Peacebuilding Fund, May 2009

Both the PBC and the PBF are supported by a Peacebuilding Support Office (PBSO) which is part of the UN Secretariat and third component of the peacebuilding architecture. The PBSO is a small non-operational office headed by an Assistant Secretary-General who reports directly to the Secretary-General. The Office supports the work of the PBC, manages the PBF, and advises the Secretary-General on UN system-wide peacebuilding strategies and policies.

Peacebuilding Architecture — A Promising Beginning

Since the Peacebuilding Architecture was only in its third year of operation as of 2009, it was too early to make a definitive assessment regarding fulfilling its mandate and meeting the high expectations that led to its creation. However, it could be said that the peacebuilding architecture has achieved some successes.

A commonly agreed to element of the PBC's added value has been its contribution to developing integrated strategies for peacebuilding, based on genuine partnerships between national and international actors. Such strategies had been completed in all four countries on the agenda of the PBC at this time. The strategies provided the basis for "compacts" between the various national actors, in particular, the government, and the international community. These have been monitored at biannual review meetings which provide a forum for inclusive dialogue amongst all partners. The PBC has also played a key role in advising operational actors on the necessary sequencing and prioritisation of peacebuilding efforts in the Central African Republic and Guinea-Bissau, in which such strategies were adopted in the period between October 2008 and May 2009.

The Commission has sought to galvanise international support for and improve coherence of peacebuilding efforts in countries on its agenda. For example, it convened the High-level Stakeholders Consultation on Sierra Leone in May 2008, at which senior representatives of member states, the UN, IFIs, the private sector, and civil society gathered and thus broadened the donor base for Sierra Leone. The Commission also played this role effectively in Burundi by keeping the spotlight on the peace process and working with regional actors to encourage both sides of the conflict to adhere to prior agreements. The Commission was also instrumental in mobilising resources to bridge the funding gaps for the November 2008 presidential elections in Guinea-Bissau and actively worked to mobilise support for economic development and security sector reforms in that country. Similarly, the Commission was engaged in promoting international support for disarmament, demobilisation, and reintegration in the Central African Republic, as an integral part of sustaining national political reconciliation and creating an enabling environment for growth and development.

The PBC's approach of sustained attention is predicated on the principles of national ownership, partnership, and mutual accountability. As Burundi, Guinea-Bissau, Central African Republic, and Sierra Leone have demonstrated, the PBC engages in active partnership with national authorities, providing a platform for incorporating and supporting their interaction with international partners. The Commission has also fostered dialogues among national authorities and local civil society actors active in peace consolidation efforts, most notably in Burundi.

Despite these initial successes in sustaining international attention for countries on its agenda, the PBC was cognisant of the challenges which must be addressed as it moved forward.

One of such challenges for the Commission will be to determine when a country "graduates" from its agenda. Emerging evidence suggests that peacebuilding results must be measured in decades or even generations, not years. The PBC has a valuable role to play in helping national and international partners build knowledge about the use of benchmarks and milestones in the peacebuilding process. A second challenge is strengthening its effort to mobilise resources for countries on its agenda, beyond allocations by the PBF.

As for the PBF, it has demonstrated its value not only as an instrument to support postconflict peacebuilding but also as a tool to address problems that could lead to potential lapse or relapse into conflict. Yet we have also learnt that the Peacebuilding Fund may have been too slow in disbursing funds. Some of its problems can be attributed to "teething," but others are systemic and related to implementing arrangements in fragile postconflict situations characterised by weak implementation capacities. However, the Fund's greatest potential is not that of a "main funder" of peacebuilding projects but that of a "catalyst" for new approaches and commitments to peacebuilding. Another significant feature of the Fund is the fact that funding decisions are decentralised to a national-level steering committee which includes government, civil society, the private sector, the UN, donors and, in most cases, the World Bank. In some cases, this has led to improved national ownership, forging new partnerships, and building a common agenda for peacebuilding.

Strengthening Partnership in Support of Postconflict Countries

Enhanced collaboration and strategic partnership between the PBC and the IFIs, and other institutional donors holds much promise. From the inception of the Commission, it was agreed that the World Bank, the International Monetary Fund, and other institutional donors should participate in all PBC meetings. The PBC provides the best platform for the World Bank to engage with other stakeholders in determining critical peacebuilding priorities, sequencing, and coordinating of peacebuilding efforts.

As a consequence of its unique composition and working methods, the PBC represents a major forum to coordinate international support to countries emerging from conflict. It is also the most suitable forum to facilitate greater collaboration between security, political, and development actors, thus advancing the World Bank's notion of "securing development". The PBC could also support the follow-up to and implementation of the World Bank-UN Partnership Framework for Crisis and Post-Crisis Situations signed in 2008 by the Secretary-General and the President of the World Bank.

The PBA has taken the important first steps to achieve its key objectives of supporting countries in transition from conflict to sustainable peace, bridging institutional gaps in the postconflict reconstruction and development within the UN, and advancing the broader international community's peacebuilding effort. Indeed, early experience suggested that the PBA was off to a promising start.

Chapter 3

The United Nations Peacebuilding Architecture: African Countries as Early Beneficiaries*

The United Nations has a long and impressive history of involvement in peacebuilding in Africa. Some of the roots of that effort are traceable to the UN role in supporting the process of decolonisation in the region; other roots lie in the peacebuilding work performed by peacekeeping missions in some African countries; and yet others are directly linked to its contemporary work in postconflict peacebuilding in the various countries emerging from conflict.

Postconflict peacebuilding, as a UN priority, began to be accorded significant recognition in the report of the Secretary-General titled "An Agenda for Peace: Preventive Diplomacy, Peacemaking and Peacebuilding", published in 1992. It gained more traction in the Report of the Panel on United Nations Peace Operations, also known as the *Brahimi Report*, published in 2000.

---

* Irene Freudenschuss-Reich & Georg Lennkh, eds.. NACHBAR AFRIKA *(Neighbour Africa): Dimensionen eines Kontinents (Dimensions of a Continent)*, (Vienna, Austria: Prassagen Verlag, 2010).

However, it was the decision in 2005 to establish the UN Peacebuilding architecture that gave a much-needed fresh impetus for postconflict peacebuilding. That decision stemmed from the recognition that many postconflict countries were repeatedly relapsing into violent conflict. In response, world leaders at their 2005 Summit at the United Nations agreed to create the United Nations peacebuilding architecture that would help provide sustained international attention to postconflict countries. The architecture consists of the Peacebuilding Commission, the Peacebuilding Fund, and the Peacebuilding Support Office.

Assessing Progress So Far

To appreciate the contribution of the peacebuilding architecture thus far is to understand the functions that were assigned to the architecture, in particular to the Peacebuilding Commission, its institutional linchpin. The Commission's key tasks include advising postconflict countries on the development of integrated strategies for postconflict peacebuilding and recovery; helping to marshal resources and ensuring predictable financing for immediate postconflict activities and sustained financial investment over the medium to longer term; and ensuring the sustained attention of the international community to post-conflict recovery.

The Peacebuilding Commission as of early 2010 had four countries on its agenda: Burundi, Central African Republic, Guinea-Bissau, and Sierra Leone. Developments in these countries seldom feature in international headline news in part because of their geopolitical location and in part because of their least-developed countries status. Yet an innovative approach to postconflict peacebuilding had began taking roots in those countries. These four African countries are thus the early beneficiaries of the work of the UN peacebuilding architecture.

Postconflict peacebuilding is a painstaking, complex, and multidimensional process: It spans the stabilisation, transitional, and consolidation phases; and it covers political, security, and development dimensions. Peacebuilding does not occur only in the postconflict context, but this is the current focus of the PBC mandate. The results of peacebuilding must be measured in decades not years. Even so, a preliminary assessment of the incremental added value of the peacebuilding architecture could be made at this point—as the peacebuilding architecture entered its fourth year since its institutionalisation and its fifth year since the decision on its creation was made. That assessment is organised around three main questions.

1. Has the engagement aided peace consolidation? As of mid-2010, the four countries on the agenda of the PBC have had their moments of turbulence since being put on the agenda of the Commission. This confirms the general view that peacebuilding is marked by progress and setbacks*: it is not a linear process. In general, the Commission has helped to sustain international attention in the countries on its agenda. The Commission brings together in a single forum all major stakeholders relevant for each country's peacebuilding process, including the United Nations, the international financial institutions; troop-contributing countries, major donor countries, the permanent members of the Security Council, neighbouring countries, and relevant regional and subregional organisations and institutions. It has articulated and adopted an integrated peacebuilding strategy (IPBS) to guide the engagement between itself and each of the four countries.

BOX 1: Key Elements of Engagement with the PBC

The PBC focuses its efforts on providing "extended attention" for the countries on its agenda through:

- Galvanising political support for the country's peacebuilding efforts;
- Mobilising financial assistance for the peacebuilding-related programmes of the country;
- Promoting the linkages between the political and development aspects of peacebuilding;
- Providing high-level political support to the joint framework/integrated strategy of the UN entities in the country.

---

* Central African Republic relapsed into violence towards the end of 2012; the reasons for and consequences of the relapse are examined in chapter 6.

Box 1 gives an idea of the key elements that "extended attention" or sustained international attention implies. The Commission seeks to ensure that the stakeholders engaged with these countries collaborate around the integrated strategy which serves as a "roadmap" for peace consolidation.

Developing the integrated strategic framework has been viewed with some scepticism. The perception that an integrated framework might not be needed has arisen from the fact that at the time the PBC began its engagement with the four countries, the governments of these countries had either developed a national recovery and development plan or a poverty-reduction strategy or both. However, none of these frameworks focused exclusively on peacebuilding challenges and priorities. Even if they did, the comprehensive consultative process among the various national stakeholders that the PBC engagement has fostered is now regarded as a positive hallmark. Thus, the process of articulation of the IPBS has not only enabled the government to assert national ownership on the determination of peacebuilding priorities, but has also given an opportunity to other national stakeholders, the UN mission, and members of the PBC to engage in serious dialogue with government on advancing those priorities. Moreover, the PBC could not reasonably be expected to undertake an engagement without an instrument of engagement, which outlines the basis of engagement and spells out the framework for mutual commitment.

An additional way that PBC engagement has aided peace consolidation is through such tools of engagement as the periodic visits of the Chairs of the country-specific configurations and of the PBC delegations. These visits, besides serving as a vehicle to review progress on agreed peacebuilding priorities, give the PBC the opportunity to interact with and encourage, support and literally cajole all key stakeholders to advance the process of peace consolidation. These visits, together with the meetings of the configurations in New York, in which senior government officials and the senior representatives of the UN missions in the country and other stakeholders participate, are thus key to the very notion of providing sustained international attention for countries on the agenda of the PBC.

2. *Have the countries received increased financial support as a consequence of engagement with the Commission?* To understand the importance of the financial support garnered by the four countries as a consequence of being on the PBC agenda, it might help to explain that countries emerging from conflict can be classified into three categories on the basis of their initial fiscal conditions and the extent of their external support when conflict ends. The first category of countries includes those that draw on their own financial resources to meet their postconflict peacebuilding needs. This was the case with a number of oil-producing countries that have emerged from conflict in the past four decades (Nigeria in 1970, Kuwait in 1991, and Angola in 2002). The second category of countries includes those that many donors are ready and willing to help. These are the postconflict countries referred to as "donor darlings." The third category comprises the postconflict countries referred to as "donor orphans", which often receive very limited external financial support. By coming on the agenda of the PBC, any postconflict country that belongs to the third category potentially stands a better chance of increased international attention, including financial support.

Yet, even where a postconflict country is financially well endowed or assured of financial support, an engagement with the PBC could potentially be beneficial. Such countries can draw on the PBC's repository of peacebuilding experiences and practices. This is part of the envisaged multitier engagement between the PBC and postconflict countries on which discussions have been launched in the PBC.

As of December 2009, each of the first four countries on the PBC agenda had received financial support from the Peacebuilding Fund — the financing arm of the architecture. By then, Burundi and Sierra Leone had each received about US$37 million, including funds from the emergency assistance facility; the Central African Republic, US$26 million; and Guinea-Bissau, US$6 million. (These figures have since risen higher for each of these countries, see table 10). These amounts may not seem much, but they were all grants and represent a significant share of official development flows to these countries. My threshold for "significant share" is if a single donor contributes up to or accounts for 5 percent of a country's net Official Development Assistance (ODA). This is because such a donor will be among the top twenty donors for that country. The allocation from the PBF to these countries calculated as a percentage of net ODA, using 2007 ODA flow as a baseline, amount to 8 percent for Burundi; 15 percent for Central African Republic; 5 percent for Guinea-Bissau, based only on first tranche allocation; and 7 percent for Sierra Leone.

As of December 2009, the allocation to the four countries on the agenda stood at 32.4 percent of the total PBF portfolio. Moreover, the ratio of PBC Agenda countries allocations to the overall amounts allocated so far stands at 57 percent (see table 4). Clearly, being placed on the agenda of the Commission has its privileges. Nonetheless, as I would argue later, these countries need more financial support.

In addition, some innovative practices for funding-raising in support of peacebuilding have emerged in the PBC. For example, a recent past Chair of the PBC negotiated with Yoko Ono, the musician, to donate to the Peacebuilding Fund the proceeds of sales from the online download of the song "Give Peace a Chance" during the months of November and December 2009. The amount of dollars collected through this arrangement may not be as important as its symbolism: it highlights the extent to which international public figures, including celebrities, show support for and endorse the work of the peacebuilding architecture.

Equally significant, the governments of developed, emerging, and developing countries on the Commission have offered additional financial and technical assistance to the four countries on the agenda of the Commission. Such offers of assistance has stemmed in part from the fact that members of the Commission feel obliged to convey their solidarity by extending support to the countries on the agenda of PBC and in part from the efforts of the Chairpersons of the various country-specific configurations who have written letters to member states requesting support for meeting funding shortfalls for specific programme activities such as elections, for in-kind contributions for police vehicles and other items, and for galvanising members of the PBC to make pledges of contributions at donor roundtables organised for countries on the agenda of the PBC.

3. *Do the countries on the Commission's agenda find the experience helpful to their peacebuilding efforts?* The engagement between the four countries and the Commission is based on the principles of national ownership, partnership, and mutual accountability. The four countries see the members of the Commission as major advocates for international support for their efforts at national political reconciliation, institutional rehabilitation, and economic recovery. In this endeavour, the successive Chairpersons of the Commission and of the various country committees as well the UN missions and departments and agencies in the countries have all played important roles. In as much as the PBC engagement has deepened the partnership and created opportunities for more collaboration among the UN key stakeholders — in the field and at headquarters — working together with the national stakeholders in each country, the UN's helping hand is magnified for the government and people of these countries striving to overcome the legacy of conflict and marching on the pathway to sustainable peace, recovery, and development. Increasingly, the helping hand that comes from being on the Commission's agenda is a highly valued asset for these countries.

Testimonies by the countries on the agenda offer useful insights on this matter. The President of Sierra Leone told the 64th session of UN General Assembly in September 2009 that "the ongoing efforts spearheaded by the PBC continue to strengthen the peace consolidation process in [his] country." The Prime Minister of the Central Africa Republic also told the same session that "the Commission has worked together with the authorities of [his country] to strengthen progress in peace and to allow the implementation of the recommendations of the Inclusive Political Dialogue, organised from 8 to 22 December 2008, notably the Disarmament Demobilisation and Re-integration project, Security Sector Reforms and the process leading to the holding of general elections in 2010."

While the first three tests explore the effectiveness and relevance of the peacebuilding architecture, there is also a test of attractiveness: Are more countries seeking to be considered by the PBC? If countries emerging from conflict consider engagement with the PBC useful, requests to be placed on the PBC agenda will increase. The first two countries — Burundi and Sierra Leone — were placed on the agenda in June 2006. Following a request from the government of Guinea-Bissau in July 2007, the Security Council referred that country for consideration by the PBC in December 2007. A country-specific configuration for Guinea-Bissau was created by the PBC on 19 December 2007. The Central African Republic requested consideration in March 2008 and was placed on the agenda of the PBC on 12 June 2008. This means that on average one country was placed on the PBC agenda every year in its first four years. This was a good record, considering that countries in conflict seldom emerge from conflict at that rate.

In a sign of the growing relevance and attractiveness of another component of the peacebuilding architecture, the Peacebuilding Fund, managed by the Peacebuilding Support Office at UN Headquarters, has extended its reach with fast, relevant and catalytic funding in fifteen countries as of December, 2009 (see table 4). In addition to providing financial assistance to the four countries on the PBC agenda, the PBF supported peacebuilding projects in Côte d'Ivoire, Guinea, Liberia, Nepal, Democratic Republic of Congo, Haiti, Timor-Leste, Kenya, Comoros and Somalia.

Identifying Some Key Challenges

Despite this evidence of progress, there are a number of challenges which need to be addressed. These may be divided into two categories: strategic challenges and operational challenges. The foremost challenge in the first category is ensuring sustainability of the peacebuilding process. Here one might note that there are a variety of perspectives on what constitutes sustainability and how it might be achieved. To some, it implies that PBC engagement would help the peacebuilding efforts so much so that it prevents the country from relapsing into conflict, in particular, avoiding periodic bouts of instability. To others, sustainability means that all efforts in support of peacebuilding initiated with help from PBC should be become self-sustaining through a process of developing national capacities to manage and resolve sources of conflict while addressing the risks factors that may threaten the peacebuilding process itself. Yet, to others, economic recovery and growth holds the key to sustaining peacebuilding. All this confirms that the PBC's role in sustaining peacebuilding must necessarily be multifaceted.

Another challenge is for the Commission to enhance its efforts in marshalling resources for countries on its agenda beyond the allocations from the PBF. Inspite of the innovations in resource mobilisation noted earlier, the countries on the agenda, like most postconflict countries, have huge financing gaps. These gaps are usually reflected in the mismatch between their internally generated revenue and the estimated costs of their peacebuilding or development programmes. The preeminent role of the PBC in marshalling resources is to contribute to closing part of the financing gap, especially on peacebuilding priorities.

Yet another challenge relates to how the Commission can provide advice to the Security Council in countries where peacekeeping operations are being planned or already in existence. Still another challenge is that the Commission determine when and under what conditions a country will "graduate" or "exit" from its agenda. And yet another challenge is that the Commission focus its efforts on providing "extended attention" to the countries on its agenda through galvanising political support for the country's peacebuilding efforts and ensuring coherence for the work of the UN system in these countries.

In the institutional category of challenges may be included such issues as: enhancing the impact in each country of the work of the country-specific configuration, in particular by developing a suitable mechanism to support PBC activities within country; promoting coherence and strengthening collaboration with the UN presence in support of agreed peacebuilding priorities; streamlining the process of developing the Integrated Peacebuilding Strategy such that it responds more flexibly to country-specific contexts–avoiding the tendency of the "one size fits all" approach. The PBC had already launched discussion on the latter issue with the aim of developing a multi-tiered engagement with postconflict countries, simplifying the process of developing the strategic framework and drawing more closely on the priorities in existing frameworks, in the new countries that will come on its agenda.

Looking Forward to the 2010 Review

This preliminary assessment of progress thus far and the challenges ahead have focused on the mandate given to the peacebuilding architecture, in particular to the PBC, in its founding resolutions. Some recent analyses and commentaries have, however, sought to call attention to other issues that the PBC should address such as helping "to prevent conflicts"; "to provide broader political support for aid reform in countries on its agenda"; and "to promote the principle of subsidiarity." Though these issues may intersect with some key functions of the PBC; they cannot be conflated with the Commission's core functions.

It speaks to the high expectations held out for the PBC that it is required to do so much. But there are at least three problems with using such criteria to assess PBC's performance. The first is that there are other UN or international bodies already working in these areas. The second is that these are clearly not within the existing mandate of the PBC. The third — closely related to the second — is that if the PBC attempted to work exclusively on these issues, it would have been accused of exceeding its mandate.

The 2010 Review of the peacebuilding architecture offers an excellent opportunity both to grapple with these challenges and to build on the lessons learnt thus far in order to give new impetus to the functioning and effectiveness of the architecture. The starting point of that review should assess the architecture against the agreed mandate and not critique what it ought to do, which that was not part of the pristine design or original mandate.

Overall, the four countries currently on the agenda of the Commission, as of mid-2010, had become pioneers of sort in a new form of engagement between the international community, through the United Nations, and postconflict countries. The experience gained and lessons learnt from this engagement will prove invaluable to the United Nations in dealing with other postconflict countries around the world.

Table 3: Peacebuilding Priorities Identified in the Strategic Framework for the First Four Countries

Country	Priorities and Challenges	Date of Bi-annual Review
Burundi (2006/2007*)	Promotion of good governance; comprehensive ceasefire agreement between Government of Burundi and PALIPEHUTU-FNL; security sector reform; justice, promotion of human rights and action to combat impunity; the land issue and socioeconomic recovery; mobilisation and coordination of international assistance; subregional dimension; and gender dimension.	June 2008 February 2009 July 2009 MARCH 2010
Sierra Leone (2006/2007*)	Youth employment and empowerment; justice and security sector reform; consolidation of democracy and good governance; capacitybuilding; energy sector; and subregional dimensions of peacebuilding.	June 2008 December 2008 June 2009**
Guinea-Bissau (2007/2008*)	Elections and institution-building for the National Electoral Commission; measures to jumpstart the economy and rehabilitate infrastructure, in particular the energy sector; security sector reform; strengthening of the justice sector, consolidating the rule of law, and fighting against drugtrafficking; public administration reform and modernisation; and social questions critical for peacebuilding.	January 2010***

| Central African Republic (2008/2009*) | Reform of the security sector and disarmament, demobilisation and reintegration; governance – rule of law; and development poles. | December 2009 |

*The first of these years is when the country was placed on the agenda of the PBC; the second is the year that the Strategic Framework was adopted between the PBC and the Country.

** This was formally a High-level Special Session that substituted for the biannual review, which produced an Outcome Document.

*** Although the biannual reviews for this country should have taken place in April 2009 and October 2009, these could not be held because of the prevailing political situation during this period. The PBC review mission to the country took place in January 2010, but the recommendations on the review were adopted on 8 February 2010.

Table 4: PBF Key Figures: Allocations and Projects Approved as of 22 December 2009

		PRF	IRF	Total allocations	PRF	IRF	Total approvals	
Countries on the PBC Agenda	Burundi	$35,000,000	$2,000,000	$37,000,000	$34,623,868	$2,000,000	$36,623,868	20
	Central African Republic*	$25,000,000	$1,000,000	$26,000,000	$10,000,000	$801,975	$10,801,975	13
	Guinea-Bissau	$6,000,000		$6,000,000	$5,793,983		$5,793,983	5
	Sierra Leone	$35,000,000	$1,946,820	$36,946,820	$34,774,102	$1,946,820	$36,720,922	24
	Sub-total	$101,000,000	$4,946,820	$105,946,820	$85,191,953	$4,748,795	$89,940,748	62
Countries not on the PBC Agenda (Priority Plan based)	Comoros	$9,000,000		$9,000,000	$950,000		$950,000	1
	Cote d'Ivoire	$5,000,000	$2,527,000	$7,527,000	$5,000,000	$2,000,000	$7,000,000	3
	DRC	$20,000,000		$20,000,000			$0	
	Guinea-Conakry	$6,000,000	$963,284	$6,963,284	100,000	963,284	$1,063,284	2
	Liberia	$15,000,000	$1,719,470	$16,719,470	$14,537,394	$1,719,470	$16,256,864	25
	Nepal	$10,000,000		$10,000,000	$6,755,830		$6,755,830	4
	Sub-total	$65,000,000	$5,209,754	$70,209,754	$27,343,224	$4,682,754	$32,025,978	35
	Total (PBC & non PBC)	$166,000,000	$10,156,574	$176,156,574	$112,535,177	$9,431,549	$121,966,726	97
Others countries (Project based)	Haiti*		$3,800,000	$3,800,000		$800,000	$800,000	2
	Kenya		$1,000,000	$1,000,000		$1,000,000	$1,000,000	1

Table 4: PBF Key Figures: Allocations and Project Approved as of December 2009

Timor-Leste		$993,625	$993,625		$993,625	$993,625	1
Somalia		$1,000,000	$1,000,000		$1,000,000	$1,000,000	1
Sri Lanka*		$3,000,000	$3,000,000			$0	1
	$0	$9,793,625	$9,793,625		$3,793,625	$3,793,625	6
Grand total	$166,000,000	$19,950,199	$185,950,199	$112,535,177	$13,225,174	$125,760,351	103

Key Indicators

Ratio of PBC Agenda Countries allocations//Overall portfolio (%)		32.4%	27.5%
Ratio of PBC Agenda Countries allocations// Allocated amount (%)		57.0%	71.5%
Ratio of PBC Agenda Countries allocations// Other countries		132.4%	251.1%

Total Portfolio	$327,316,550

* - These were new PBF allocations at the time

SOURCE: *Peacebuilding Fund December 2009.*

Chapter 4

Leading the Peacebuilding Commission: An Institutional History in the Making*

Introduction

As the work of the PBC[1] has evolved, a frequently encountered question is what role does the Chair of the PBC play. A simple answer to this question is that the Chair, at best, serves as "the conductor of a symphony orchestra" — an orchestra that consists of what the founding resolution describes as the PBC configurations. These include the Organisational Committee, the Country-specific Configurations (they are currently six, one each for six countries on the agenda of the PBC) and the Working Group on Lessons Learnt (WGLL). The Organisational Committee is the body that serves, more or less, as the plenary of the PBC. The Country-specific configuration is the forum where issues pertaining to the individual countries are discussed. The origin and functions of the Working Group on Lessons Learnt are discussed in the next section.

---

* Originally published by Global Governance Institute (GGI) "Views from Practice" no.1/2013, March 2013 (Brussels: Global Governance Institute).

Some of the Chairs interviewed for this chapter expressed the view that they saw their role as extending beyond "the conductor of a symphony orchestra". They also saw their role as "proactive leader" taking initiatives on a range of issues, facilitating various negotiations on practices that have been adopted by PBC and managing the web of relationships among the PBC configurations and between the PBC as well as other inter-governmental bodies and international institutions with which the PBC developed partnerships during their tenures.

Leading the various configurations is a shared responsibility among the Chair of the PBC, assisted by the Vice-chairs, and the Chair of the WGLL, as well as the Chairs of the various configurations. This chapter, however, focuses only on the leadership of the organisational committee (see table 5 for the list of the past Chairs and Vice-chairs of the PBC). The role and the contributions of the country-specific configurations have been detailed by the author in other chapters of this book.[2] For this reason, the list does not include the Chairs of the country-specific configurations.

This chapter represents the first attempt in the literature on PBC to examine the main highlights of the Commission's work under successive Chairs of the PBC, reflecting their individual priorities and contributions, since the PBC's inauguration in June 2006. This is essentially an unexplored issue in the growing literature on the PBC. This chapter examines the first six years of the PBC (2006-2012), and its approach is to highlight three main contributions of each chair during their tenure.

The chapter is predicated on the belief that the growth of any new intergovernmental institution critically depends on the creative adjustments made by the successive leadership, as the institution evolves. Such adjustments are necessarily incremental, borne out of persistent experimentation. This assessment drew on the insights of those who were and have been present since the establishment of the PBC, on the annual reports of the PBC and on other related documents, and from conversations with the successive Chairpersons themselves. The author was fortunate that all the Chairpersons of the Organisational Committee of the PBC for the period covered in this chapter were still serving in one capacity or the other in New York when the author interviewed them.

Laying the Foundation: June 2006 to June 2007

The first year of the PBC was devoted to laying the foundation for the work of the Commission. Much of that effort concentrated on designing the institutional processes to ensure the effective functioning of the Commission. The three most significant contributions during the tenure of the first Chair were: (1) making a decision to admit institutional donors pursuant to paragraph 9 of the founding resolution; (2) establishing the Working Group on Lessons Learnt; and (3) drawing attention to the need to make funding available for PBC field visits.

In paragraph 9 of the founding resolution establishing the PBC, it was stated that "representatives from the World Bank and the International Monetary Fund and other institutional donors shall be invited to participate in all meetings of the Commission." Selecting the other institutional donors was one of the major decisions of this period. The Chair led the consultations that resulted in the agreement to invite the European Union and the Organisation of Islamic Cooperation as the two other organisations that met the criteria of institutional donors and allowed them to participate in the formal meetings of the OC and the configurations, (as non-voting members).

Brokered by the Chair, the creation of the Working Group on Lessons Learnt was both an act of institutional innovation and a consolation prize. It was an innovation because the Working Group was not explicitly envisaged in the founding resolution. Once created, it became a vehicle for giving practical effect to the founding resolution's requirement "to develop the best practices" for peacebuilding, a function envisioned for the Commission in paragraph 1(c) and for the Peacebuilding Support Office in paragraph 23. It was a consolation prize because the decision to establish the Working Group and assign it to one of the Vice-chairs came after that Vice-chair failed to secure the position of Chair of the country-specific configuration for Sierra Leone. Once selected, the first Chair of the Working Group held the position for three-and-half years(mid-2006 to end of 2009). The issues that the Working Group focused on during that period are contained in the publication titled "Emerging Lessons and Practices in Peacebuilding, 2007-2009".[3]

In its first year of work, experience showed the usefulness of PBC field visits to the countries on its agenda. Such visits not only gave the members of the Commission an opportunity to interact with the key stakeholders in the country but also enabled them to assess progress in peacebuilding. Field visits were designed to realize the objectives that the modality of videoconferencing suggested in paragraph 19 of the founding resolution could not. The first annual report on the work of the PBC, negotiated under the guidance of the Chair's team, at the end of the first session of the PBC laid the foundation for financing of PBC visits from the regular budget. In it, the Commission argued that as part of its working methods, the Commission had "decided to organise field missions to the countries under consideration, and in light of their usefulness for the work of the Commission, it intended to continue undertaking such missions...in that context, the Commission wished to bring to the attention of the Assembly the fact that the issue of financing such missions needed to be appropriately considered, and that such consideration could include all options, taking into account the fact that the Commission was a new body."[4] The task of taking this proposal forward fell on the next chair of the PBC.

During this year of laying the foundation for the PBC, the Chair recognised — and emphasised — that two considerations must guide the work of the Commission for it to be credible: (1) strengthening the national ownership of the peacebuilding efforts by the countries on the agenda; and (2) ensuring that its work was results-oriented to build the confidence of both the countries on the agenda and the partner countries, both developed and developing, that make various contributions to support the agenda countries.

Pushing the Envelope: July 2007 to December 2008

This period, July 2007 to December 2008, the longest by any Chair, witnessed the pushing of the envelope, both literally and figuratively, on many fronts. The key actions included ensuring that PBC field visits were funded from the regular budget rather than from individual contributions by Chairs of configurations; mobilising resources from private organisations; and initiating discussion on developing criteria for placing more countries on the agenda of PBC.

As a follow-up to the first annual report, the Chair of the PBC, during this period, wrote to the President of the General Assembly, bringing to the latter's attention the need for the question of financing of the PBC field missions to be allocated to the Fifth Committee for consideration.[5] This letter was referred to the fifth Committee for discussion, which in turn requested the Secretary-General to produce a report.[6]

The Secretary-General's note provided not only the cost estimates for the field missions for the biennium but also proposed the number and composition of the PBC field visits that have governed those visits up till now. It suggested one field visit by a PBC delegation comprising of seven members: the Chair of the configuration, one member each from the five regional groups, and the representative of the country on the agenda. Allowance was also made for the Chairs of the country-specific configurations to undertake solo visits, as "certain circumstances may warrant." The sum of $676, 300 was proposed in the 2008-2009 biennium[7] for the field visits. This opened the way to financing this core work of the PBC from the regular budget and eliminated the need to fund these by self-financing or other forms of contribution that would have considerably weakened this important modality of the PBC's work.

As part of the effort to fulfill the PBC mandate on resource mobilisation, the Organisational Committee held a discussion on the theme "The Role of the Private Sector in Peacebuilding: Contribution by the Peacebuilding Commission." The Chair assigned a Facilitator to lead a working level discussion to "focus on tangible ways that the Commission could contribute to strengthening of the role of private sector in post-conflict peacebuilding...with consideration given to three specific areas: microfinance, remittances and partnerships with foundations."[8] The Facilitator (Indonesia) produced a report entitled *The Outcome of the PBC Task Force on Private Sector*, dated 2 April 2008, which made a number of proposals on how PBC can strengthen its links with the private sector with a view to attracting private capital to countries on the agenda.

The Chair explained that his focus on the role of the private sector, as a source of resource mobilisation, and his efforts to develop partnerships with the international financial institutions (he was the first PBC Chair to visit the IMF on 14 February 2008 and the World Bank on 31 March 2008)[9] reflected his strong belief and deeply-felt commitment to highlight the importance of the economic dimension of peacebuilding. This was at a time when some members of the PBC argued that the focus of its work should be on the political rather than the economic dimension.

With more countries requesting placement on the agenda during this period, there was a keenly-felt need to reflect further on the criteria for considering such requests. In as much as paragraph 12 of the founding resolution had outlined the routes through which a country could be referred to the PBC, it did not indicate what criteria should be used in making the decision on the referrals.

The Chair convened two informal discussions on the subject on 16 October and 19 November 2007 and subsequently produced an informal paper[10] for discussion at the Organisational Committee. The paper set out two sets of criteria: procedural considerations and country-specific considerations. Concerning the former, the paper suggested that the number of countries that the PBC places on its agenda should be based on the capacity of the PBC and the PBSO; the PBC should be kept fully apprised by the referring bodies mentioned in paragraph 12 of the founding resolution; and each referral should focus on specific peacebuilding challenges appropriate for each country. In so far as country-specific considerations are concerned, the paper proposed that the requesting country demonstrate willingness, ownership, and determination to work with PBC; and the expectations of the requesting countries concerning the nature and scope of PBC support (value added) should be mutually agreed upon and spelt out in the instrument of engagement between the PBC and the requesting country.

Broadening the PBC's Outreach and Improving its Engagement Process: 2009

The three most significant highlights of the year 2009 were developing the PBC's partnerships with regional organisations, extending the outreach to Philanthropic Foundations, and improving the country-engagement process of the county-specific configurations.

The main initiative on broadening partnerships related to the Chair's visits to three regional institutions: the Organisation of American States in March 2009, the European Union Commission in May 2009, and the Chairs Group visit to Africa Union in November 2009. Each of these visits marked the first time that the Chair of the Commission or the Chair's Group travelled to those institutions for policy dialogue. The PBC leadership's main message in all those policy dialogues was similar, namely to advocate that leaders and senior officials of those institutions work closely with the PBC in advancing the cause of peacebuilding.

In the case of the visit to the African Union, the Chair's Group held a formal meeting with the AU Peace and Security Council (AU-PSC). At that meeting the member states of the AU-PSC, while expressing appreciation for inclusion of four African countries — at that time — on the agenda of the PBC, called on the PBC to take on more African countries. Thus, in the press statement issued at the end of the meeting, the AU-PSC "reiterated its encouragement to the Peacebuilding Commission to pursue and intensify its efforts in order to effectively contribute to the consolidation of peace in Africa and the recovery of countries of countries emerging from conflict....and encouraged the PBC to consider expanding its activities to other African countries in postconflict situations."[11] The meeting also produced an agreement on holding "an annual joint meeting of the Commission and the Peace and Security Council of the African Union [which] would be held back to back with the annual consultative meetings between members of the Security Council and the Peace and Security Council."[12] The need for a strong partnership between the AU and the PBC was well recognised by the AU, when it urged for the establishment of "a relationship between the UN Peacebuilding Commission and the AU with regard to the AU's Postconflict Reconstruction and Development (PRCD) programmes on the continent ...[and]... institutionalised partnership between the AU Multidimensional Committee on PRCD and the United Nations Peacebuilding

Commission, the Peacebuilding Support Office at the UN Secretariat, and other concerned departments of the UN."[13]

The idea that the PBC should work with and benefit from philanthropic foundations began to take hold during this period. The seeds of those efforts were sown when the Chair made contacts with prominent individuals in the arts and music. Foremost were his several meetings with Yoko Ono, whom he met on 3 March and 3 December 2009. The Chair stated that "following his conversations with artist and pro-peace activist Yoko Ono, she had partnered with EMI Music, Sony/ATV Music Publishing and iTunes to donate to the Peacebuilding Fund all proceeds from the sale, in the last quarter of 2009, of a commemorative fortieth anniversary digital single of the song 'Give Peace a Chance', written by her late husband, John Lennon."[14]

Four countries had come on the agenda by 2009: Burundi (2006), Sierra Leone (2006), Guinea-Bissau (2007), and the Central African Republic (2008). The coming on the PBC agenda of more countries prompted a reflection on how to reduce the transaction costs of their international engagement. In response, the PBSO prepared a paper[15] on improving the process of PBC engagement for discussion at the Organisational Committee. The paper focused on four key issues aimed at reducing the transaction costs of engagement both to the PBC and to the countries on the agenda: reducing the frequency and number of PBC meetings and especially of the country configurations (see table 6 for the declining trends in number of meetings); reducing the timeline for developing and completing the instrument of engagement; simplifying the instrument of engagement by focusing on a few, selected peacebuilding priorities; and improving the sequencing of some the activities of the country-specific configurations, for example, between the allocation of the PBF and the development of the instrument of engagement.

The discussion on these issues, conducted under the leadership of the Chair, subsequently resulted in the first round of changes to the process of engagement between the PBC and the countries on its agenda. The changes included, for example, replacing the strategic framework for peacebuilding with the statement of mutual commitments as the instrument of engagement between the PBC and the countries on its agenda; reducing the number of peacebuilding priorities in the statement of mutual commitments; increasing the timeline for the periodic review of the instrument of engagement; and significantly reducing the time devoted to developing and adopting the instrument of engagement. The progress made on the last component is reflected in table 7 — which shows that it took about one-third of the time for completing the development of the instruments of engagement for the last two countries that came on the agenda (Liberia in 2010 and Guinea in 2011) compared with that of the first four countries. Taken together, these changes represented the first steps in moving the PBC towards what is now commonly referred to as a "light PBC engagement". Even so, there was growing recognition that more needed to be done in improving the process — a theme that the cofacilitators of the 2010 Review highlighted in their report.

The Year of the First Quintennial Review of the Peacebuilding Architecture and its Follow-up: 2010

The PBC annual report covering this period put it best when it stated that 2010 "coincided with the mandated five-year review of the United Nations peacebuilding architecture. While the review process was distinct from the ongoing work of the Commission, the latter focused its activities on key issues which have been subsequently highlighted [in] the Review Recommendations."[16]

The 2010 Review of the UN peacebuilding architecture was led by a team of three facilitators — consisting of the three Permanent Representatives to the United Nations from Ireland, Mexico, and South Africa — appointed jointly by the UN General Assembly and the Security Council. They submitted their report to the President of the General Assembly and the President of the Security Council in a letter dated 19 July 2010.[17] By the time the report was submitted in July 2010, the Commission was half way through its work for the year. Nonetheless, the orientation of the Commission's work not only cohered with the main findings of the 2010 Review but was also subsequently inspired by its recommendations.

The three major highlights of the Commission's work during this year included a policy discussion on Partnerships for peacebuilding; strengthening interactions with the Security Council; and developing an annual roadmap for the implementation of the 2010 Review.

On 23 March 2010, the PBC Chair convened a policy discussion on Partnerships for Peacebuilding to which he invited the African Union, the European Union, the International Monetary Fund, the Organisation of Islamic Conference, and the World Bank. "The discussion centred on four types of partnerships, namely, partnership for a common vision for engagement in a country; partnership for improved coordination; partnership for advocacy and political support; and partnership for financial resources mobilisation. On 23 June, the Chair followed up by convening a discussion with the World Bank …to address a number of critical issues on the basis of which the Commission and the bank could build on their evolving partnerships in the countries on the agenda."[18]

The Chair also devoted much time and effort to cultivating ties with the Security Council and the General Assembly. Thus, the Chair was invited to and addressed the Security Council during the debates on transition and exit strategies (12 February); postconflict peacebuilding (16 April); and the Secretary-General's progress report on peacebuilding in the immediate aftermath of conflict (13 October). He also participated in an informal Security Council retreat hosted by the government of Turkey and the International Peace Institute on the theme "At Crossroads of Peacekeeping, Peacemaking, and Peacebuilding" held in Istanbul on 25 and 26 June, 2010. The Chair also participated in the high-level thematic debate organised by the General Assembly to mark the tenth anniversary of the report of the Panel on United Nations Peace Operations (Brahimi Panel report) on 22 June 2010.[19] These efforts anticipated and were consistent with one of the recommendations of the 2010 Review relating to strengthening relationships with the principal organs of the UN.

Recognising the importance of taking forward the recommendations from the 2010 Review of the United Nations peacebuilding architecture, the Chair suggested, towards the end of that year, developing an annual Roadmap of Actions for their implementation beginning in 2011. The recommendations emanating from the Review were wide ranging, covering such issues as national capacity building; intensifying resource mobilisation efforts; lightening the administrative burden of PBC engagements; focusing on the developmental aspects of peacebuilding; enhancing coherence and coordination among various actors; improving the working methods of the organisational committee; clarifying the rationale for discussions in the working group on lessons learnt; developing approaches for multitiered engagement; articulating entry and exit criteria for PBC engagement; strengthening key relationships with the Security Council, the General Assembly, and the Economic and Social Council; and enhancing partnerships with key regional and international actors, etc.

The articulation of an annual Roadmap of Actions for implementing the recommendations of the 2010 Review not only gave a sharper focus to the work of the Commission but also imposed stricter prioritisation in the annual programme of the Commission's work. In many important respects, 2010 was a turning point in the work of the PBC because the issues that it addressed that year — from defining partnerships to strengthening relationships with principal organs to developing an annual Roadmap of Actions for 2010 — have become the touchstone of PBC work in subsequent years.

Taking Forward the 2010 Review: 2011

The 2011 Roadmap of Actions[20] marked the first year of the beginning of what would be a multiyear effort to implement the recommendations of the 2010 Review. The Chairperson for 2011 focused on three key issues: national capacity building; sharing experiences in lessons learnt in postconflict peacebuilding; and building partnership and resource mobilisation.

The Chair convened two meetings of the Organisational Committee to focus on national capacity development. One meeting provided an opportunity for the Organisational Committee to dialogue with the Senior Advisory Group on the Review of Civilian Capacity in the Aftermath of Conflict; and the other, for a discussion between the Organisational Committee and the UNDP. In regard to the former, the PBC "expressed interest in at least one of the countries on the agenda [of PBC] becoming a pilot for implementation of partnership arrangements that draw on the capacities from the global South."[21] In the dialogue with the latter, PBC members "stressed the need for a United Nations system-wide approach to capacity development for peacebuilding and such an approach would give balanced attention to strengthening security and economic capacities in countries emerging from conflict."[22]

Providing a platform for sharing experiences in postconflict peacebuilding is one of the most important contributions that PBC can make to peacebuilding. Seeking to advance this aspect of PBC work, the Chair encouraged his government to convene the High-Level Meeting on Peace and Statebuilding: The Rwandan Experience which was held in Kigali on 8-9 November 2011. The event was organised by the Government of Rwanda, in collaboration with the PBC and the AfDB. The meeting "represented an innovative effort by the Commission to serve as a platform for promoting experience-sharing between countries that have undergone peacebuilding and statebuilding processes and those engaged in or embarking on similar process...the meeting focused on critical peacebuilding challenges, such as inclusive ownership; innovative approaches to nation-building and socio-economic development; and strategic use of aid."[23] Participants at that meeting were drawn from the countries on the PBC agenda as well as non–PBC agenda countries.

Another major highlight of PBC work during this year was the first ever visit by the Chairs Group to the temporary headquarters of the African Development Bank in Tunis in November 2011. Initiated by the Chair, this visit was made possible in part because of the personal friendship between the President of the AfDB and the Chair of PBC, who are compatriots. The major objective of the visit was to develop and "deepen collaboration between the PBC and the AfDB and explore how both institutions could jointly support peacebuilding priorities in African countries on the Commission's agenda."[24] The visit was a "path-breaking" event that has produced consequential results. A key outcome of the visit was the adoption of a Minutes of Consultations between the PBC and the AfDB that identified specific areas of collaboration.

In the follow-up to that visit, the AfDB and the PBC have supported and participated in the Donors Conference on Burundi held in Geneva, Switzerland, on 29-30 October 2012; the AfDB has invited the PBSO to comment on their country-strategy paper for the Central African Republic and has agreed to collaborate with PBSO in providing support to Guinea-Conakry in natural resources management. In Liberia, the PBC and AfDB have agreed to collaborate in supporting decentralisation, including revenue generation and public financial management at sub-national levels; disarmament, demobilisation, and reintegration; youth employment creation; regional integration and trade; and natural resources management and transparency and accountability in extractive industries; and strengthening political dialogue for programme purposes.[25]

The Implementation of 2010 Review Enters its Second Year: 2012

The 2012 Annual Roadmap for the implementation of the recommendations of the 2010 Review carried forward a number of the issues that were in the 2011 Roadmap for Actions. This reflected the emphasis that the 2010 Review had placed on such issues. For example, the Review called on the PBC to "intensify [its] overall resource mobilisation efforts."[26] Thus two of the three major highlights during this year were resource mobilisation and building partnerships with IFIs.

The first major highlight related to the effort to further develop the PBC's work in the area of resource mobilisation. Although the Organisational Committee of the PBC has had discussions on some aspects of resource mobilisation in 2008 and 2009; and the Working Group on Lessons Learnt had also organised discussions in 2010 and 2011; the PBC's policy discussion on resource mobilisation on 9 July 2012 was the first time that it undertook an in-depth and comprehensive review of the topic.

The panel discussion convened by the Chair had before it a paper prepared by the PBSO[27] which covered a wide range of issues, including enhancing national ownership and leadership in resource mobilisation, developing new approaches to mapping of peacebuilding finance, forging partnerships and coordination,

> **Box 2: Improved Synergy Between the PBC and the PBF**
>
> The synergy between the PBC and the PBF has improved considerably over the years. In the 2009 revision of the PBF Terms of Reference, automatic eligibility for PBF funding by countries on PBC agenda was agreed.[1] More recently, PBSO has worked to more closely align peacebuilding priorities in PBC's instruments of engagement and PBF programme support. The extent of progress in the improved synergy is highlighted by their on-going work in Liberia. There, the PBF and the PBC experimented with a new approach, which was to encourage the design of a larger Peacebuilding Programme, to which the PBF would provide catalytic support. The Liberia Peacebuilding Programme mirrors the priorities in the PBC's Statement of Mutual Commitments. Similarly in Guinea-Conakry, the PBF's strategy followed closely on the heels of the Statement of Mutual Commitments produced in mid-2011. The PBSO is also improving its standard operating procedures to increase synergies. For example in its new guidelines, the PBF has added systematic consultation of the PBC Chairs of Country Specific Configurations on programme decisions, and opportunities have been sought for the PBF staff to accompany the Chairs of Configurations on their country visits. A new dimension to strengthening PBC-PBF synergy is the growing recognition of the need to empower Chairs of the PBC country configurations to discuss with the missions the peacebuilding priorities that the PBF can fund in the countries on the agenda. As of December 2012, the six countries on the agenda of the PBC have received approximately 60 percent of the cumulative allocations from the PBF.
>
> ---
>
> [1] This is based on the Terms of Reference of the PBF; see (A/63/818; 13 April 2009, TOR 3.1, page 6).

engaging the private sector, supporting the local private sector, strengthening intermediation the role of local financial institutions, south-south cooperation, outreach to philanthropic foundations, and leveraging the PBC-Peacebuilding Fund (PBF) synergy (see box 2 on this issue).

The discussion itself at the OC led to a "general acknowledgement of the need to map resource flows as a tool which could help in identifying gaps and stimulate the development of effective national aid management and coordination systems. Other areas identified included the support of the Commission for the organisation of donor conferences and the engagement with other donors, such as foundations and philanthropic organisations."[28]

The second major highlight was related to deepening the partnership between the PBC and the World Bank. Although two of the previous Chairs of the PBC and most of the Chairs of the PBC country configurations had visited the World Bank to hold discussions with senior officials at that institution, there had been no meeting with the Executive Board. The Chair successfully pressed for a meeting between the PBC Chairs Group and selected Executive Directors on 13 September 2012 at the World Bank in Washington DC; the first time the PBC and the World Bank met at the level of their inter-governmental bodies. The meeting agreed on several specific measures to deepen collaboration between the two entities, most notably to strengthen policy-level dialogue between the PBC and the World Bank management and Board of Directors at headquarters level; to identify specific examples of existing collaboration that would be further scaled-up; to explore ways to strengthen alignment between the PBC's Statement of Mutual Commitments and the World Bank's Country Assistance Strategy.[29]

Reflecting the shared commitment to strengthen policy-level dialogue between the two institutions, a follow-up meeting that brought together the PBC Chair's Group and selected World Bank Executive Directors was held in New York on 3 December, 2012. The New York meeting agreed on a few specific actions to take the collaboration forward, including developing a joint calendar of events/activities; undertaking follow-up actions on a range of sector-specific issues in Liberia (youth employment, mining and public finance management); Sierra Leone (addressing gaps which might emerge after the prospective draw-down of United Nations Integrated Peacebuilding Mission in Sierra Leone); and Guinea-Bissau (extending the pilot work on Global Employment Facility to this country).[30]

The Third major highlight was the Chair's decision to convene a high level Event on 25 September, 2012 in the margins of the 67th session of the United Nations General Assembly under the theme "Peacebuilding: The Way Towards Sustainable Peace and Security." The theme of the meeting had been foreshadowed in the inaugural speech of the PBC Chair in January 2012, when he said that "we look forward to meet your expectations and more importantly, to achieve sustaining peace and stability on the ground."[31]

When the Chair first mooted the idea of a high level event, it encountered some scepticism as regards its value and purpose. However, the meeting eventually attracted the participation of a number of Heads of State and governments, and several Ministers of Foreign Affairs as well as senior officials from the capitals. The meeting achieved its two stated objectives: to engage political leaders and high-ranking officials from capitals in peacebuilding efforts, and to provide a platform for UN member states to reaffirm their political commitment to peacebuilding and to encourage their active participation in PBC. Thus, in the Political Declaration adopted at the end of the meeting, the leaders "re-affirm our commitment to addressing the short- and long-term needs of postconflict countries towards achieving sustainable peace through security and development."[32] The Declaration also underlined the need to adhere to a number of key principles which experience has shown are essential to successful peacebuilding efforts to avoid costly relapse into conflict. Equally important, the convening of the high-level event opened the possibility of holding an annual session of the PBC with the participation senior officials' from capital cities, an idea that subsequently gained much traction among some members of the PBC.[33]

Conclusions: Some Major Institutional Issues

This chapter would be incomplete if it did not highlight some current or anticipate possible institutional challenges that lie ahead. The term institutional challenge is used here, in a very broad sense, to refer to any issue that will affect the effectiveness, functioning, and impact of the PBC. Following the pattern adopted in this chapter, I want to identify three such challenges, in no particular order of priority.

It is now a standard cliché that an important measure of the PBC's effectiveness will be its impact in the field — that is in the countries on its agenda. There are many ways that the impact of the PBC can be created or magnified. One of them is by working with the Joint Steering Committee (JSC) — an institutional mechanism that will help the PBC achieve policy coherence and programme coordination in the countries on its agenda. Although the first generation of JSCs was established as tools for managing PBF-funded projects, they have increasingly become mechanisms for broad-based discussion on peacebuilding priorities. The JSC mechanisms have proven to be an important local counterpart to the PBC in some country contexts. In so far as the JSC is typically cochaired by the ranking UN representative in the country, it is also another vehicle for deepening the interface between the PBC country-configurations and the Secretary-General's most senior representative in country. A JSC can also serve as a useful forum for reflecting on evolving peacebuilding priorities and monitoring PBF projects performance as well as developing progress reports on PBC instruments of engagement.

Financing is key to peacebuilding. Several representatives of the governments of the countries on the agenda as well as heads of UN missions have argued that well-articulated peacebuilding strategies are meaningless, if not adequately funded. The PBC, however, faces a two-fold financing challenge: (1)being able to mobilise adequate financial resources for the agreed upon peacebuilding priorities for countries on its agenda, well beyond what the PBF can provide; and (2) coping with the dwindling regular budgetary outlays for its field visits. Without much success on the former, progress in peacebuilding will be limited and without adequate funding for the latter function, the ability of PBC to interact with key national stakeholders, to assess progress in peacebuilding, and to bring its support to bear on national efforts will be reduced. The onset of the global economic and financial crisis in 2007, so soon after the PBC was established in 2006, created an unfavourable backdrop for the PBC to fully realise its full potential in mobilising resources for countries on its agenda. At the same time, the severe budgetary constraint under which the United Nations has operated might make it increasingly difficult for the PBC to perform some of its mandated functions, in particular the field visits to countries on the agenda and to the international financial institutions.

Of all the principal organs of the United Nations, the Security Council is the one that the PBC has historically sought to deepen relationships. The PBC needs to sustain those efforts. There is a very practical reason for this: so far five of the six countries on the agenda of the PBC were referred through the Security Council. The sixth – Guinea-Conakry – applied directly to the PBC. There is an additional consideration which was articulated in the 2010 Review when it noted that "there is a widely held view that Security Council deliberations would benefit from the Commission's advice at an early stage in framing of peacekeeping mandates, on relevant aspects during the lifetime of missions and as drawdown approaches."[34] This is in line with the role envisaged for the Commission in paragraph 16 of the founding resolution.

As this chapter has shown, beginning with the 2010 Review, the PBC has intensified its efforts to actively cultivate the Security Council. The Security Council has reciprocated that gesture by inviting both the Chair of the PBC and of the country configurations to its formal deliberations on relevant themes and countries. As peacebuilding issues increasingly loom large on peacekeeping missions and special political missions, the Security Council should assign specific tasks to the PBC on which it needs advice of PBC. This approach of specifically tasking the PBC to report on particular issues in countries on its agenda, which was applied during the German presidency in September 2012 in the invitation to the Chairs of Liberia and Sierra Leone, is a model that holds much promise in fulfilling the mutual expectations of both bodies.

Table 5. List of PBC Chairpersons and Vice-Chairs (2006-2012)

Chairpersons and Vice-chairs	Term
Chair: H.E. Mr. Ismael A. Gaspar Martins (Angola); Vice-chairs: H.E. Mrs. Carmen Gallardo Hernandez (El Salvador), H.E Mr. Johan Løvald (Norway)	23 June 2006 - 22 June 2007
Chair: H.E. Mr. Yukio Takasu (Japan); Vice-chairs: H.E. Mrs. Carmen Gallardo Hernandez (El Salvador), H.E. Mr. Leslie Kojo Christian (Ghana)	23 June 2007 - 31 December 2008
Chair: H.E. Mr. Heraldo Muñoz (Chile); Vice -chairs: H.E. Mr. Park In-kook (Republic of Korea)	1 January 2009 - 31 December 2009
Chair: H.E. Mr. Peter Wittig (Germany); Vice-chairs: H.E. Mr. Martin Palouš (Czech Republic), H.E. Mr. Jean-Francois Zinsou (Benin)	1 January 2010 - 31 December 2010
Chair: H.E. Mr. Eugène-Richard Gasana (Rwanda); Vice-chairs: H.E. Mr. Gert Rosenthal (Guatemala), H.E. Mr. Yuri Sergeyev (Ukraine)	1 January 2011 - 31 December 2011
Chair: H.E. Mr. Abulkalam Abdul Momen (Bangladesh); Vice-chairs: H. E. Mr. Ranko Vilović (Croatia), H.E. Ms. Mwaba Patricia Kasese-Bota (Zambia)	1 January - 31 December 2012

Source: UN Peacebuilding Support Office.

Table 6. Number of PBC Meetings (2006-2012)

Configuration/ Years	2006/ 2007	2007/ 2008	2009	2010	2011	2012	Total
OC (total)	19	25	15	10	13	11	93
Informal OC	6	17	10	7	10	8	58
Formal OC	13	8	5	3	3	3	35
WGLL	3	12	4	4	4	2	29
CSCs (total)	23	65	22	22	29	21	182
Informal CSCs	13	50	19	18	26	17	143
Formal CSCs	10	15	3	4	3	4	39
Number of Countries on PBC Agenda	2	4	4	5	6	6	
Total	45	102	41	36	46	34	304

Source: Compiled from documents at UN Peacebuilding Support Office.

The number of PBC formal and informal meetings per annum have declined over time both in absolute and relative terms. In relative terms, the way to confirm this is to calculate the number of meetings per PBC configuration per annum. The formula to apply is: 2+nc=, where 2 stands for OC and WGLL and nc= number of countries on the agenda. Thus we use the gross total of meetings of OC, WGLL, and CSC meetings divided by the number of the configurations at the time. This will yield for 2006-2007, 45/4=11.2 meeting per configuration for that year; 2007-2008, 102/6=17; 2009, 41/6=6.8; 2010, 36/7=5.1; 2011, 46/8=5.75; and 2012, 34/8 =4.2.

[Note also that the uptick in the 2007-2008 period was because the session was for 18 not 12 months.]

Table 7. Comparative Timeline for Completing Instruments of Engagement — Strategic Framework/Statement of Mutual Commitments

Country	Number of Months		Date of Adoption
	Informal Adoption	Final Adoption	
Burundi (SF)	8*	14	(20 June 2007)
Sierra Leone (PCF)	(-)	14 **	(12 December 2007)
Guinea-Bissau (SF)	6	8	(1 October 2008)
Central African Republic (SF)	7.75	10	(6 May 2009)

....

*Strategic framework formally adopted without monitoring mechanism.
** The preparation of the SF was suspended during period leading to the 2007 elections.
(-) There was no informal adoption.
....

Average   7.25 (3 countries)   11.5

Liberia (SMC) + 21 days = (0.70 month)   1.30 (15 November 2010)
+ Between dates that PBC mission report was presented to,
  and its informal/formal adoption, by the country configuration
Guinea (SMC)+ (Between Chair's mission and adoption) 4.5 (23 Sept. 2011)

Average for first 4 countries: 11.5 months; and for 6 countries: 8.63 months.

Abbreviations:
SF= Strategic Framework for Peacebuilding
PCF= Peacebuilding Cooperation Framework
SMC= Statement of Mutual Commitment on Peacebuilding

Source: Compiled from data at UN Peacebuilding Support Office.

Notes to Chapter 4. *Leading The Peacebuilding Commission: An Institutional History in the Making*

1. Although the decision to create the PBC was agreed in the World Summit Outcome Document (A/60/1 of 24 October 2005) and the enabling resolutions establishing the body were adopted by General Assembly in Resolution A/60/180 and Security Council in Resolution S/1645 (2005) on 20 December 2005; the inaugural meeting of the PBC was held on 23 June 2006.
2. see, for example, chapters 1, 2, and 5 of this book..
3. see Report on the Working Group on Lessons Learnt of the Peacebuilding Commission, May 2010.
4. see Report of the Peacebuilding Commission on its first session, UN Doc.A/62/137-S/2007/458, 25 July 2007 page 16.
5. This letter is contained in UN Doc. A/62/493 dated 18 October 2007
6 see Financing field missions of the Peacebuilding Commission: Note by Secretary-General,,(A/62/670 of 31 January 2008.
7. The actual expenditure for the field visits for 2008-009 was US$593,200 but in in subsequent biennia the allocations were US$495,000 for 2010-2011 and US$455,000 for 2012-2013 (see Supplementary Financial Information for Advisory Committee on Administrative and Budgetary Questions: Proposed Programme Budget for 2012-2013 in UN Doc. A/66/6(section 3 of 31 May 2011, page 44.
8. Report of the Peacebuilding Commission on its second session , A/63/92-S/2008/417 of 24 June 2008, page 5.
9. Ibid,, page 4.
10. This paragraph draws on the Chairman's non-paper entitled "Points To Be Cconsidered for Adding a New Country to the Peacebuilding Commission agenda", 26 November 2007.
11. See AU PSC Press Statement (PSC/PR/BR/CCVIII) issued at the end of its 208th Meeting on 9 November 2009.
12. Report of the Peacebuilding Commission on its fourth session, UN Doc. A/65/701- S/2011/41 of 28 January 2011, page 22.
13. See para.6 of the AU Executive Council Decision on the AU Policy Framework on Postconflict Reconstruction and Development, EX.CL/274(1X0 of July 2006 in Banjul, The Gambia.
14. Report of the Peacebuilding Commission on its third session, UN Doc. A/64/341-S/2009/444 of 8 September 2009, page 4 and Report of the Peacebuilding Commission on its fourth session, UN Doc. A/65/701-S/2011/41 of 28 January 2011, page 5.
15. The paper was entitled "Improving the Country Specific Meetings: A New Approach for New Countries Coming on the agenda of PBC", dated 9 October, 2009.

16. Report of the Peacebuilding Commission on its fourth session, UN Doc. A/65/701- S/2011/41 of 28 January 2011, page 1.
17. Review of the United Nations Peacebuilding Architecture, UN Doc. A/64/868-S/2010/393 of 21 July 2010)
18. Report of the Peacebuilding Commission on its fourth session, Un Doc. A/65/701- S/2011/41 of 28 January 2011, page 3.
19. Ibid., page 21.
20. The 2011 Roadmap of Actions was adopted by the Organisational Committee of the PBC on 25 January 2011 -- see Report of the PBC at its Fifth session, UN Doc. A/66/675-S/2012/70 of 30 January 2012,.page 2
21. Ibid., page 3.
22. Ibid.
23. Ibid, page 5.
24 Ibid.
25. The decisions on Guinea are reflected in the Summary of the Meeting in New York between the AfDB Vice-President for country and regional programme and policy and the Assistant Secretary-General for the PBSO on 26 September 2012 and the one on Liberia are reflected in the Aide Memoire dated 19 October 2012 signed between the Chair of the PBC Liberia configuration and the First Vice-President of AfDB during the former's visit to Tunis.
26. Review of the United Nations peacebuilding architecture, UN Doc. A/64/868-S/2010/393 of 21 July 2010, page 18.
27. An updated version of the paper entitled "Resource Mobilisation for Peacebuilding Priorities: The Role of the Peacebuilding Commission" is available at http://www.un.org/en/peacebuilding/pdf/resource-mobilisation
28. See Report of the Peacebuilding Commission on its sixth session, UN Doc. A/67/715 – S/2013/63 of 29 January 2013, page 4.
29. The issues of agreement highlighted in this paragraph draws on the summary of the discussion and outcome of the PBC Chairs Visit to the World Bank on 13 September 2012.
30. The issues of agreement highlighted in this paragraph draws on the summary of the discussion and outcome of the Executive Directors Visit to the UN Headquarters on 3rd December 2012.
31 Speech by Ambassador Abdulkalam Abdul Momen of Bangladesh to the Organisational Committee of PBC on 25 January 2012, page 1.
32. See PBC Declaration on Peacebuilding: The Way Towards Sustainable Peace and Security (PBC/6/OC/6) of 25 September 2012.
33. The first annual session of PBC was held in 2014 and second scheduled for 23 June 20115.
34.. Review of the United Nations Peacebuilding Architecture, UN Doc. A/64/868-S/2010/393 of 21 July 2010, para 110.

Chapter 5

Facts, Fictions, and Frustrations with the Functioning of the Peacebuilding Commission*

Every new institution grapples with the challenge of fulfilling expectations. The Peacebuilding Commission is not an exception. Performance expectations arise — or are cast — not only in relation to stated objectives of institutions but also from the presumptions of what various stakeholders think a particular institution ought to do. Where such stakeholders are very diverse, as in the case of PBC, it begs the question of whose views should be regarded as the most valid in assessing its performance: the country on the agenda, the members of the PBC, the UN mission/country team or independent experts? The question of the extent to which PBC has fulfilled its stated objectives was the subject of the 2010 Review.[1]

The starting point of assessing whether the PBC is fulfilling its expectations is to examine the stated objectives set for

---

* This chapter will be published as a book chapter in Adekeye Adebajo, ed. (Forthcoming, 2015), *Pax Africana: Making, Keeping, and Building Peace in Post Cold War Africa*.

the institution in the founding resolutions. The 2010 Review noted that "the principal reference point is General Assembly resolution 60/180 and Security Council resolution 1645 (2005) adopted simultaneously in 2005."[2] It then adds that the "hopes that accompanied the founding resolution establishing the PBC have yet to be realised,[3] [nonetheless] this is not to understate what has been accomplished and certainly not to devalue the unfailing commitment shown by many dedicated Member State representatives, especially those with chairing responsibilities."[4] This statement represented a summons to action for the PBC to work towards realising its full potential.

There is a strong link between the goal of achieving an institution's full potential and expectations about improvement in institutional performance. Carefully designed and sustained improvements in performance hold the keys to the realisation of full institutional potentials. Yet, it is hard to exaggerate the extent to which expectations about performance can be driven by theoretical or normative prescriptions, as the experience in other disciplines have shown. As the relatively young field or discipline of peacebuilding has evolved, normative frameworks have begun to shape its practices and expectations. Three normative or descriptive frameworks for peacebuilding have emerged in the literature on peacebuilding. These are well summarized in a recent publication[5] as: liberal peacebuilding; peacebuilding as stabilization; and peacebuilding as social justice. The following explanation is offered about the linkages between the three frameworks:

> There are at least three main frameworks for understanding peacebuilding that are prevalent in the literature. Although there are important areas of overlap between these positions, they rest on different conceptions of power and politics in Africa. Each of these views contains important normative assumptions about the nature of peace and about the identity and motivations of peace builders. They lead to different conclusions about the role of the state in peacebuilding, the type of economic policies best suited to recovery, the appropriate ways of encouraging societal reconciliation, and how best to ensure security.[6]

A synopsis of the key elements of these three normative frameworks as outlined in that publication runs as follows: "Liberal peacebuilding is [seen] to be part of a global project of liberal governance, promoted by international and regional institutions and other actors...liberal governance relies more extensively on building institutions and markets."[7] On the other hand, advocates of peacebuilding as stabilization "shares the liberal peacebuilding concern with order"[8] .... places emphasis on "creation of stable, secure states with well-policed borders,"[9] and "relies heavily on coercion and building the coercive apparatus of the state."[10] By contrast, proponents of peacebuilding as social justice "believe that peacebuilding can and should be based on social justice rather than liberal governance or stabilisation ...peacebuilding therefore involves programmes to encourage inclusive access to resources and institutions, to empower marginalized groups, to end discrimination against women and other disadvantaged groups, and to redistribute income and land ownership."[11]

The experience of the PBC confirms a critical insight in the excerpts above, namely, that there are important areas of overlap between the three normative frameworks for peacebuilding. Indeed, the PBC's engagement with the countries on its agenda — Burundi, the Central Africa Republic, Guinea, Guinea-Bissau, Liberia, and Sierra Leone — shows that the key themes highlighted by each of the three normative frameworks are marked by considerable interlinkages. Equally important, PBC's experience has also revealed that much of peacebuilding work is driven mostly by pragmatic imperatives rather than particular ideological prescriptions or motivations.

This chapter is offered as a contribution to separating the facts from the fictions in the experience of PBC and, by so doing, sheds light on practical results, possible challenges, and potential constraints in peacebuilding. It concludes by highlighting some key issues in the future of PBC.

Facts

PBC work straddles security and development enabling it to fulfill its mandate: The ability of the PBC to provide support to countries on its agenda in ways that link security and development issues is one of the important features and strengths of the PBC in its design and actual performance.[12] Indeed, "it is the only body that explicitly links the political, security and economic functions of the Organisation."[13] PBC has given practical effect to this advantage in two well-documented instances. In Sierra Leone, in the initial phase of engagement with that country, the PBC accepted the government's argument that restoration of electric power supply was not only a national emergency but an important peacebuilding priority. This led the PBC to include energy among the initial five peacebuilding priorities in the Peacebuilding Cooperation Framework.[14] An independent study has noted that "the incorporation of energy as a priority in the framework highlights an important principle: specifically, that economic risk can be as significant a threat to peace as security or political risks. In this case, the PBC fostered negotiations among the relevant stakeholders to garner political support for inclusion of energy — normally considered a medium-to-long-term development concern — in a framework of peace consolidation."[15]

The effort of the first Chair of the Burundi configuration in helping to persuade the IMF to lift its ban on 6th Review of the replenishment for Burundi is usually seen as case study in the advocacy work by the PBC. On closer examination it can also be viewed as a striking illustration of how PBC's work straddles security and development.[16] The Chair's demarche to the IMF took place in the context of what was referred to "the triple obstacles" — perhaps, more appropriately as "the triple threats" to peace consolidation in Burundi at the time. These were the decision of the opposition to boycott Parliament because of the disagreement between the main opposition parties and the government on the implementation of power-sharing principles contained in the various Peace Accords; the Front Nationale du Liberation (FNL) withdrawal from the Joint Verification and Monitoring Mechanism on 21 July 2007; and the delay by the IMF in concluding the 6th Review to Burundi, without which donors withheld their budgetary support to the Government of Burundi. Into this breach stepped the Chair, who made the argument to the IMF Board, through the Executive Director representing the constituency, which his country belongs, that if the IMF did not provide the financial support for the 6th Review, Burundi risked relapsing into conflict, given that Burundi was in the midst of the two other political crises. The Chair well recognised the link between the financial relief and the political situation, when "he underlined the importance of concluding the IMF Review at early stage and in way that could enable the Government to deal decisively with the political and socio-economic situation."[17]

PBC work in resource mobilisation is progressing slowly but steadily. One of the most difficult responsibilities entrusted to the PBC is mobilising resources to support postconflict peacebuilding. Coming to grips with the nature and scope of the role that the PBC is expected to play in this area has been bedevilled as much by the definition of the task as by operational details. In the founding resolution that responsibility was stated in these terms: "to bring together all relevant actors to marshal resources and to advise on and propose in integrated strategies for postconflict peacebuilding and recovery....and to help to ensure predictable financing for early recovery activities."[18] The term *marshal* is imprecise, lacking in operational guidance. At the same time, the loosely applied term *funding raising* is very limiting and limited in scope.

The appropriate interpretation of the role has to be mobilising financial and technical expertise and harnessing ongoing funding efforts in support of peacebuilding priorities. Absent that element of prioritisation linked to peacebuilding and the PBC's resource mobilisation work begins to resemble traditional development assistance. This conception of the role of the PBC in resource mobilisation has validation in the 2010 Review, which remarked that "PBC role is essentially one of advocacy, a relentless advocacy for allocation of adequate resources to certain critical and urgent issues, which if left addressed or unfunded, have the potential to threaten peace."[19] The Review noted that "the record of as regards resource mobilisation is mixed" and called on the PBC "to intensify overall mobilisation efforts [and] ensure that they are steadily attuned to development challenges with political implications."[20]

In response to the recommendation of the 2010 Review, PBC has focused its efforts on three aspects of resource mobilisation: mobilising financial support through donors' roundtables and for elections; developing partnerships with the international financial institutions; and promoting partnership with the private sector. Since the first of these issues is detailed in the next two sub-sections in this section, I will concentrate on the last two areas here.

Developing and deepening partnerships with international financial institutions has ranked high on the agenda of the PBC. This is precisely because the PBC recognised that the IFIs are not only major players in most postconflict countries but also because PBC believed that partnerships with IFIs — in particular AfDB and the World Bank — will generate complementarities to the benefit of the countries on the PBC agenda.

Just as the PBC recognised very early the need to work with IFIs, so it did with the private sector. I have provided the narrative of PBC's early efforts in articulating an orientation for its work with the private sector.[21] The new momentum for action in outreach to the private sector arose from the PBC policy discussion in July 2012 centered on a paper titled *Resource Mobilization for Peacebuilding Priorities: The Role of the Peacebuilding Commission*. Subsequently, the PBC decided that renewed emphasis should be placed on more outreach to the private sector. This led to convening in June 2013 the high-level event organised by PBC and Global Compact on the theme of *Business for Peacebuilding: The Role of Private Sector*. A major outcome of this event was the realisation that individual country configurations should identify practical entry points for the PBC in support of the efforts of the countries on the agenda to develop its local private sector and its local systems to manage and use natural resources, and to attract responsible investment. Moreover, where private sector investment flows occur, the impact will show up not only in money but the sharing of organisational and technological expertise that goes with it.

A careful review of the evidence of the PBC record in resource mobilisation, explained above and described later, reveals that the PBC may be have initially been very slow in this area, but has clearly intensified its efforts to fulfill this aspect of its mandate. The evidence also shows that not all efforts in resource mobilisation need lead to financial resources in terms of "money on the table". Rather, some of the efforts might result in complementary actions, for example, actions by the AfDB to support relevant infrastructure projects that will help in the regional justice and security hubs aimed at increasing citizens access to legal and security services in Liberia. [For more discussion on relations with the IFIs, see the section on fictions below in particular, the sub-section on the PBC accepts the priorities of the IFIs approaches, despite long-standing criticisms of those approaches].

Country specific configurations give focused attention to countries on the agenda. The pristine purpose of the institutional vehicle of the country-specific configuration was to serve as "a group-of-friends-of-sorts" consisting of member states of the organisational committee of the PBC as well as other interested member states willing and able to provide political, financial and technical support for peacebuilding efforts for the countries on the Commission's agenda. The composition of the configurations has the advantage of bringing together a diverse membership that can be quickly mobilised to address issues. One area where that rapid mobilisation has been particularly successful and has exemplified the focused attention by the CSCs is in the contributions by members for meeting the funding gaps of the electoral budgets of the countries on the agenda of the Commission.

Member States of the relevant country configurations have made financial contribution for funding gaps in the electoral budgets of countries on the agenda. In all cases, and at the behest of the government and ranking UN representative in the country, the Chairs of the country configurations addressed letters to members of the configurations soliciting financial support to cover the financial gap in the election budget. Through this approach, the members of the Central African Republic country configuration bridged the funding gap of US$7.5 million in the electoral budget of the 2011 presidential and general elections in that country. Similarly, members of the Guinea-Bissau country configuration contributed the sum of US$4.5 million to bridge the funding gap for the election budget of the 2008 parliamentary election; US$1.03 million for the 2009 presidential elections; and US$3.4 million for the first round of presidential elections in March 2012.[22] The second round (run-off) of that election, scheduled for 29 April 2012, was disrupted by the coup d'etat of 12 April,

2012. In addition to financial contributions, several members of the various configurations have provided technical assistance for elections.

While the ability of the PBC to mobilise financial resources for elections plays to the strength of its size, it has not escaped notice that the relatively large size of the country specific configurations creates its own problems: it has often times made it difficult to task members to take on specific assignments in support of the country. There is a growing realisation that whereas size has its advantages; the current configurations may have become too unwieldy for focused discussion and quick decision, hence the desire to establish steering groups of limited size. [See the section below on Frustrations, where a sub-section discusses the lack of flexibility in the "one size fits all" format of the country configurations].

The Chair of the country-specific configurations plays an important role in the work of PBC. Neither the founding resolution nor the PBC's rules of procedures explicitly made provision for the position of an independent Chair of the country configuration that is separate from the PBC Chair and Vice-chairs. The PBC Rules of Procedure simply stated that "The Chair or the Vice-Chairs of the Commission shall preside over both the Organisational Committee and the country-specific meetings, unless the Organisational Committee decides otherwise."[23] Indeed, the first Chair of the Burundi configuration was selected for that position by virtue of being a Vice-chair of the PBC. However, the selection of the independent Chairs for the other configurations reflected a practical adaptation to the reality that as more countries came on the agenda, it became impractical for the Chair and the two Vice-chairs of PBC to serve simultaneously in those positions and be assigned chairing responsibilities for the country configurations. But there is no question that the country configuration occupies a central position in the work of the PBC.

Reflecting on his experience, an adviser to the first Chair of the PBC country configuration for Sierra Leone has described the country configurations in these terms: "the country-specific meetings of the PBC have proved to be the engine rooms where its peacebuilding mandate was given operational meaning."[24] If so, the chair of the country of the configuration is the "chief engineer" — the Chair ensures that the "engine" functions optimally to achieve desired results. While this analogy may sound too mechanical and a bit of a stretch, it conveys the essential point that the position of the Chair of the country configuration is of crucial importance in the work of the configuration. The Chair is the lodestar around which the work of the country configuration rotates.

The roles of the Chair can be summed up as an advocate, a resource mobiliser, and a facilitator. These roles are directly derived from the key functions of the PBC itself, which can be summed up in the mnemonic: ARC which stands for Advocacy, Resource Mobilisation and (fostering) Coherence. Few as they may be, some of the key achievements of the PBC to date are attributable to how individual Chairs of the country configurations have played each of these roles.

Thus, the first Chair of the Liberian configuration championed the development of the regional justice and security hubs aimed at extending state authority in Liberia. Writing on the occasion of the inauguration of the Gbarnga hub, the first of five regional justice and security hubs, the Minister of Justice of Liberia, and the Assistant Secretary-General for Peacebuilding Support noted that "each hub is designed to increase citizens' access to justice and security by co-locating police, courts, and immigration departments — creating, in effect, a "one stop shop" for their services. The hubs will also enhance the government's efforts to extend the provision of these services from the capital to outlying and previously neglected areas of the country."[25] In addition to ensuring that the work on the second and third hubs is initiated, the successor chair of the configuration intensified efforts to support the government's work on national reconciliation.

Similarly, the Chair of the Sierra Leone configuration had issued a statement commending the people and institutions of Sierra Leone on the successful conduct and conclusion of presidential, parliamentary, district, and local elections.[26] The Chair of the Guinea configuration has offered much encouragement for the political process in that country, in particular by issuing statements at critical turning points. The Chair of the Guinea configuration of the PBC issued statements welcoming the Accord of 3 July 2013 among the political parties,[27] encouraging them to conduct fair, peaceful, and transparent elections,[28] and congratulating the people of Guinea for their peaceful participation in the 2013 legislative elections.[29]

Political advocacy work is not a one-way street, with Chairs of the country configurations always supporting of efforts of governments of countries on the agenda. There have been important moments when the Chairs of a country configuration have had to deliver "tough messages" to these governments. A striking illustration is provided in the letter written by the Chair of the Guinea-Bissau country configuration to the Minister of Foreign Affairs of Guinea-Bissau in May 2010 expressing the deep concern of the PBC about the so-called 1st April, 2010 incident in which the Prime Minister was briefly detained and the Chief of Armed Forces of Guinea-Bissau and other officers were illegally detained for some time after 1 April 2010.[30] The Chair demanded assurances from the government of Guinea-Bissau that such actions would not occur in the future. The Minister of Foreign Affairs replied two weeks later, offering the needed assurances.[31] The political fragility in that country was underlined by the fact that exactly two years after that incident; the military staged a coup on 12 April 2012 to halt the second round of the presidential elections. The Chair of the configuration issued a statement condemning in the "strongest terms the forcible seizure of power from the legitimate government of Guinea-Bissau that took place on April 12, 2012."[32]

The Chair of the Guinea configuration has also issued statements expressing concern about attacks on the residence of President Conde[33] and the increase in violence around issues related to legislative elections.[34] In his speech to the second sectoral conference on government PRSP priorities, the Chair of the Burundi configuration recalled the outcome of the 2012 Partners' Conference in Geneva, where Burundi succeeded in making positive headlines and noted that while the spirit of Geneva still lives on, the enthusiasm has somewhat faded. Positive developments, including the workshops of March and May 2013 on the elections and the return of leaders of the political opposition, have to a certain extent been thwarted by less positive ones like the adoption of the new media law or the sense that political space is at times restricted.[35]

The successive Chairs of the Burundi country configuration have led the efforts in organising donor conferences in support of Burundi. It has been noted that "US$655.6 million in funds pledged from international donors to Burundi in May 2007 would probably have been much lower if it had not been for the Commission, in particular the influence of Norway's Ambassador to the United Nations, John Lovald, who chairs the Commission's Burundi configuration."[36] In 2012, the Chair of the Burundi configuration supported the government of Burundi in organising the donors conference held in October 2012 in Geneva, Switzerland, that resulted in a pledges of US$2.5 billion for Burundi's second Poverty Reduction Strategy 2013-2016. The Chair of the Central African Republic country configuration had also supported the government of that country to organise a partners roundtable in Brussels, Belgium, in June 2011 to raise awareness about the funding needs of the second PRSP 2012-2016.

The fact that the Chairs of various configurations have organised or cosponsored donor conferences in support of PRSPs shows that PBC instruments are not in competition with PRSPs but, rather, are complementary. The PBC's instruments of engagement which have evolved from the Strategic Framework for Peacebuilding to Statement of Mutual Commitments on Peacebuilding cannot be in competition with PRSPs any more than the World Bank's Country Assistance Strategy or the African Development's Country Strategy Paper is in competition with PRSPs. Indeed, where a country has already developed a peacebuilding sensitive PRSP or a New Deal Compact, the PBC's instrument of engagement should be very brief Statement of Mutual Commitments outlining areas of peacebuilding support and what the PBC intends to achieve in each agreed priority area.

One important example of the political facilitation role of the Chair of configuration is provided by the work of the Sierra Leone configuration. There, the PBC offered a political platform for endorsing[37] the *Joint Vision of the UN Family in support of Agenda for Change* in Sierra Leone, thus giving additional encouragement to the work of UN system for supporting of the country and for rallying donors around the *Agenda for Change* in Sierra Leone, thereby fostering a more coherent approach.

To appreciate how difficult it is for a configuration to function without a Chair, we need look no further than the experience of the PBC country configuration for Central African Republic (CAR). The Chair of CAR configuration resigned effective 1 June 2012. The configuration seemed rudderless between the resignation of the first Chair of the configuration and the election of his successor in June 2014. The problem of lack of direction for a configuration, in the absence of a Chair, has been accentuated by the fact that the country configurations do not as yet have an institutional position of Vice-Chair, who would take over even temporarily in the absence of a Chair. Indeed, the failure of the 2010 Review to recommend the creation of the position of a Vice-chair for the country configurations was one of the unfulfilled expectations of that Review. Whether the PBC retains the system of country-specific configurations or move to a system of country meetings directly under the organisational committee of the PBC, whoever leads the arrangement — Chair or Coordinator — will play an equally important role, especially at the transition phase of PBC engagement with a country, before the PBC exits.

There is increasing synergy and coherence between PBC work and PBF programmatic support for countries on the agenda of the Commission. The founding resolutions that established both the PBC and PBF were silent on the relationship between these two new bodies of the UN peacebuilding architecture. But this relationship was clarified in the terms of reference of the PBF. In both the original[38] and revised[39] terms of reference of the PBF, it was stated that:

> In principle, any country before the Peacebuilding Commission should be considered a possible recipient of Peacebuilding Fund support. The Commission would advise the Secretary-General that the country under consideration should be considered eligible for funding, which will then formally trigger the allocation and disbursement process. The Commission is expected to make this determination early on in its deliberations to ensure that support through the Fund can be provided in a timely manner.

The Commission will be provided with regular updates and have the opportunity to provide, at the initial stage of priority plan formulation, strategic advice on overall funding priorities on the basis of the Commission's strategic engagement in the country concerned.

This wording shows that member states intended that the two instruments should play mutually reinforcing roles. However, a major criticism leveled against the PBC and the PBF in their early days, based on the experience of the first two countries that came on the agenda of PBC — was that "the PBF was a lot of money with no analysis, whilst the Compact [PBC Strategic Framework for Peacebuilding] was a lot of analysis with no money."[40] This observation reflected the fact that the PBF financial allocations were made before the instrument of engagement between the PBC and the first two countries on the agenda were completed and adopted, and after the instrument of engagement was adopted between the PBC and the two countries, additional money did not materialise. Indeed, the announcement on the allocation of PBF grants to these two was made in January 2007, when the PBC was still in the midst of negotiating the instruments of engagement (the Strategic Framework for Peacebuilding in Burundi and the Peacebuilding Cooperation Framework for Sierra Leone which were subsequently adopted respectively on 20 June 2007 and 12 December 2007). It was much later, after PBF introduced its "renewal policy" — the practice of giving more money after the first allocation, that these countries got more money in 2010.

The synergy between PBC and PBF has improved considerably over the years.[41] More recently, PBSO has worked more closely to align peacebuilding priorities in PBC's instruments of engagement and PBF programme support. The extent of progress in the improved synergy is highlighted by their ongoing work in Liberia. There, the PBF and the PBC experimented with a new approach, which was to encourage the design of a larger Peacebuilding Programme, to which the PBF would provide catalytic support. The Liberia Peacebuilding Programme mirrors the priorities in the PBC's Statement of Mutual Commitments. Similarly in Guinea, the PBF's strategy followed closely on the heels of the

Statement of Mutual Commitments produced in mid-2011. The PBSO is also improving its standard operating procedures to increase synergies. For example, in its new guidelines, the PBF has added systematic consultation of the Chairs of PBC Country Specific Configurations on programme decisions. Moreover, the PBF staff are increasingly encouraged to accompany the Chairs of Configurations on their country visits. A new dimension to strengthening PBC-PBF synergy is the growing recognition of the need to empower Chairs of the PBC country configurations to discuss with the missions the peacebuilding priorities that the PBF can fund in the countries on the agenda.

Moreover, "PBSO is actively seeking the joint advice of the Chair and UN leadership on the ground as to how the Fund can be best used to achieve the peacebuilding objectives. In seeking such joint views on priorities, the PBSO intends for those undertaking the critical advocacy work on policy — the Commission and the UN on the ground — to be able to draw upon the (modest) additional leverage that may be associated with the Fund's investments. Arguably, the Fund's impact is quite dependent, in fact, upon such ownership of the priorities by the Commission and the UN leadership on the ground in order to be successful."[42]

One measure of this growing synergy between the PBC and the PBF as of 31 December 2014 the six countries on the agenda of the PBC have received 53.67 percent of the cumulative allocations from the PBF out of a total of thirty one countries that have received allocations from PBF (see table 8). These huge allocations to the countries on the agenda shows that being on the agenda of PBC confers financial privileges, in so far as PBF is concerned.[43]

The PBC is a new body striving to add value in a crowded field. Peacebuilding is a field where many actors are involved. By nature, postconflict settings cry out for action and support across a spectrum spanning peacemaking, humanitarian assistance, development and in some country contexts, peacekeeping. Peacebuilding involves many actors including the government of the country, civil society, women and youth, private sector agents in the country as well as entities of the UN system, international financial institutions, bilateral donor/partners and international nongovernmental organisations. Into this already crowded field steps in the PBC which was created in 2005 and inaugurated in 2006.

Member states recognised the reality of the crowded field in which the PBC would operate, when, in the founding resolution, requested the PBC "to provide recommendations and information to improve the coordination of all relevant actors within and outside the United Nations."[44] This legislative directive has provided the basis of PBC efforts to promote and deepen collaboration with a range of actors in the countries on its agenda. In practice those efforts have manifested themselves in deepening partnerships with IFIs, in particular the AfDB and the World Bank; in strengthening the relations with regional and subregional organisations, especially the AU and Mano River Union, as well as working closely with the Special or Executive Representatives of the Secretary-General and lead UN Departments at headquarters and cultivating the private sector in support of peacebuilding efforts. The nature and intensity of PBC relations with each of these category of actors vary, reflecting the scale and scope of their activities in the countries and responsive to the principle of national ownership and leadership of the country itself.

A real assertion of the national ownership and leadership of peacebuilding efforts holds the key to ensuring that the PBC brings value in such a crowded field of actors in peacebuilding, especially working closely with UN missions/country teams and the national governments. At a minimum, the government should be ready, willing, and able to discuss and agree with the PBC not only on the specific peacebuilding priorities that the PBC should focus on but also convey its expectations of how the PBC should contribute to achieving the agreed-upon priorities. It is often thought that postconflict and fragile states are so bereft of expertise that they would be unable to implement some key peacebuilding activities. Yet, such a view conflates decision making on peacebuilding priorities with implementation ability. The PBC's ability to add value in the crowded field will depend as much on the commitment of the members to support the country, as on the clarity of the expectations that the government holds in regard to the PBC engagement. Various instances where senior representatives of governments of countries on the agenda and the ranking UN officials in the country have presented sharply contrasting views of the value added of PBC underline a point made at the beginning of this chapter: whose views should be regarded as valid in assessing the performance of PBC?

Multiple stakeholders have differing views of what PBC should do and achieve. There are many actors involved in peacebuilding, as the preceding sub-section has shown. This multiplicity of actors creates a situation in which various stakeholders have different expectations of what a particular institution ought to do. This problem is particularly pronounced in the case of the PBC not least because of its relatively wide remit. The expectations may be classified into two categories: those about the appropriate process(es) that PBC should use to achieve its results and the outcomes that it should aim for.

There are considerable differences on issues of processes as there are about issues of outcomes. Some expect the PBC to focus on root causes of conflict rather than on risk factors for relapse in the countries on the agenda. Such an expectation conveniently ignores the length of time dimension implied in the former approach. Still, others believe that the PBC should focus more on the "tangible" (for example, building infrastructure, rehabilitating institutions, mobilising financial resources for peacebuilding programmes) rather than on "intangibles" (for example, processes to launch and nurture national reconciliation; advocacy and diplomatic and political processes to overcome the eruption of conflict or tension). As a practical matter, PBC's work has encompassed both intangible and tangible aspects of peacebuilding. The notion that PBC's work should somehow be always tangible prompted the famous observation attributed to a Security Council mission to Liberia and Sierra Leone in 2012 that "the impact of PBC was not visible."

Even on such peacebuilding issues as security sector reforms, experts are divided between those who advise that the PBC should focus on helping the executive and legislative arms of government to strengthen civilian oversight and accountability of armed forces and security forces, and those who support professional training of armed forces and other security forces. At the same time, while there is broad agreement on the need for "institution building efforts necessary for recovery from conflict,"[45] there is no agreement on which institutions should be prioritized — security sector or economic management issues. Complicating the task of PBC, there is also no consensus on whether some issues can be neatly categorized as peacebuilding or development; for example: natural resources management, youth unemployment, and provision of energy in postconflict contexts. These divergent perspectives on what the PBC should do reflect in part the complexity of the field of peacebuilding, and in part the fact that peacebuilding is marked by a multiplicity of definitions[46] but also have resulted in exaggerated expectations from and criticisms of the institution.

Fictions

The exclusion of preventive work from the remit of PBC is an important limitation. The notion that PBC's remit excludes prevention work is traceable to the fact that the Secretary-General proposed in his report that he did "not believe that such a body should have an early warning or monitoring function"[47] in conflict situations. The decision of the Secretary General to excise the "early warning and monitoring function" from the PBC, contrary to the recommendation of the High Level Panel on Threats, Challenges and Change, was intended more to avoid giving a global role to the PBC — a role that the Security Council already performs — rather than precluding the Commission from performing that role in the countries on its agenda.

However, one analyst has noted that "the PBC is aimed at preventing a relapse into conflict in states that have recently emerged from a period of internal strife....it is an undisputed fact that activities aimed at building peace (reinforcing a given country's recovery and sustainable development) are instrumental to preventing conflict in the longer term."[48] Indeed, the strategic intent behind the creation of the PBC was to enhance the international community's ability to prevent the instances of repeated relapse into conflict by many countries. That is a broad and multifaceted task that requires the PBC to actively and effectively fulfill the functions set out in the founding resolution. The real issue, then, is not so much that the PBC lacks the remit to do preventive work but how to ensure that its work can contribute to preventing countries on its agenda from relapsing into conflict.

The PBC is dominated by the permanent members of the Security Council, the principal donors of UN system and the largest troop contributors, which make up half of the Organisational Committee. The idea of creating one category for principal donors and another for troop contributing countries in the organisational committee has been described as a reward for "global good citizenship."[49] The contrary view is that principal donors and largest troop contributing countries, along with the permanent members of Security Council, dominate the PBC.[50] Although the concept of domination was not clarified, we can usefully examine it from three dimensions: that these three category of countries (Security Council permanent members, largest troop contributing countries, and principal donors) are taking a leading role by assuming responsibility of chairing the country configurations; that they are very actively engaged in the work of PBC, including leading the efforts in generating initiatives; and that they can dictate the tune in peacebuilding in the countries on the agenda of the PBC because they make huge contributions to financing of peacebuilding, especially to the PBF.

Using these criteria to assess the domination by the three categories of countries shows that the notion of domination is a fiction. For example, none of the P5 member states of the Security Council has taken on a chairing role either of the organisational committee or the country configuration or the Working Group on Lessons Learnt. It is true that most the Chairs of the country configurations are from developed countries, but there have been a few from developing countries that do not fit the definition of major donor countries. Moreover, none of the largest troop countries but one has assumed the chair of the country configuration and only one major troop-contributing country has been elected to the Chair of the organisational committee. The major donor countries that have been elected to the chair of the organisational committee have done so as a consequence of the rotation to their regional group.

In so far as generating initiatives are concerned, the record confounds the view of domination. Some of the important initiatives that have emerged in the PBC, excluding the key roles of the Chairs of the country configurations noted earlier, have not been from the P5 members of the Security Council. Thus, the idea of financing PBC field trips and working closely with the private sector was pushed by Japan; strengthening relations with regional organisations and outreach to philanthropic organisations was pushed by Chile; enhancing relations with the AfDB by Rwanda; proposing annual sessions of the PBC by Indonesia, in addition to serving as a facilitator in 2008 for the Task Force on Private Sector.

As regards contribution to the PBF is concerned, as of December 2014, one of the P5 members of the Security Council has made no contribution to the PBF since the Fund was established, another has contributed less than US$3 million, another has made a total contribution of US$8 million, still another has contributed a total of US$14 million and only one has topped the charts by making a commitment of over US$141 million. In contrast to the view of domination, one report has noted that "it is also worth recording the concern of several PBC members that participation by the P5, with the exception of the UK, has tended to be intermittent and comparatively low level."[51] Of course, the criticism or observation that permanent members of the Security Council dominate the PBC can be sustained, if domination is by inaction, the tendency to be hesitant in giving greater policy and institutional space to the PBC. The real problem with the Security Council permanent members' attitude towards the PBC is not one of domination but of neglect or indifference. One final issue to consider — which minimizes the possibility of domination by one group or another — is that the resolution establishing the PBC explicitly states " that the Commission shall act in all matters on the basis of consensus of its members"[52] — a very unusual stipulation for an intergovernmental body — but one that potentially limits the extent to which any member state can dominate the PBC.

The PBC accepts the priorities of the IFIs approaches, despite long-standing criticisms of those approaches. This assertion has been coupled by a warning by some analysts that "without wholesale changes to the policies and initiatives of IFIs, their strong involvement with the PBC will likely give preeminence to a market-driven development approach with scant regard for local contexts."[53] The experience of PBC engagement in the six countries lends no validity to any of these claims. Indeed, the IFIs, in particular the African Development Bank and the World Bank have both been good advocates for and supporters of the work of the PBC. For example, during the first visit of the Chair of the PBC Sierra Leone configuration to that country, in 2007, as part of the fact-finding mission to articulate the Peacebuilding Cooperation Framework (PCF), the country representatives of the World Bank and the AfDB supported the government's insistence on making energy a peacebuilding priority. This expression of support by AfDB and the World Bank strengthened the hand of the Chair in convincing member states of the configuration in including energy among the five peacebuilding priorities for Sierra Leone — at a time when there was doubt and hesitation among some developed country member states about the wisdom of including energy in the PCF.

In the Statement of Mutual Commitments for Peacebuilding in Liberia, the government made a commitment to "increase budgetary allocations for institutions central to security and the rule of law, including the Armed Forces of Liberia, Liberia National Police, Bureau of Immigration and Naturalization and Corrections."[54] Subsequently, a report[55] on public expenditure review jointly financed by the World Bank and the UN Partnership Trust Fund recommended that the government of Liberia should increase its budgetary allocations on the security sector to 6 percent of the GDP from the current level of 4.9 percent. This recommendation provided encouragement for the Government to increase allocations to the security sector, even if the proposed target will take time to accomplish. Another example of collaboration involved the World Bank and the PBF "[joining] efforts to pay the salaries of civil servants from May through August 2014, contributing to reestablishment of core public services in the Central African Republic."[56] PBF paid the salaries of the police and gendarmerie and the World Bank paid for the rest of the public servants.

Both the AfDB and the World Bank have been supporters and active participants in the donor conferences highlighted in the first section of this chapter. The picture that emerges from this review is one in which the PBC and the IFIs are making good-faith efforts to take coordinated actions, where necessary, and complementary measures, where possible, to support countries marked by conflict and fragility. The peacebuilding priorities that the PBC supports in the countries on its agenda are a product of negotiations between the Commission and the government of the country concerned: IFIs neither drives those negotiations nor impose market–driven solutions. The PBC and the IFIs adopt pragmatic approaches to peacebuilding priority setting and implementation.

The results of the PBC's work should always be tangible and visible. As explained earlier, as the field of peacebuilding has evolved, the expectations of what the field should accomplish have grown, reflecting the fact that peacebuilding draws upon and indeed stands at the intersection of many disciplines. It should not come as a surprise that the work of the PBC is marked by multiple expectations of what it should be. One such expectation is that the work of the PBC must be tangible and visible. But one needs look no further than the main remit of the PBC — advocacy; resource mobilisation, and fostering coherence — to realise that some of the PBC's work will not show up as tangibles — if tangible is defined as money and institution building, such as the regional justice and security hubs in Liberia, that were referred to in the section above on Facts. As an illustration, advocacy and support for training of soldiers to accept civilian control of the armed forces will show up in behavioural or attitudinal change over time but will not be tangible. The same is true when PBC encourages and supports processes of national reconciliation.

PBC has overlooked developing partnerships with UN field operations and acts in parallel with UN peace missions. PBC places great importance on working with UN missions in the field. This is consistent with the guidance provided in the founding resolution which includes "the senior United Nations representative in the field and other relevant UN representatives"[57] in the discussions of the PBC country configurations. Cultivating the relationship between the PBC and the UN missions/UN Country Teams, on one hand, and the Chair of the country configurations and the Special/Executive Representatives of the Secretary-General(S/

ERSGs), on the other, has been a central feature of the PBC's engagement in the countries on the agenda.

Efforts to deepen these sets of partnerships have taken several forms. The S/ERSGs and the Heads of country teams have been deeply involved in articulating the instruments of engagements between the PBC and the countries on the agenda. The Chairs of the PBC country configurations frequently consult the Heads of the UN missions on all topical political, economic, and social developments in the countries on the agenda.

Moreover, at the initiative of the PBC, an annual Chair's Group and S/ERSG meeting was inaugurated in 2011 to provide an opportunity to discuss issues of common interest. There is growing recognition that this forum offers a dedicated platform to address critical peacebuilding-related issues. The first two meetings addressed issues of broadening the donor base by bringing in new and nontraditional donors that are not represented at the country-level; ensuring coordinated messages of the UN and the international community to the Government; supporting and complementing the process of the UN mission draw-down to be accomplished by bringing in support from the PBF to ensure that certain national and UN capacities are in place; and sustaining the attention of the international community and the Security Council with a view to addressing conflict-drivers beyond the draw-down of missions.

The PBC has failed to anticipate crises in the countries on its agenda. The specific instance cited to illustrate this case is the coup d'etat of 12 April 2012 in Guinea-Bissau which halted the presidential run-off elections.[58] There are three intriguing aspects to this comment. First, as the analysis in sub-section one under the Facts section above has shown, the PBC has, at least in the case of Burundi in 2007, intervened to ensure that political crisis did not spiral out of control leading to a relapse into conflict. Second, there is much expectation — indeed demand — for PBC to play an important "signaling function" in crisis management, if not prevention. Third, what has not been known till now is that on the day that the coup took place in Guinea-Bissau, the Chair of the Guinea-Bissau configuration had completed review of a letter she was to send to Ambassador Susan Rice, President of the Security Council for the month of April, 2012. In the opening paragraph of that letter dated 12 April, the Chair wrote "to call your attention to the recent political and security developments in Guinea-Bissau, including possible threats to political stability of that country."[59] That was a code word for the coup that was seen to be in the making. This showed that the PBC anticipated the coup, but the situation evolved so rapidly between the draft of that letter, written on 11 April, and its dispatch to the Security Council, that it was overtaken by events. The PBC's performance in Guinea-Bissau was not so much a failure of anticipation as it was a very rapid evolution of the situation in the country itself that overtook the "signaling" to the Security Council. History is replete with many such instances. And what about the relapse in the Central African Republic? There are two issues to note here. First, the relapse in the Central African Republic was a slow moving event that did not catch anyone by surprise, except the ensuing, initial ferocity of the fight among the various factions. Second, the PBC issued two statements — one before and the other after the transition authorities had been installed — calling attention respectively to the deteriorating situation and asking the international community to support the transitional authorities to implement the roadmap for the restoration of constitutional order in CAR.[60]

Frustrations

The PBC holds too many meetings which focus more on process than outcome. The number of meetings held by the various configurations of the PBC has reduced considerably,[61] falling from a peak of 17 meetings per configuration per year in 2007-2008 to 4.2 meetings per configuration per year in 2012 (See table 6 in chapter 4). Nonetheless, there remains a pervasive sense that many PBC meetings continue to focus more on process rather than outcome. To overcome this source of frustration with the PBC, it is important that the outcome the PBC seeks to achieve be well defined as part of preparations for every meeting. It bears emphasis, however, that as an intergovernmental body of member states, that goal may occasionally prove elusive.

The PBC does not "show us the money". The expectation that the PBC should be helping to mobilise resources for the countries on the agenda, beyond what the PBF provides, is very high. As I have indicated elsewhere, "several representatives of the governments of countries on the agenda and heads of UN missions have underlined that well-articulated peacebuilding strategies are meaningless if not adequately funded."[61] The PBC's role in mobilising resources goes beyond money, and includes mobilising technical expertise from within and outside the membership to tackle peacebuilding issues. More importantly, the disappointed expectations about the PBC performance in this area can be attributed partly to the belief that the PBC ought to mobilise financial resources for priorities in the broader development agenda in the country and partly due to the hope that PBC resource mobilisation efforts will yield revenue for the in-country Development Trust Fund. Even without fulfilling any of these expectations, if PBC's successes in Burundi could be replicated in other country contexts, the persisting frustrations on lack of resource mobilisation would be attenuated.

The Chairs of the PBC configurations are not working in harmony with or even competing S/ERSGs. There is no question that this pair of critical relationships has not functioned optimally. Mutual mis-comprehension of each other's role has been a factor that has afflicted this relationship. The notion of competition has arisen both from the lack of clear and legislated delineation of roles and responsibilities and from the rather difficult interpersonal relationships between some of the Chairs and the S/ERSGs. The countries on the agenda have much to gain when the United Nations, as represented by the Head of the UN mission and the Chair of the PBC country configuration, can work as one cohesive team. The key elements for strengthening this relationship are beginning to fall in place. Notably, these include the annual meetings between the PBC Chairs Group and the E/SRSGs, the growing recognition that both the Chairs of PBC configurations and the Heads of the UN missions are all working to support the country on the agenda, and the acknowledgement that the Chairs have to recognise the lead role of the Heads of mission in the country; while the Heads of missions should rely on the diplomatic and political support of the Chairs in New York.

Membership commitments are not as strong and effective as they should be – leaving the Chairs sometimes feeling lonely. A frequently encountered observation is that the Chairs are shouldering the burden of the work of PBC engagement in the countries on the agenda. Members of the PBC have offered support on a range of issues, as the analyses in the first two sections above show. Even so, there is a sense that the members ought to do more to strengthen the impact of the PBC to support the countries on the agenda. The expectations are that such support should manifest itself in at least three ways: in the active participation of member states in peacebuilding problem solving whenever problems arise in the countries on the agenda; providing financial and technical resources; and mobilising political and diplomatic support for the Chair in his/her engagement with the country on the agenda. The composition of the PBC was designed to enable individual member States to bring their unique strengths to bear on fulfilling the PBC's commitment to the countries on the agenda. Members states have not always been forthcoming in providing the needed support in response to appeals by the Chairs. One particularly disappointing event occurred when the chair of the Sierra Leone configuration wrote a letter[63] requesting members of that configuration to assist in providing in-kind support of police vehicles (cabin vehicles, pick-up vehicles, and small trucks) to strengthen the police capacity to patrol the waters and territory of the country, in order to curb drug trafficking – a priority that the PBC had undertaken to help in the Outcome Document of June 2009.[64] The failure of this appeal caused much embarrassment to the PBC and left the Chair of the configuration in the lurch.

Neither the Organisation Committee nor the Working Group on Lessons Learnt is serving as a forum of reflections on peacebuilding and sharing lessons and experiences. The pristine expectation associated with the Organisational Committee (OC) was that it would serve both as a plenary forum for the PBC and for serious discussion on peacebuilding on UN system-wide basis. On the other hand, although the Working Group on Lessons Learnt (WGLL) "was not explicitly envisaged in the founding resolution, once created, it became a vehicle for giving practical effect to the founding resolution's requirement to develop "best practices" for peacebuilding, a function envisioned for the Commission in paragraph 1(c) and for the Peacebuilding Support Office in paragraph 23."[65]

There is a growing sense that these two bodies are not fulfilling their expected functions to the fullest extent possible. The OC is viewed as having focused more on procedural issues relating to the effective functioning of the PBC rather than on a forum for serious, sustained, and in-depth discussion on peacebuilding issues globally. In so far as the WGLL is concerned, there is now a realisation that a body consisting of member states might not be the appropriate forum to distill or disseminate lessons learnt. Instead, such a body, which will be periodically convened for such a purpose, should ideally be composed of a few experts, even if drawn on a geographic basis.

The "one- size- fits-all" format of the country configurations lacks flexibility. One of the issues that PBC has had to grapple with in the early years of its creation was how to make the configurations more adaptive or responsive to the diverse needs of different country contexts. There are many complaints about the current configuration formats. Their relatively large size is viewed as being too unwieldy, making the discussions less focused. Some members are not showing as much interest as required, prompting the consideration of composing configurations with a sort of coalition of the willing and able to help the country on the agenda — something that the steering committees for three of the six configurations have begun to experiment with. The current configuration format appears not to be particularly suitable for engagement with a country that is seeking support of the PBC in one or two areas of peacebuilding or its advice in learning from its lessons of experience in peacebuilding in the countries on its agenda.

Such considerations turn critically on how best to design an institutional approach for attracting new countries to the PBC. Three set of ideas are beginning to emerge on how PBC can imbue its engagement with new countries with more flexibility. First, designate a co-coordinator from the membership of the PBC who reports directly to the organisational committee (plenary) of the PBC — to lead the process of supporting new countries. Second, the coordinator will work with a few, selected members ("a Steering Group" instead of a configuration) who are really interested in the country moving forward the agenda of peacebuilding. Third, where a new country seeks advice on learning from the lessons of the PBC experience, a few member States and experts with relevant experience can be put at the service of such a country for the agreed duration of engagement.

The PBC should focus not on "hard" but "soft" issues in peacebuilding. Given the expansive nature of peacebuilding, it should not come as a surprise that the PBC's engagement in the countries on its agenda has spanned both the so-called "hardware" and "software" issues. However, there is a growing belief that PBC is highly unlikely to make great impact on the "hardware" issues — resource mobilisation, natural resources management and support for institutional infrastructure. As such PBC should focus on "software" issues, such as reconciliation, transitional justice, supporting inclusive political dialogue, and civil society engagement in peacebuilding. This debate harks back to the contending perspectives between the three normative frameworks, to the "tangibles vs. intangibles" controversy, and to the definition of peacebuilding — all three issues grappled with in various parts of this chapter. Yet, the stress on "software" issues is a recognition that some of the impacts by PBC are reflected in intangible issues such as behavioural or attitudinal changes that are not amenable to quantitative measurement. There is no easy way to resolve this dilemma of "software vs. "hardware" issues. But it bears special emphasis that respecting the peacebuilding priorities proposed to the PBC by the country will be a crucial determining factor in overcoming this tension.

Future of the PBC

In the previous chapter, the author argued that the way the PBC manages three issues holds the key to its future success: The PBC's relations with the field, defined to mean support for and actions in the countries on the agenda through appropriate institutional arrangements; its ability to contribute to financing peacebuilding priorities in the countries on the agenda; and its relations with the Security Council. It is easy enough to make the point that all these issues are "means to an end". That end is laying the foundation for sustainable peace and development, a process that we all recognise can be long and arduous.

At one level, getting the PBC processes right is fundamental to creating the impact that PBC seeks to achieve and that everyone expects it to achieve. Hence, improving the processes is essential. There is more to improving the processes of the PBC than those three issues. A careful review of the areas of frustrations outlined above highlights the scope of improvements required. In fact, making improvements in any of those areas will contribute significantly to the functioning and effectiveness of the PBC.

At a deeper level, there is a need to develop some commonly agreed upon criteria under the auspices of the Organisational Committee of the PBC on how its impact should be measured. The lack of such criteria has led to conflicting assessments or judgements on PBC's performance. As is the case in other disciplines, it be important that the "guess work" be taken out of measuring PBC's performance. If there is one contribution that can be made to improving the performance of PBC, it is precisely to develop a common measurement or criteria for success of PBC's work.

The future of the PBC will ride on the commitment of its members to support the countries on its agenda; on the flexibility and adaptability of its working methods; on developing and strengthening partnerships that help it to deliver desired results; on agreements on how its impact should be measured; and on the willingness and sustained commitment of the countries on the agenda to pursue the policies and measures that enable them to overcome the legacy of conflict and fragility and lay the foundation for peace and development.

Table 8. PBF Country Summary of PRF and IRF Allocations as at 31 December, 2014

	[in U.S. Dollars]		
	PRF	IRF	TOTALS
PBC Countries	Total Amount Allocated	Total Amount Allocated	
Burundi	55,850,000.00	5,888,725.00	61,738,725.00
CAR	30,000,000.00	17,754,388.00	47,754,388.00
Guinea	45,233,382.28	12,059,229.62	57,292,611.90
Guinea-Bissau	22,800,000.00	5,724,337.88	28,524,337.88
Liberia	50,154,000.05	1,719,470.00	51,873,470.05
Sierra Leone	43,700,000.00	8.457,979.00	52,157,979.00
Total - PBC	247,737,383.33	51,604,129.50	299,341,511.83
Non-PBC Countries			
Bosnia & Herzegovina	--	2,000,000	2,000,000.00
Chad	--	4,788,011.00	4,788,011.00
Colombia		2,000,000.00	2,000,000.00
Comoros	11,500,000.00	400,000.00	11,900,000.00
Cote d'Ivoire	25,150,000.00	7,577,750.00	32,727,750.00
DRC	20,000,000.00	7,999,967.00	27,999,967.00
Guatemala	10,000,000.00	1,000,000.00	11,000,000.00
Haiti	--	3,800,000.00	3,800,000.00
Kenya	--	1,000,000.00	1,000,000.00
Kyrgyzstan	15,100,000.00	9,999,948.30	25,099,948.30
Lebanon	--	3,008,472.00	3,008,472.00
Libya	--	2,283,308.00	2,283,308.00
Mali	--	10,932,168.00	10,932,168
Myanmar	--	3,630,192.64	3,630,192.64
Nepal	18,000,000.00	2,475,402.00	20,475,402.00
Niger	--	2,999,650.00	2,999,650.00
Papua New Guinea	7,300,000.00	352,637.13	7,652,637.13
Philippines	--	2,999,570.00	2,999,570.00

Somalia	--	3,995,100.00	3,955,100.00
South Sudan	10,000,000.00	6,521,.990.00	16,521,990.00
Sri Lanka	--	3,000,000.00	3,000,000.00
Sudan, Republic of	--	19,074,513.00	19,074,513.00
Timor-Leste	--	993,625.00	993,625.00
Uganda	14,000,000.00	1,461,162.00	15,461,162.00
Yemen	13,100,000.00	7,603,554.00	20,703,554.00
United Nations	--	2,294,294.00	2,294,294.00
Total - nonPBC	144,150,000.00	114,188,314.07	258,338,314.07
TOTALS	391,887,382.33	165,792,443.57	557,679,825.90

Percentage PBC/non-PBC	115%
Percentage PBC /Overall Allocation	53.67%
Percentage non-PBC / Overall Allocation	46.32%

Notes on Chapter 5: *Facts, Fictions, and Frustrations with the Peacebuilding Commission and Issues for the Future.*

1. Review of United Nations peacebuilding architecture, UN Doc. A/64/868-S/2010/393) of 21 July 2010.
2. Ibid., page 8.
3. Ibid., page 3.
4. Ibid., page 8..
5. See Devon Curtis and Gwinyayi A. Dzinesa, eds. Peacebuilding, Power, and Politics in Africa (Johannesburg: Wits University Press, 2013).
6. Ibid., page 9.
7. Ibid., page 9 and 14.
8..Ibid., page 11.
9..Ibid., page 12.
10 Ibid., page 14.
11. Ibid.
12. See Funmi Olonisakin and Eka Ikpe (2013)" The United Nations Peacebuilding Commission: Problems and Prospects", in Devon Curtis and Gwinyayi A. Dzinesa, eds, Peacebuilding, Power and Politics in Africa (Johannesburg: Wits University Press 2013), page 144.
13. Center on International Cooperation and International Peace Institute, Taking Stock, Looking Forward: A Strategic Review of the Peacebuilding Commission: An Independent Study commissioned by the Permanent Mission of Denmark to the UN, New York, 2008, page 28.
14. See Peacebuilding Cooperation Framework, UN Doc. PBC/2/SLE/1 of 3 December 2007, page 7-8.
15. Center on International Cooperation and International Peace Institute, 2008, Page 3.
16. The Center on International Cooperation and International Peace Institute, highlights this view on the security-development of the work by the Chair of Burundi configuration, 2008, page 2-3.
17. See Report of the Fact-Finding mission of the Chairman of the Burundi Specific Meeting of the Peacebuilding Commission to Burundi, 5 to 7 September 2007, page 4.
18. See para. 2 (a) and (c) of UN General Assembly Resolution 60/180 and Security Council Resolution 1645(2005).
19. See Review of UN peacebuilding architecture, page 11.
20. Ibid., page 18.
21. See Ejeviome Eloho Otobo "Leading the Peacebuilding Commission: An Institutional History in the Making", 'Views from Practice' no. 1/2013, March 2013, Brussels: Global Governance Institute, reproduced in chapter 4.

22. The letters of solicitation from the Chair to the Members of the configuration for the elections of 2008, 2009, and 2012 are respectively dated 8 May 2008, 3 June 2009, and 14 February 2012.

23. See PBC Rules of Procedure in UN Doc. PBC/1/OC/3/Rev.1 of 5 December, 2012.

24. See Bartjan Wegter, "Emerging from the Crib: The Difficult First Steps of the Newly Born UN Peacebuilding Commission", *International Organisation Law Review, 12/2008 4(2) page 343-355.*

25. See Christiana Tah and Judy Cheng-Hopkins, "Rebuilding Liberia, One Hub at a Time", *Mail and Guardian,* South Africa, 10 February 2013.

26. See Statement by the Sierra Leone configuration of the Peacebuilding Commission, 19 December 2012.

27. See Statement issued by the Chair of PBC Guinea configuration on 8 July 2013.

28. See Statement issued by the Chair of PBC Guinea configuration on 17 September 2013.

29. See Statement issued by the Chair of PBC Guinea configuration on 24 October 2013.

30. See Letter from Chair of the Guinea-Bissau configuration to the Minister of Foreign Affairs dated 6 May, 2010.

31. The reply from the Minister of Foreign Affairs of Guinea-Bissau was dated 21 May 2010.

32. See Statement issued by the Chair of PBC Guinea-Bissau configuration on 13 April 2012.

33. See Statement issued by the Chair of PBC Guinea configuration on 19 July, 2011.

34. See Statement by Chair of PBC Guinea configuration on 6 March 2013.

35. see The Statement of the Chair of Burundi configuration to the second sectoral conference devoted to governance on 28 October 2013 in Bujumbura. (The First sectoral conference of the Burundi PRSP II, devoted to Infrastructure development, was held in July 2013).

36. See Security Council Report, October, 2007 page 8.

37. See PBC Outcome of the Peacebuilding Commission High-level Special Session on Sierra Leone, PBC/3/SLE/2 of 10 June 2009.

38. Secretary-General Report on the arrangements for establishing the Peacebuilding Fund, UN Doc.A/60/984, 22 August 2006.

39. Secretary-General Report on Arrangements for the revision of the Terms of Reference of the Peacebuilding Fund (PBF), UN Doc. A/63/818, 13 April 2009.

40. Actionaid, CAFOD and CARE International (2007), Consolidating The Peace?: Views from Sierra Leone and Burundi on the United Nations Peacebuilding Commission, London. Page 14 and 25.

41. This section draws on the box on PBC and PBF synergy in Ejeviome Eloho Otobo, "Leading the Peacebuilding Commission: An Institutional History in the Making", chapter 4.

42. See PBSO (2013) Background Note on Synergies between the PBC and the PBF prepared for the PBF Advisory Group Meeting 7-8 October 2013. p.2.

43. See Otobo "The UN Peacebuilding Architecture: African Countries as Early Beneficiaries", in chapter 3.

44. See paragraph (2) of UN Document General Assembly Resolution A/RES/60/180 of 20 December 2005.

45. See UN General Assembly Resolution on PBC A/60/180, para. 2(c).

46. For a recent review of definitions and approaches to peacebuilding, see Alliance for Peacebuilding (2012) Peacebuilding 2.0: Mapping Boundaries of an Expanding Field.

47. In Larger Freedom Towards Development, Security and Human Rights for All, Report of the UN Secretary-General, para. 115.

48. See Bartjan Wegter, "Emerging from the Crib: The Difficult First Steps of the Newly Born UN Peacebuilding Commission", *International Organisation Law Review,12/2008 4(2)* page 345-346.

49. Mark Malloch-Brown, "Holmes Lecture: Can the UN Be Reformed?" Annual Meeting of the Academic Council on the UN System (ACUNS), 7 June 2007, 7.

50. See Olonisakin and Ikpe (2013)" The United Nations Peacebuilding Commission: Problems and Prospects", page 149.

51. See CIC and IPI, page 19.

52. See UN General Assembly Resolution A/68/180 of 20 December 2005, operative para. 18.

53. See Olonisakin and Ikpe, page 150.

54. See Statement of Mutual Commitments for Peacebuilding to Liberia (A/PBC/4/LBR/1 of 16 November 2010, page 8.

55. Geopolicity (2012) Public Expenditure and Needs Assessment Review of the Security Sector in Liberia: Establishing A Sustainable Security Sector in View of UNMIL Transition, page 10.

56. See paragraph 15 of Report of the Peacebuilding Commission on its eighth session. UN Doc. PBC/8/OC/L./1/17 December, 2014.

57. See UN General Assembly resolution A/60/180 of 20 December 2005, operative para. 7(d).

58. See Security Council Report [the NGO] (2013): The Security Council and the Peacebuilding Commission, Special Research Report, page 6.

59. See unpublished letter from Chair of the Guinea-Bissau configuration to the President of Security Council for month of April, dated 12 April 2012.

60. See Statement by the PBC the Central African Republic configuration dated 24 December 2012 and 21 May 2013.

61. For figures on this, see chapter 4.
62. Ibid.
63. See Letter by the Chair of the PBC configuration for Sierra Leone, dated 27 October 2009, page 4.
64. See Outcome of the Peacebuilding Commission High-level Special Session on Sierra Leone, PBC/3/SLE/2 of 10 June 2009.
65. See Chapter 4.

Chapter 6

Reflections on Three Important Questions Concerning the Performance of the Peacebuilding Commission

The pristine purpose for creating the Peacebuilding Commission was first articulated in the report of the High Level Panel on Threats, Challenges and Change. The panel observed that "our analysis has identified a key institutional gap: there is no place in the United Nations system explicitly designed to avoid State collapse and the slide to war or to assist countries in their transition from war to peace."[1]

In order to fill that void in the institutional architecture of the United Nations, the panel recommended the creation of a new body to be called the Peacebuilding Commission and entrusted it with the key functions "to assist in the planning for transitions between conflict and postconflict peacebuilding; and in particular sustain the efforts of international community in postconflict peacebuilding over whatever period may be necessary."[2] There are three key elements in that sentence that should be borne in mind as we reflect on the role of the PBC: assisting in planning for the transition, sustaining international support, and possibly contending with a long period of engagement.

Although, the proposal of the High Level Panel relating to the establishment of the PBC went through various modifications, from the report of the Secretary-General[3] through the World Summit Outcome document[4] to the concurrent resolutions of the UN General Assembly and Security Council[5]; the notion that the PBC is a body to assist countries in their transition from war to peace remained intact. Instead, the focus of the subsequent changes to the proposal was whether the PBC should have a role in early warning or monitoring functions, how the membership should be composed, whether the PBC should report to ECOSOC and the Security Council; and whether the PBC should wholly be a subsidiary of the Security Council or whether it should have a joint "parentage" of the UN General Assembly and the Security Council — which is what it is today.

The idea that the PBC is an important instrument of the United Nations for supporting the transition of countries emerging from war to peace puts its work in a broader strategic context. In particular, that raises the question, what are the most appropriate ways for members of the Commission to undertake such an important task? This cuts to the heart of how the PBC should engage with the countries on its agenda. The work and the results of the PBC as well as its shortcomings have been detailed in many of the preceding chapters, especially chapter 5.

This chapter examines three issues that have often been overlooked in many of the reviews or assessments of the functioning and effectiveness of the PBC. These are, namely; Why have some countries on the agenda of PBC done relatively better than others? Was the PBC willed enough means to achieve the desired ends? And has the position and the authority of the PBC in the constellation of UN bodies and processes affected its effectiveness? Most assessments of PBC tend to take for granted the last two of these three issues in particular. That does not seem a reasonable assumption any longer.

In examining these questions, it helps to remember that there is no single lever to be pulled by national authorities or their partners for postconflict peacebuilding to happen. Peacebuilding success depends on a composite of measures, including the commitment of the national authorities, the individual country context, careful targeting of interventions and the scale and scope of international support. It is the positive interactions among these factors that create a positive dynamic for peacebuilding.

A. Why Have Some Countries Done Relatively Better Than Others?

The six countries on the agenda of the PBC came at different times and with different agreed upon peacebuilding priorities between the PBC and the country concerned. These are detailed in table 9. Although the countries on the agenda share many economic, political and social characteristics (see table 10), each country exhibits certain unique features that have affected the pace and progress of peacebuilding in their individual countries.

To understand how those differences in national conditions have impacted national peacebuilding efforts, it helps to focus on three set of issues: historical political antecedents of the conflict in each country; how these antecedents shape the environment for PBC engagement with each country; and the expectations of what the PBC should do to help to advance peacebuilding in each country. By examining these issues, it is possible to classify the six countries on the agenda of the PBC into three categories as follows: the first two countries on the agenda, Burundi and Sierra Leone — where considerable progress has been made; the next two countries — Guinea-Bissau and the Central African Republic — which have continued to be marked by much travail; and the two latest entrants on the agenda of PBC — Liberia and Guinea — which hold much promise.

The Progress of the First Two Countries on the Agenda of the PBC: Burundi and Sierra Leone

Burundi and Sierra Leone, the first two countries to come on the agenda, went through very traumatic conflict experiences which were brought to an end after lengthy negotiations, between the governments and the rebel factions, resulting in peace agreements. Subsequently, both countries received regional or subregional intervention missions that were replaced by United Nations peacekeeping operations before their engagement with the PBC.

Historical Political Antecedents in Burundi

The civil war in Burundi lasted from 1993 to 2005. Although the immediate trigger for the conflict that erupted in Burundi in 1993 was the killing of the first democratically elected Hutu President, Melchior Ndadaye, the conflict followed a pattern of interethnic violence between the two major ethnic groups stretching back many decades. Less than a year later, the successor to President Ndadaye was killed in a plane crash with the leader of Rwanda, a development that further exacerbated the mutual antagonism and violence between the two ethnic groups. To de-escalate the violence, a power-sharing arrangement was devised in which the two ethnic groups — the Hutu and the Tutsi — alternated power until 1996, when Pierre Buyoya, a Tutsi, staged a coup, thus putting an end to that arrangement.

In June 1998, the Arusha peace negotiations were launched, led initially by Tanzania's Julius Nyerere and later by Nelson Mandela, after he stepped down as President of South Africa. These negotiations culminated in the Arusha Peace and Reconciliation Agreement of 2000, which was signed by the government and the three Tutsi groups. The Hutu groups declined to sign. The Forces for Defense of Democracy (FDD), the National Liberation Forces (FNL), the armed factions of the National Council for Defense of Democracy (CNDD), and the Party for the Liberation of the Hutu People (Palipehutu) did not sign the Arusha Accords. The CNDD-FDD later signed the ceasefire and power-sharing agreements with the government in 2003 and the Palipehutu-FNL signed a comprehensive ceasefire agreement with the government in 2006.

To support the implementation of the Arusha Agreement and to demonstrate regional solidarity with the peace process, an African Union Mission in Burundi (AMIB) was deployed in February 2003. This paved the way for Pierre Buyoya to hand over leadership to his deputy in May 2003. The Arusha Agreement was supplemented by the Pretoria Protocols on political, defence, and security power sharing, which was signed by the government and the CNDD-FDD in November 2003. The United Nations Operations in Burundi (ONUB) replaced the African Mission in Burundi (AMIB) in June 2004. The year 2005 witnessed many important developments in Burundi: a law was signed on the establishment of a new national army composed of the Tutsi military and Hutu rebel groups; a new constitution was approved in a national referendum; parliamentary and presidential elections were held, with the FDD winning the majority seats and Pierre Nkurunziza was elected president. The ONUB was in turn replaced by the Integrated Office in Burundi (BINUB) on 1 January 2007, which was in turn replaced by the BNUB in 2011 that was closed in December 2014.

Historical Political Antecedents in Sierra Leone

The civil war in Sierra Leone broke out in March 1991, when the fighters of the Revolutionary United Front (RUF) led by Foday Sankoh crossed from Liberia to launch attacks in Sierra Leone, with the active support and encouragement of Charles Taylor, then President of Liberia, who had a made deal to supply arms to Sankoh in exchange for diamonds from Sierra Leone. It is widely commented that Sankoh's rebellion was motivated mainly by the desire to have access to Sierra Leone's mineral wealth, perhaps a striking illustration of a "war of greed". Underscoring the access to natural resources motivation, during the peace talks in 1999, Sankoh insisted on and was appointed as the Head of the Commission for Management of Strategic Resources. Shortly after Sankoh's incursion from Liberia, the government in power was overthrown in 1992 and the successor government was in turn overthrown in 1996. Following elections in March 1996, Ahmed Tejan Kabbah was elected President. In response to the overthrow of Kabbah in May 1997, the Economic Community of West African States Ceasefire and Monitoring Group (ECOMOG) intervened in March 1998 to reinstate President Kabbah.

In July 1999, the Lome Agreement was signed between the Kabbah government and the RUF, paving the way for the withdrawal of ECOMOG and the establishment of a UN Assistance Mission (UNAMSIL) in November 1999. Sankoh was granted amnesty as part of the Lome Peace Agreement and appointed to a senior level position in the government. Foday Sankoh, who launched the 1991 attack and Major Johnny Paul Koroma, who overthrew Tejan Kabbah government in May 1997, were indicted for war crimes by the International Special Court for Sierra Leone in 2003. Sankoh died in detention before the end of the trial. United Nations involvement in Sierra Leone began with the appointment of a Special Envoy and this was followed in 1998 by UNOMSIL – a UN Monitoring Mission, which was replaced by the United Nations Assistance Mission in Sierra Leone(UNAMSIL) in October, 1999. UNMASIL was in turn succeeded by the UN Integrated Office in Sierra Leone (UNIOSIL) on 1 January 2006; and in January 2008, UNIOSIL was replaced by UNIPSIL, which closed in March 2014. Since the end of the civil war in 1999, the country has held elections in 2002, 2007, and 2012. The election of 2007 witnessed the alternation of power from Sierra Leone Peoples Party to the All Peoples Congress.

How the Political Antecedents Shaped the Environment for PBC Engagement

Having highlighted the historical political antecedents of the conflict in the two countries, we turn next to examining how the antecedents shaped the engagement of the PBC, including in particular the expectations that the governments had of the PBC both at the initial phase and subsequently. In doing so, it is worth emphasising the importance of the role of contingent and idiosyncratic factors in each country context. In retrospect, it is possible to argue that the environment for postconflict peacebuilding appears more fertile in these two countries for a variety of reasons.

In Burundi, although the antagonisms between the government and the FNL posed the ever-present risk of relapse into conflict – and there were moments when that risk was high – one mitigating factor has been war weariness among the population. Indeed, at the time of PBC engagement in 2007, both the government and the opposition parties grasped the opportunity afforded by the articulation of the PBC instrument of engagement to engage in reasonably serious dialogue on peacebuilding priorities in the country. Another important factor that had contributed to creating a propitious environment was the reform of the army – which had been dominated by the minority Tutsi from independence to 1995 – which successfully integrated elements from the two former rebel movements, the CNDD-FDD and the FNL and adhered to the Arusha principle of ethnic balance: with the majority Hutu getting 60 percent and minority Tutsi, 40 percent. Still another factor was the role regional actors played both in supporting Burundi to join the regional economic integration group — East African Community — and in emphasising the need for unity. On the last point, Kofi Annan has recalled that "in brokering a power sharing agreement between Burundi's squabbling parties, Mandela's admonition to them [that] — *the way you are behaving makes me feel ashamed to be an African* — carried a force that no militia, however misguided, could ignore."[6]

In Sierra Leone, a confluence of factors contributed to a relatively propitious environment for peacebuilding at the time of PBC engagement. Some of the "key spoilers", Foday Sankoh and Charles Taylor, were no longer in the scene: the former had died in during his trial; the latter had left for exile in Nigeria, from where he was taken to The Hague for trial and subsequent conviction. Despite occasional flashes of disputes and tensions between the government and opposition parties — of which the political violence of March 2009 was the most serious — all sides recognised the need to make the transition from war to peace a success. One indication of that commitment is the fact that Sierra Leone has held three relatively successful elections since the Lome Accords in 1999, with alternation of power between the parties, a very rare development in postconflict countries. The civil society groups, especially the cross-parties' women and youth groups have played an important part in this transition, in particular by rallying the electorate to embrace the ethics of peaceful, fair, and orderly elections. Another indication is what appears to be a growing cross party consensus that Sierra Leone needs to put the past behind and focus national efforts on economic development and transformation — a spirit reflected in the two titles of the country's postconflict poverty reduction plans: *Agenda for Change and Agenda for Prosperity*.

Expectations Concerning PBC Engagement

Against this backdrop, what were the expectations of the government, and also of the UN missions regarding PBC engagement in these two countries? In addressing this question, it bears emphasis that the expectations of key national stakeholders evolved overtime. Though the instrument of engagement between the PBC and the two countries identified a number of peacebuilding issues (see table 9), the key national stakeholders had specific expectations concerning what the PBC should do to advance peacebuilding in their countries.

In Burundi, the opposition parties believed that the PBC should join the efforts of the UN Mission and the AU to ensure that the government gave political space to and recognised the rights of the opposition parties to organise for elections. The government, for its part, desirous to make the people see and feel the dividends of peace, had continually urged the PBC to mobilise resources both for sustainable socioeconomic reintegration of ex-combatants and internally displaced persons into the local communities and for the broader postconflict recovery and development efforts, as reflected in the successive poverty-reduction plans. In response to these requests and as a result of Burundi's placement on the agenda of the PBC, the Peacebuilding Fund made financial allocation to support the government's economic and social reintegration programme. The PBC response to the country's request has also taken the form of active support and involvement in successfully organising two donor round conferences: the first in Bujumbura in May 2007 and the second in Geneva in October 2012.

In Sierra Leone, a major initial expectation of the government was that the PBC would support the newly elected government — (from the August 2007 elections) — in its declaration to improve energy supply as an emergency. This resulted in the inclusion of energy as one of the peacebuilding priorities in the Peacebuilding Cooperation Framework, which enabled the government to receive financial allocation from the PBF to purchase fuel for generating electricity supply. The government also expected and requested the PBC to provide in-kind support of police vehicles (cabin vehicles, pick-up vehicles, and small trucks) to strengthen the police capacity to patrol the waters and territories of the country in order to curb drug trafficking. This appeal failed (see chapter 5 for details). The UN mission also expected that, in addition to providing political and diplomatic support for its work, the PBC would contribute to a Multi-Donor Trust Fund to support the activities of the Joint Vision of the United Nations in support of Sierra Leone's *Agenda for Change*. This expectation was not realised.

The Two Most Difficult Cases: Guinea-Bissau and the Central African Republic

Historical Political Antecedents in Guinea-Bissau

In its forty years of postindependence (1974-2014) history, Guinea-Bissau has lurched from one political crisis to another, marked by a brief civil war from 1998 to 1999 and intermittent violent coup d'etats interspersed with elections. The brief civil war was brought to an end by peace negotiations under the auspices of ECOWAS which resulted in the Abuja Agreement of November 1998. Subsequently, the UN Security Council, in March 1999, authorised the establishment of the United Nations Peacebuilding Support Office in Guinea-Bissau (UNOGBIS) to monitor the general elections and the implementation of the Abuja Agreement. UNOGBIS was subsequently replaced by the United Nations Integrated Peacebuilding Support Office (UNIOGBIS) in January 2010.

As a follow-up to the Abuja Agreement, an election was held in January 2000, and Kumba Yala was elected President; but he was overthrown in a coup in September 2003 and followed by another coup in 2004. This was followed by elections in 2005 in which Joao Bernardo Vieira was elected president and he led the country until he was brutally assassinated in March 2009. The presidential elections held in September 2009 were won by Malam Bacai Sanha. In April 2010, a group of military officers briefly detained Prime Minister Carlos Gomes, Jr; and replaced Admiral Zamora Induta, the Chief of General Staff of the Armed Forces with General Antonio Indjai. On 26 December 2011, there was an incident that was widely described as a failed coup attempt. Following the death of President Malam Bacai Sanha in January 2011, Raimundo Pereira was appointed interim President, a position he held until 12 April 2012, when the Military High Command staged a coup overthrowing the government a few days before the second round of presidential elections that had been scheduled for 29 April 2012.

Following the 12 April coup, power was transferred to an Interim President, Manuel Serifo Nhamadjo, who had placed third among the presidential candidates in the first round of the presidential elections of 18 March. As part of the effort to manage the transition, an ECOWAS Mission in Guinea-Bissau (ECOMIB) was deployed in replacement to the Angolan Technical Military Cooperation Mission (MISSANG) that had been deployed during the previous government. A series of political developments followed. The UN Security Council imposed a travel ban on five of officers "who played a leading role in the coup d'etat of 12 April 2012 and who aim, through their actions, at undermining the rule of law, curtailing the primacy of civilian power and furthering impunity and instability in the country."[7] A Political Transition Pact was signed in May 2012 by many of the political parties except the African Party for the Independence of Guinea and Cape Verde (PAIGC). On 17 January 2013, PAIGC signed the Political Transition Pact. A Memorandum towards the realisation of an inclusive government was signed by (PAIGC) and Social Renovation Party (PRS) on 17 May 2013, paving the way for the formation of an inclusive government on 6 June 2013. The elections to end the transitional government were held in April 2014.

Historical Political Antecedents in Central African Republic

The Central African Republic postindependence history has been marked by chronic instability, reflected in serial coup d'etats and almost constant rebellion, with elections far and few in between. One major indicator of the instability in that country is that of the nine Heads of State since independence in 1960, six came to power by military coups or rebellion, with one of those leaders having come to power twice. After a period of prolonged military rule, the first democratic elections were held in 1993, which saw Ange-Felix Patasse elected as President. In 1996, three years into his tenure, the country witnessed three mutinies by soldiers ostensibly because of salary arrears and unequal treatment of military officers from different ethnic groups. In an effort to tackle the crisis, an Inter-African Mission to Monitor the Implementation of the Bangui Accords (MISAB) was deployed in 1997. The Bangui Accords were signed in January 1997 under the mediation of General Amadou Toumani Toure of Mali.

The MISAB was subsequently replaced by the UN Mission in Central African Republic (MINURCA) in 1998, which stayed till February 2000. The key mandate of the MINURCA was to support the legislative elections of December 1998 and the presidential elections of 1999 as well as to support the reform of the security sector. Ange-Felix Patasse won the presidential elections. In April 2000, the MINURCA was replaced by the UN Political Office in Central African Republic (BONUCA) and later by UN Integrated Peacebuilding Office in Central African Republic (BINUCA) in 2009. Following an unsuccessful coup attempt in May 2001, in which he was implicated, Francois Bozize fled the country and returned in 2003 to seize power. In 2002, the Economic and Monetary Community of Central Africa (CEMAC) established a subregion Multinational Force in Central Africa (FOMUC), which consisted of troops from Cameroon, Chad, Gabon, and the Republic of Congo. The operational responsibilities over FOMUC were formally transferred to the Economic Community of Central African States (ECCAS) on 12 July 2008, and the subregional peacekeeping force, called MICOPAX, became operational in January 2009.

In the 2005 general and presidential elections, François Bozizé was elected president and his government committed to an Inclusive Political Dialogue, in an attempt to put an end to the country's recurrent political and security crises. The Dialogue's Preparatory Committee (CPDPI), formed in December 2007, brought together representatives from the government, the opposition, civil society, and the armed groups to elaborate a consensual framework for an inclusive political dialogue. In that spirit, the government concluded separate peace agreements with the Democratic and Popular Forces of the CAR (FDPC) in Syrte, Libya in February 2007, and with the Union of Democratic and Republican Forces (UFDR) in Birao in April 2007. The government's separate peace agreement with the Popular Army for the Restoration of Democracy (APRD) was signed in Libreville, in May 2008. The Government concluded a Comprehensive Peace Agreement with APRD and the UFDR in Libreville in June 2008. The Inclusive Political Dialogue was finally held in December 2008.

The results of President Bozize's reelection in January 2011, on the platform of the National Convergence Kwa Na Kwa (KNK) party, were rejected by the three other candidates who contested in those elections. Almost two years after those elections, in December 2012, violence erupted in the northeast of the country led by a rebel alliance called Seleka consisting of the Union of Democratic and Republican Forces (UFDR), the Convention of Patriots for Justice and Peace(CPJP), and the Wa Kodro Salute Patriotic Convention (CPSK). Mediation efforts under the auspices of the Economic Community for Central African States (ECCAS) resulted in the signing of the Libreville Agreement between the Seleka Alliance and the government of President Bozize in January 2013.

Under the terms of the Libreville Agreement, Bozize was allowed to remain in power until 2016 and Nicolas Tiangaye was named as the new Prime Minister and Michel Djotodia, Head of the Seleka Alliance, was named First Deputy Prime Minister. However, on 24 March 2013, in defiance of the Libreville Agreement, the Seleka Alliance marched into Bangui and overthrew Bozize, whom the Seleka claimed had not honoured the commitments he made in Libreville. Michel Djotodia, then, proclaimed himself Head of State of the Transitional Government. In April 2013, Ndjamena Roadmap was adopted that reaffirmed the key understandings of the Libreville Agreement. Despite the various accords, widespread acts of violence erupted in various parts of the country involving fighting not only among the various factions of the Seleka Alliance but also between Seleka fighters, many of them Muslims and initially regarded as local self-defence groups, and the Christian militias referred to as "anti-balaka" or "anti-machete."

Indeed, a disturbing trend in the conflict in the Central African Republic was that it assumed a sectarian character, with Christian and Muslims launching reprisal attacks on each other. In response to the intensifying violence, France sent an intervention force of

1600 soldiers to work alongside an AU African-led International Support Mission in CAR (MISCA) of about 6000 soldiers that took over from ECCAS's MICOPAX force on 19 December 2013. On 10 January 2014, nine months after they came to power, Michel Djotodia and Nicolas Tiangaye, his Prime Minister, were forced to resign at a meeting of the Heads of State of ECCAS in Ndjamena, on the grounds that they had failed to curb the growing violence. His successor, Mr. Alexandre Ferdinand Nguendet, the Parliament leader, was named as an Interim President and, thus, became the 8th Head of State in the chequered history that country. Within fifteen days, he was replaced by Catherine Samba-Panza, who was elected as the new Head of the Transition. The UN Security Council voted on 10 April 2014 to authorise a 12, 000 strong peacekeeping force into the Central African Republic mainly to protect civilians in that country.

How the Political Antecedents Shaped the Environment for PBC Engagement

No two countries on the PBC agenda better illustrates the difficulties the PBC has encountered in supporting postconflict peacebuilding than Guinea-Bissau and the Central African Republic. In both cases, PBC engagement began at a period of relative lull from the pattern of chronic instability, raising hopes that the domestic country contexts were auspicious for peacebuilding and that this time would be different. This expectation proved to be both false and short-lived. In no time, both countries reverted to their usual patterns; eruption into political crisis or violence that manifested in different forms.

In the first five years of being placed on the agenda (2007-2012), Guinea-Bissau witnessed one convulsing political episode after another. Thus, in 2008 there was an unsuccessful coup attempt in August of that year, resulting in the fleeing from the country of the senior naval officer, José Américo Bubo Na Tchuto who was accused of masterminding it. In March 2009, President Joao Bernardo Vieira and General Batista Tagme Na Waie, the Chief of the General Staff of the Armed Forces, were killed. In April 2010, a group of military officers briefly detained Prime Minister Carlos Gomes, Jr., and replaced Admiral Zamora Induta, the Chief of

General Staff of the Armed Forces with General Antonio Indjai. On 26 December 2011, there was an incident that was widely described as a failed coup attempt. On 12 April 2012, the Military High Command staged a coup overthrowing the government of Interim President Raimundo Pereira in the lead to the second round of presidential elections.

Two key factors have exacerbated the instability and fragility in Guinea-Bissau. The first factor is the deeply entrenched belief among a segment of the military, especially the "old generation of soldiers" who fought in the liberation struggle, that they have an inherited right to lead or at the very least to call the political tunes in the country. Closely linked to that belief is the problem of how to retire the "old generation of soldiers". As General Batista Tagme Na Waie, the late Chief of the General Staff of the Armed Forces, was used to saying, the old soldiers must be "retired with dignity", meaning that they need to receive national recognition for their contribution to the national liberation struggle and a good retirement package as an incentive. This requires adequate financial remuneration which neither the government nor its partners have been able to provide. The situation may be changing with renewed financial support by ECOWAS for security sector reforms in Guinea-Bissau, and by the international community, reflected in the pledge of €1.15 billion in aid over ten years at the 25 March, 2015 Donor Conference in Brussels.

The second factor that had complicated the situation in Guinea-Bissau was the growing use of that country as a transit point for trade in illegal drugs that originates from Latin America to European markets. There is a widely held belief that the political upheavals in Guinea-Bissau were increasingly partly linked to the competition among the military elites for control of a greater share of the illicit drug trade. Three senior military officers have been accused of complicity in drug trafficking and blacklisted by the US government. One of them José Américo Bubo Na Tchuto was arrested in a sting operation by the US Drug Enforcement Agency on 2 April 2013. Drug traffickers appear to have settled on Guinea-Bissau as country of transit because of its weak institutions, especially in the security and justice sectors. In many important respects, therefore, drug trafficking had become both a cause and a consequence of Guinea-Bissau's political turbulence.

In the Central African Republic, three main factors have historically conspired to frustrate sustained peacebuilding efforts. The first factor is what amounts to a state of permanent rebellion in that country: one group is always sufficiently aggrieved to lead a rebellion against the government of the day. At the time of PBC engagement in 2008, peace agreements had been signed between the government and the various politico-military groups, as they are referred to in the country. But many of these agreements were honoured more in breach than in observance. Indeed, the Seleka Rebellion was launched in December 2012 ostensibly because the government of President Bozize was seen as defaulting on critical aspects of agreements previously signed between it and factions of the Seleka Alliance and as preparing to breach the constitutional provision on two terms by contemplating a run for a third term in 2016.

The second factor has been the failure of successive governments to provide basic safety as well as social and administrative services to the people in a huge swathe of the country, coincidentally the areas mainly inhabited by the Muslim population. A striking illustration of this is that, although CAR has approximately the same geographic size as France, even if the population size differs, before the onset of the Seleka Rebellion in December 2012, the Central African Armed Forces (FACA) had an estimated strength of 6,000 soldiers, a police force of 1,750 and gendarmerie of 2,000 personnel. This lack of institutional capacity by the state to exercise authority over its geographic space has prompted the labeling of the Central African Republic as "phantom State."[8]

The third factor that compounds the state weakness is that, although the military serves as a tool of repression and maintenance of law and order, it has suffered serial neglect, which in turn makes it ill-equipped to defend the country, instead of the regime of the day. Indeed, the President was always in fear of his own army overthrowing him.

Expectations Concerning PBC Engagement

Against this backdrop, what were the expectations of the governments of these two countries regarding PBC engagement? Before answering that question, it will be useful to answer another question repeatedly asked about PBC engagement in those two countries, namely, why did the PBC agree to the requests of these two countries to come on the agenda, given the historic instability in both countries? The response to the latter question comes in two parts: first was the hope that PBC's engagement would help to rally international support for the key peacebuilding challenges in the two countries. Second was that given the lull in the violence or the absence of political crisis at the time of PBC engagement, it was felt that the PBC had a window of opportunity for serious engagement. Or to put it differently, there was the feeling that the demons that haunted both countries had been banished but, sadly, they returned in no time. In any case, rejecting the request from these countries — which were the third and fourth countries, after Burundi and Sierra Leone — would have sent the wrong signal that the PBC was not keen to welcome more countries to its fold or on its agenda.

The governments of both countries had specific expectations of the PBC. At the time of PBC engagement in Guinea-Bissau, the government expected the PBC to support its effort in security-sector reforms, an issue that had proved particularly elusive. The main planks of SSR were obvious: to modernise the military and to retire the soldiers, who were generally believed to have reached or passed retirement age. Any serious modernisation had to grapple with the inverted pyramidal structure of the army, which had a high ratio of officers to the non-officer corps, and with ensuring the "retirement of soldiers with dignity." Strong political will and adequate financial support were central to tackling both issues, but these were lacking — an effort that saw little progress not least because of the lack of support within the military for the retirement exercise. The PBC's efforts to focus on the issue of mobilising resources for military pension fund was undercut by the political turbulence in that country. The other expectation was that PBC engagement might contribute to supporting national, regional, and international efforts to curb the growing incidence of drug trafficking in the country. There again, the effort by the PBC aided by the PBF to provide financial support to build institutional capacity, by rehabilitating prisons to incarcerate drug traffickers and strengthening the national anti-drug unit, made little headway mainly because of the political situation.

In Central African Republic, the government had three main expectations concerning PBC engagement. First, the government looked to the PBC for diplomatic and financial support to the inclusive political dialogue that was underway at the initial phase of PBC engagement. In response to the latter, the PBF made financial allocation to support the political dialogue. Second, the government put much premium on helping to mobilise financial support for the disarmament, demobilisation, and reintegration programme as a way to ease the transition of many ex-combatants into society. While the PBF provided financial support for DDR in the northwest part of the country, with salutary effects; funding for the DDR in the north-east was not forthcoming from other donors. This prompted the SRSG to convene a Group of Friends meeting in New York in April 2012 to mobilise financial support for the DDR in that region. Third, the government also had expectations that PBC would support its efforts to mobilise resources for the second generation poverty reduction plan. This led the PBC both to organise a high-level event in New York in September 2010 and support the convening of a partner's roundtable in Brussels in August 2011.

Experiences in these two countries crystallise the problems that the PBC must grapple with in its efforts to support the fragile countries on its agenda. Those experiences serve as a cautionary tale in dealing with most postonflict contexts, even when we should acknowledge that the cases are extreme.

The Promise of the Two Latest Entrants on the Agenda: Liberia and Guinea

Historical Political Antecedents in Liberia

The civil war in Liberia mutated from a rebellion launched by the National Patriotic Front of Liberia (NPLF) and was led by

Charles Taylor in 1989 to overthrow Samuel Doe, who had himself overthrown the elected government of President William Tolbert. ECOMOG intervened in 1990 to halt the conflict, disarm Liberia's warring factions, restore peace, and organise elections, which Charles Taylor won in 1997. The ECOMOG intervention lasted from 1990 to 1998. As in Sierra Leone, one motivation for the rebellion was the desire to gain access to the natural resource wealth of the country — rubber, timber, and iron ore. The dictatorial style of Charles Taylor coupled with the desire of other factions to have access to power and resources, provoked another rebellion launched from Guinea in 1999 by the Liberians United for Reconciliation and Democracy (LURD).

Following a very brutal fight that killed many people in 2003, Charles Taylor was forced into exile and the Accra Comprehensive Peace Agreement was signed in August 2003, paving the way for a transition government. An ECOWAS Mission in Liberia (ECOMIL) was deployed which became part of, and was eventually replaced by, the UN Mission in Liberia (UNMIL) in October 2003. With the help of UNMIL, elections were conducted in November 2005, and Ellen Johnson Sirleaf was elected president. Almost immediately thereafter, the newly elected President requested that Charles Taylor, who had been living in exile in Nigeria, should be sent for trial at the International Special Court for Sierra Leone and was subsequently transferred to The Hague for trial. The International Criminal Court convicted Charles Taylor in May 2012 of aiding and abetting war crimes. Meanwhile the second postconflict elections were held in November 2012 at which Ellen Johnson Sirleaf was reelected president.

Historical Political Antecedents in Guinea

Of the six countries on the agenda of the PBC, Guinea is the only one that had not fought a civil war and the only one that has not had a peacekeeping or special political mission. The Statement of Mutual Commitments — the instrument of engagement — between the PBC and the government of Guinea put it very well, when it observed that ["Guinea's need for national reconciliation is not the result of a civil conflict. Instead, it is the cumulative effect of several decades of authoritarian rule and military dictatorship which has left a legacy of fractured civilian-military relationships, a population that has lost all confidence in those that govern it, gross human rights violations and deep interethnic rivalry, exacerbated during the 2010 presidential elections. As Guineans have said, "We have not lived through violent conflict, but we face the same challenges as a country emerging from violent conflict."[9]

Guinea's authoritarian rule manifested itself in three phases: from 1958-1984, under the leadership of Sekou Toure, who assumed the reins of power at independence; from 1984 - 2008, under Lasana Conte, who seized power after the death of Sekou Toure; and from 2008-2010, under Moussa Dadis Camara, who also seized power soon after the death of Conte. Two adverse developments that occurred in rapid succession contributed to cutting short the rule of Camara. First was the massive protest on 28 September 2009 at which soldiers fired ammunition on opposition supporters in the national stadium, resulting in the death of over 150 persons and injuring a large number of others. Second was the failed assassination attempt, on 3 December 2009, on the life of Camara, which led to his medical evacuation and handing over power to General Sekouba Konate as an Interim President. Following mediation by President Blaise Comparore of Burkina Faso, the Joint Declaration of Ouagadougou was signed in January 2010, which led to installing a six-month transitional government that supervised the presidential elections, won by Alpha Conde, to whom power was handed over on 21 December 2010. Moreover, after several postponements, the legislative elections were held in September 2013, completing the transition from authoritarian rule to democratic civilian rule.

How the Historical Antecedents Shaped the Environment for PBC Engagement

The historical political antecedents in both countries have shaped the environment for PBC engagement in distinct ways. Liberia is the first country with an active peacekeeping mission to be placed on the agenda of the PBC. The Statement of Mutual Commitments (SMC) identified three priorities: security-sector reforms, rule of law, and national reconciliation. The SMC also noted that "further support [in those three areas] will facilitate a smooth transfer from UNMIL, with the close collaboration of the United Nations country team, to the Government of Liberia in security management."[10] Moreover, at the time of PBC engagement, a Truth and Reconciliation Commission had issued its report and recommendations on how to advance the process of national reconciliation in the country. The departure for exile and subsequent trial in The Hague of Charles Taylor meant that one "spoiler" was longer in the political scene to cause more problems.

By the time the PBC began its engagement in Guinea, the democratically elected government had determined that security sector reform would be accorded high priority. By then, a Security Sector Roadmap for the country had been prepared by the government in collaboration with the African Union, ECOWAS, and the United Nations. The emphasis on the SSR reflected a political commitment to overcome the legacy of prolonged periods of authoritarian rule by rejuvenating the military, including retiring officers, some of whom have participated as agents or instigators of human rights violations. A closely related effort was launching a broad-based national reconciliation effort in a country that has become riven with political or ethnic tensions and crises.

Expectations Concerning PBC Engagement

The Presidents of Liberia and Guinea have not only shown their strong commitment to the process of engagement with the PBC but have been very clear about what the PBC should do to support the peacebuilding process in their respective countries. Both evinced their commitment to engagement with PBC by personally participating in the meeting at which the Statements of Mutual Commitments were adopted: President Ellen Johnson Sirleaf joined, through Video Tele-Conference, the meeting of the PBC Liberia configuration held on 16 November 2010; and President Alpha Conde personally attended the PBC Guinea configuration on 23 September held in New York.

The specific expectations of the government of Liberia included support for the establishment of the regional justice and security hubs in Liberia. The regional hubs are designed to achieve three goals: support the UNMIL transition by helping the government to assume some of the functions currently being performed by the UNMIL; increase citizens' access to justice and security services by locating police, courts and immigration services at the hubs; and enhance the government's efforts to decentralize the provision of those services from the national capital to various parts of the country. Five regional hubs will be built to serve the fifteen counties in the country; each regional hub will serve three counties. The first of the regional justice and security hubs is located in Gbarnga in Bong County and was commissioned by the President of Liberia in February 2013. Work has started on the next two hubs to be located in Harper and Zwedru. The fourth and fifth regional hubs will be located in Tubmanburg and Buchanan. At the same time, the PBC has offered support for the development of a Roadmap for National Reconciliation.

Reflecting his determination to draw maximum benefits from the PBC engagement, the President of Guinea had written twice to the Secretary-General to clearly indicate the areas where assistance should be offered to his government to advance peacebuilding in his country. In his first letter, he requested financial assistance for paying retirement benefits (mainly in the form of a lump sum) for 3928 soldiers and for recruiting a high-level adviser on SSR to advise the government on the reform of the defence and security sector. The Peacebuilding Fund paid for part of the retirement benefits and fully for the services of the high level adviser. The President has also written to solicit support in reforming the criminal justice system of the country. The UN is coordinating its response with the European Commission, which is the main donor in this area.

We now return to the central question of this section. *Why have some countries on the agenda of the PBC done relatively better than others?* We examine that question through the prism of commitment of the national authorities, the individual country context, and the scale and scope of international support. In proffering an explanation to this question, a few points bear particular emphasis. No two countries are alike or should be treated alike when it comes to national peacebuilding efforts. Historical political antecedents shape the outcomes of peacebuilding efforts.

The foregoing review of the experience of the six countries on the agenda of the PBC has shown that those countries which have made progress or showing much promise in peacebuilding are marked by the strong commitment of national stakeholders, especially of the political leadership to peacebuilding. That may seem a stylized fact, but it does not mean that it is an easy attribute, which is why it cannot be taken for granted. Another critical factor is the degree to which the influence of "spoilers" have been significantly curtailed or eliminated in the countries doing relatively well. The progress in Sierra Leone, Liberia, and Burundi can be attributed to the confluence of these factors as well as the fairly significant international support that was given these countries at important turning points in their peace-consolidation efforts.

Even so, in the case of Burundi, there is growing concern that the elections scheduled for the period May to August 2015 could generate a new bout of instability, if the president runs for a third five-year term. The resulting political confrontations and popular protests would set back peacebuilding efforts in that country.

The factors that have provided the underpinning of stability in the other countries have been lacking in the Central African Republic and Guinea-Bissau. In both countries, especially the latter, the military has become a sort of permanent "spoiler" to the consolidation of democratic traditions. Guinea-Bissau and Central African Republic which have been respectively wracked by serial coups and rebellion, have been least able to stay the course of peacebuilding compared to the other four countries. This is not a reason for despair about such situations but a cause for reflection on how best the international community, including the PBC should engage such countries. It is also the case that there has been tardiness of international response to critical political developments in these two countries, a major contributory factor for events spiralling out of control in both countries. It remains unclear the extent to which the elections of April 2014 will mark a positive, major turning point in the political evolution of Guinea-Bissau. In the Central African Republic, hope remains that the current effort to stabilise the country with the support and active military presence of the United Nations, which replaced the African Union forces, would lay the foundation for long term stability and economic recovery.

B. Was the PBC Willed Enough Means to Achieve the Desired Ends?

The desired end for PBC work was well reflected in the founding resolution, which recommended that one of the main purposes of Commission was "to focus attention on the reconstruction and institution building efforts necessary for recovery from conflict and to support the development of integrated strategies in order to lay the foundation for sustainable development."[11] This paragraph recognised that PBC was established to support reconstruction, contribute to recovery, and lay the foundation for, rather than promote, development. This suggests that while PBC engagement would inevitably be temporary, it must be focused on certain targeted interventions.

Assessing whether the PBC was willed enough means to achieve the desired ends turns critically on three issues: Was it endowed with sufficient institutional authority as a new institution to undertake the tasks assigned to it? Was it endowed with a robust funding arrangement to support the countries on its agenda? And does it have staying power in the countries on its agenda? This section addresses the last two questions, as the first question is addressed separately in the next section which discusses the position and authority of the PBC among the constellation of UN bodies and processes.

As I have noted in chapter 3, countries emerging from conflict can be classified into three categories on the basis of their initial fiscal conditions and extent of their external support when the conflict ends. The first category of countries includes those that draw on their own financial resources to meet their postconflict peacebuilding needs. This has been the case with a number of oil producing countries that have emerged from conflict in the past four decades (Nigeria in 1970; Kuwait in 1991; and Angola in 2002). The second category of countries includes those that many donors are ready and willing to help. These are the postconflict countries referred to as "donor darlings". The seventeen countries of Europe that benefited from the Marshall Plan from 3 April, 1948 – 30 June, 1951 and, in contemporary terms, Afghanistan belong to this category. The third category is the postconflict countries referred to as "donor-orphans", which often receive very limited external financial support. By coming on the agenda of the PBC, any postconflict country that belongs to the third category potentially stands a better chance of increased international attention, including financial support.

The major shortcoming of not willing enough means to the PBC, in terms of financial arrangement, can be traced to the report of the High Level Panel that neither proposed a funding mechanism for peacebuilding nor assigned it any responsibility for "marshalling resources" — to use the term of art subsequently reflected in the founding resolution. The ensuing Secretary-General's report did a little better by suggesting that the PBC should "help to ensure predictable financing for early recovery activities, in part by providing an overview of assessed, voluntary and standing funding mechanisms."[12] Even that report did not contain the idea of the Peacebuilding Fund — which emerged from the negotiations on the World Summit Outcome Document.

Yet, the importance of providing financial support for postconflict reconstruction was well recognised in the historically most important postconflict reconstruction effort[13] in modern times: The Marshall Plan. George Marshall said in his famous Harvard address of 5 June 1947: "that truth of the matter is that Europe's requirements for the next three or four years of food and other essential products — principally from America — are much greater than her present ability to pay, that she must have *substantial additional help,* or face economic, social and political deterioration of a very grave character."[14] The emphasis on substantial additional help is significant. The Marshall Plan eventually provided the sum of US$12.5 billion (equal to the annualized 1.2 percent of the US gross domestic product at that time) during the period that the plan was in effect.

A prominent scholar of the Marshall Plan has noted that the US motive for organising the Marshall Plan was more than altruistic–what Marshall himself declaimed as a [fight] "against hunger, poverty, desperation and chaos". Rather, as Diane Kunz has noted, "charitable considerations played a large role in the Marshall Plan, but strategic concerns were equally important". She explained that the strategic consideration was containing communism and noted that there were also domestic considerations (tackling nascent recession in US economy by increasing exports to Europe) and national security consideration (that Marshall Plan would make Europe safe for capitalism as New Deal had done the same for the US).[15] Today, if we substitute combating terrorism for containing communism, as the strategic consideration, it becomes obvious why a country like Afghanistan has received so much international support compared with the post-conflict and fragile African states on the agenda of the PBC. The scale and scope of international support for Afghanistan is reflected in table 11. It is beyond dispute that scale and scope of international support for all six countries is much far less than that of Afghanistan.

With the possible exception of Burundi, where significant international support has been evinced at the two donor conferences, financial support has been less than forthcoming at critical junctures in the peacebuilding of many of the countries on PBC agenda. On closer examination, however, most of the countries currently on the agenda fail the strategic considerations test on two counts: None of them is as yet a haven for terrorists, and they appear to lack geostrategic significance. But we must ponder whether the conditions in these countries have to deteriorate to the point of being failed states, at which point they could be a haven for terrorists before international community would spring into action. The phrase "a stitch in time saves nine" should apply: The situations in these countries should not be allowed to relapse or deteriorate because of inadequate international support.

The PBC's staying power in the countries on its agenda can be examined from three perspectives: the length of engagement with the country; the outcomes of the engagement; and the response to eruption of crisis or violence. There was no precise guidance from either the report of the High Level Panel or the Secretary-General or the founding resolution on how long PBC engagement with a country should last. The High Level Panel proposed only that "the efforts of international community in postconflict peacebuilding over whatever period may be necessary". The founding resolution recommended that the PBC should "contribute to recovery and help lay the foundations for sustainable development."

But we know that around 40 percent of postconflict countries relapse into violence within a decade.[16] Based on this observed trend, Paul Collier has argued that aid to postconflict countries should be "sustained for a decade, not just the first couple of years,"[17] noting later that "post-conflict recovery was the initial rationale for international aid agencies."[18] Meanwhile, the PBC itself has not developed any guidelines on the issue of length of engagement, cognisant of the differences in each country context. The two countries that have remained longest on its agenda are Burundi and Sierra Leone, both of which came on the agenda in 2006. However, the finding that postconflict countries relapse within a decade must be borne in mind in determining of how long the PBC should be engaged in any country. Even so, other considerations will include the views of the government as well as the purpose of continued engagement.

The added value and the outcomes of PBC engagement will ineluctably evolve over time. The longer the PBC engages with a country, the more carefully targeted the interventions that national stakeholders, especially the government, will expect of the PBC. Indeed, the areas where the PBC should direct its support for national peacebuilding efforts have to be a subject of agreement between the government and the PBC, consistent with the principle of national ownership and leadership of the peacebuilding process. The extent of progress that has been made in the original peacebuilding priorities, spelt out in the instrument of engagement, and the ability to address new and emerging priorities, especially in situations of exit by a mission, will be key determinants of the PBC's prolonged engagement. The nature, scope, and length of the PBC's engagement in a country after the withdrawal of peacekeeping or special political missions — where they had existed — will be a major test of its staying power. In any case, the outcome of a sustained PBC engagement must respond to and conform with the expectation that the country is making discernible progress and showing its commitment to laying the foundation for durable peace.

A critical test of PBC staying power is how it responds to outbreaks of political crisis or the eruption of violence. The nature of its response will naturally have to be calibrated to the type of crisis. It is possible to envisage three types of political crises situations: inter-party disputes that could potentially lead to political violence; an unconstitutional change of government; and a full-scale rebellion or insurrection that leads to a change of government. Although it might be possible to anticipate the first and third types of crises, the second type could evolve so rapidly as to make any meaningful response possible. The PBC's record to date shows that while it could help in ameliorating the first type of crisis, the second and the third types have proven problematic not only for the PBC but also for the Security Council. In any case, it is far from clear that the PBC has the tools to address the second and third types of situations.

This brief review of the issues in this section has shown that it is hard to come to any conclusion other than that the PBC was not willed enough financial means to do its work and its staying power in the countries on the agenda is still a work in progress.

C. Has the Position and Authority of the PBC in the Constellation of United Nations Bodies and Processes Affected its Effectiveness?

Although created under the joint authority of the UN General Assembly and the Security Council, there were scarcely any institutional adjustments in the constellation of UN bodies and processes as a consequence of its creation. How would such institutional adjustments have looked? Starting from the premise that PBC was designed, among other things, to improve coherence and coordination in peacebuilding in the United Nations, as envisaged in the founding resolution, there were at least three specific ways that such adjustments should have unfolded.

The first institutional adjustment should have been to transfer the portfolio of work from the ECOSOC Ad Hoc Advisory Group on Countries Emerging from Conflict to the PBC. The Advisory Group was created at a time when there was no institution within the UN intergovernmental architecture to address the needs of the group of countries that the Advisory Group handled. The creation of the Advisory Group was predicated on the same consideration that inspired the establishment of the PBC, with the added advantage that the PBC has more comprehensive remit. Although two of the countries (Burundi and Guinea-Bissau) on the agenda of the Advisory Group later transferred to the PBC and asked to be taken off the agenda of the Advisory Group, this was not a part of creative institutional adjustment in response to the establishment of PBC. Instead, it was at the initiative of the two concerned governments. Today, the Advisory Group exists alongside the PBC, conforming to a commonly observed pattern in the UN where old bodies continue to exist even though new ones have overtaken their purpose.

The second institutional adjustment pertains to PBC relations with the Security Council. This relationship is important not only because the Security Council is one of the routes through which countries are referred to the PBC but also because the Security Council is one of the "joint parents" of the PBC. Indeed, the original recommendation of the High Level Panel was that the PBC will be "chaired by a member approved by the Security Council". A number of institutional adjustments by the Security Council would have put the PBC on a firmer footing than it has turned out to be. One such adjustment would have included tasking the PBC to report on specific issues and by so doing strengthen the Council's ability to respond to developments in the countries on the PBC agenda. Another adjustment would have been a clearer guidance on the roles of the Chairs of PBC country configurations and the Special Executive/Representatives of the Secretary General (E/SRSGs). In the event, these two issues were left to evolve through a process of "learning by doing" rather than by deliberate design. There is nothing wrong with "learning by doing", except that in the context of new intergovernmental institutions; it not only creates more anxiety and problems than is necessary, but it lacks the legitimacy of orderly design. The initial lack of effort on clarifying the relationship between the Chairs of the country configurations and the E/SRSGs created problems in those relationships and gave the unfortunate impression that the two were in competition. A strong and effective partnership between the Chairs of the country configurations and the E/SRSGs is fundamental to the UN effort in supporting peacebuilding.

There is a third way that institutional adjustment should have been made: By linking the Post-Conflict Needs Assessment (PCNA) process to the work of PBC. Introduced since 2003, three years before the inception of the PBC in 2006, the PCNA is an important tool for conducting postconflict needs assessments in order to better appreciate the challenges and needs of countries emerging from conflict. It combines conflict analysis and sector priority settings in each country context. PCNAs have been conducted in Iraq (2003); Afghanistan (2004); Liberia (2004-2005); Timor-Leste (2006); Haiti (2006); Somalia (2006); Sudan — North and South (2006); Georgia (2008) and Yemen (2010 and 2012).

The PCNA is supported by a partnership consisting of the United Nations, the World Bank and the European Commission. In 2008, these three institutions signed a Joint Declaration on Post-Crisis Assessments and Recovery Planning in which these institutions decided to coordinate crisis response frameworks and "agreed upon a common platform to enhance country resilience to crises, answer to recovery needs of vulnerable populations and strengthen the capacity of national institutions for effective response and prevention."[19] A Project Advisory group has also been established comprising one representative each from the European Commission, the World Bank, the African Development Bank, three representatives of the UN Development Group (UNDP, UNICEF and UN Habitat), and three representatives of the UN Secretariat(PBSO, DPA, and DPKO).

Both the World Bank and the European Commission, which are the main partners with the UN in the PCNA, are members of the organisational and country specific configurations of the PBC. The main institutional adjustment that should have been made would be to use the PCNA as tool for supporting the PBC's work on conflict analysis and priority setting in the lead up to the adoption of the instrument of engagement between the PBC and the country on the agenda. The second way that the PCNA would have contributed to PBC work is to make the PCNA provide all its assessments to the PBC, so that a discussion could be had on how PBC could support the countries where the PCNA has been completed. In that way, there would be a potentially bigger portfolio of countries on the PBC agenda, in as much as the countries would come not only through referral procedures set out in the founding resolution but also through links with the PCNA process.

Concluding Reflections

While countries on the PBC agenda cannot realistically expect to be accorded the same level of financial support or attention like post-World War II Europe or present-day Afghanistan, they should have a reasonable hope that international support would be more forthcoming than the present record shows. But is such a hope realistic? Not so much. This is because the international community's generosity is being stretched to the limit. The UN peacekeeping budget stands at US$7.54 9 billion per year; the humanitarian appeal for 2014 was US$13 billion — a Marshall Plan size amount (half of which was meant for Syria); and many traditional donor developed countries are just beginning to recover from the global economic and financial crisis that broke out in 2008.

Yet, it is hard to imagine how serious peacebuilding can be undertaken without adequate financial support. If the Marshall Plan cannot be used as a standard for gauging international support for countries on the PBC agenda because they lack strategic significance, international support for Afghanistan can serve as a benchmark. If, as it has become increasingly clear that failed states can be haven for terrorists and failing peacebuilding efforts are a major contributory factor for many of the humanitarian emergencies, the time may be ripe to give serious thought to the need for enhanced support for peacebuilding. But, then again none of the countries on the agenda of the PBC has served as a haven for terrorists to warrant anguished international debate and political anxiety on how to support them. The fact that the scale and scope of international funding to countries on PBC agenda is less than was required is one proof that PBC was not willed enough means to achieve its desired ends. This has important implications for the work of the PBC: it must focus on a very limited set of peacebuilding priorities that it can reasonably deliver on.

This reflection on the performance of the PBC in African countries would not be complete without commenting on the impact of the outbreak of the Ebola Virus Disease on the peacebuilding efforts in the three worst-affected countries in West Africa: Guinea, Liberia, and Sierra Leone, all of which are on the agenda of the PBC. The outbreak of Ebola began in Guinea in December 2013 and spread to Liberia in March 2014 and Sierra Leone in May 2014. As of 8 March, 2015, a total of 24,247 people have been infected by the virus in these three countries of which 9,961 had died.[20] This is represents an aggregate mortality rate of 41.08 percent.

In addition to the horrific loss of lives, the economic impact of Ebola on these three countries has been severe. The IMF estimated that economic growth in Liberia and Sierra Leone would decline by 3-4 per cent in 2014 and in Guinea by 1.5 per cent in 2014. Separately, the World Bank had estimated in October 2014 that the two-year regional financial impact for West Africa could reach US$32.6 billion by the end of 2015 and under a medium-term high-impact scenario. This estimate was revised down to $4 billion on 19 November 2014. The lost GDP stemming from Ebola in the three countries could by 2015 reach US$815 million, consisting of US$142 million for Guinea, US$234 million for Liberia, and US$439 million for Sierra Leone.[21]

The sudden outbreak of Ebola illustrates how an entirely unexpected event can intrude into and set back peacebuilding efforts in countries emerging from conflict. It is a rude reminder that the PBC will sometimes be confronted with, and will be required to respond to, a range of crises — from political crisis, to economic crisis, to epidemic crisis, and to natural (earthquake or hurricane) or man-made disasters — in the countries on the agenda. This means that the crises the PBC might confront in course of its engagement with a country will not be the same and neither should PBC's response to them.

In deciding on the response of the PBC to the Ebola pandemic, it is useful to remember that Ebola is, firstly a health issue, albeit one with dire consequences for the politics, economy, and society of the affected countries. The effects of Ebola on peacebuilding efforts have manifested themselves through three main channels:

reduced economic growth with implications for employment and government revenue; fraying social cohesion and trust; and further withering of the institutional capacity of the state in many sectors.

The PBC efforts to play a role in this context have to begin with the realisation that there are many international actors well placed to tackle the various consequences of the Ebola crisis. Thus, WHO and UNICEF have been handling the health issues; the AfDB, the ECA, the World Bank, and other IFIs have undertaken the economic analyses; and the IFIs and a host of bilateral development partners have offered technical and financial resources.

Indeed, the need to play a sharply focused role in the aftermath of and in response to the ravages of Ebola in the three countries noted above had been well recognised by PBC member states, when they affirmed "the need to focus on peacebuilding needs and requirements which will emerge in the aftermath of the epidemic and emphasised the need for PBC to focus on the epidemic's impact on social cohesion, security and political institutions and continued improvements in governance."[22]

Against this backdrop, the role of and response by the PBC has to be guided by three principles: It has to focus on an area where its own previous efforts may have been undercut by the Ebola crisis; such an area must be one that is not already being addressed in an assistance programme of development partners in the context of the Ebola crisis; and it must be area that helps the government to maintain stability. The one area that meets these criteria is the security sector and rule of law institutions.

The role of the PBC here will be threefold: work with relevant departments of the UN to undertake Institutional Resilience Assessment of the key institutions in the security and rule of law sector by ascertaining the loss of capacity by death or departures of staff as a result of Ebola; by estimating the cost of rebuilding that capacity; and by mobilising international efforts to train and recruit to cover the lost capacity. In the midst of the panic and anxiety over Ebola, the task of such an assessment might not look urgent but it is important. The ability of these countries to recover and rebuild — which is what resilience is about — their institutional capacities for effective rule of law and robust security in the aftermath of the Ebola crisis will critically depend on this type of work by the PBC. Undertaking Institutional Resilience Assessment, along the lines spelt out above, in the relevant sector(s) in a post-crisis situation, whatever the crisis may be, could be a major value added for the PBC

Although the number of active conflicts in Africa is at a historic low, the challenges of peacebuilding in the region remain enormous. As such, Africa will now be a proving ground for the PBC — it can only do so, if it well supported by the international community. The explanation for the relatively better performance of some countries than others on the agenda of the PBC shows that historical political antecedents shape PBC engagement but also determines the outcomes of peacebuilding efforts. The degree of the commitment of national stakeholders, especially of the political leadership, is a critical factor in peacebuilding outcomes. That may seem a stylized fact, but it does not mean that it is an easy attribute, which is why it cannot be taken for granted. This review shows that it is hard to come to any conclusion other than that the PBC was not willed enough financial means to do its work. At the same time its staying power in the countries on the agenda is still a work progress. The 2015 Review of the PBC must grapple not only with the "mechanics" of PBC operations but structural reforms to anchor the PBC on a solid institutional foundation.

Table 9: Details on PBC Engagement with Countries on the Agenda

Country	Date Placed on PBC Agenda	Date of Adoption of Instrument of engagement	Agreed Peacebuilding Priorities	Date of Periodic Reviews	Chairs of the Configuration with Dates
Burundi	23 June 2006	20 June 2007	*Areas of current focus: Consolidation of democracy & dialogue; good governance; human rights & rule of law; support to PRSP & socio-economic reintegration of the vulnerable groups; regional integration	June 2008. February 2009. July 2009. March 2010. April 2011. July 2012.	Ambassador Johan Lovald (Norway), June 2006 to June 2008. Ambassador Anders Liden (Sweden), July 2008 to June 2009. Ambassador Peter Maurer (Switzerland), July 2009- May 2010. Ambassador Paul Seger (Switzerland), June 2010 to present.

Sierra Leone	23 June 2006	12 Dec 2007	*Areas of current focus: Tackling drug trafficking; youth employment and empowerment; improving governance.	June 2008. December. 2008. June 2009. September 2010. October. 2012.	Ambassador Frank Majoor (Netherlands), June 2006 to March 2009. Ambassador John McNee (Canada), April 2009 to July 2011. Ambassador Guillermo Rishchynski (Canada), September 2011 to present.
Guinea-Bissau	19 Dec 2007	1 October 2008	Elections & institution-building for the National Electoral Commission; measures to jump-start the economy & rehabilitate infrastructure, in particular the energy sector; security sector reform; strengthening of the justice sector; consolidating the rule of law & fighting drug trafficking; public administration reform & modernization; & social questions critical to peacebuilding.	January 2010	Ambassador Maria Luiza Ribeiro Viotti (Brazil), December 2007 to May 2013. Ambassador Luiz Alberto Figueiredo Machado (Brazil), June 2013-August 2013. Ambassador Antonio de Aguiar Patriota (Brazil) – September 2013 to present.

Central African Republic	12 June 2008	6 May 2009	Reform of the security sector reform and disarmament, demobilisation, reintegration; governance – rule of law; and development policies.	December 2009 August 2011 November 2011	Ambassador Jan Grauls (Belgium), June 2008 to May 2012. Ambassador Mohammed Loulichki (Morocco), June 2014 to present.
Liberia	16 Sept 2010	15 Nov 2010	Strengthening the rule of law; supporting security sector reform and promoting national reconciliation.	March 2012 March 2013 March 2014	Prince Zeid Ra'ad Al Hussein (Jordan), September 2010 to March 2012 Ambassador Staffan Tillander (Sweden), April 2012 to June 2014 Ambassador Marten Grundit (Sweden), July 2014 to January 2015. Ambassador Olof Skoog (Sweden), February 2015 to present.
Guinea	23 February 2011	23 Sept 2011	Promotion of national reconciliation; security sector reforms and defence reforms; youth and women employment policies.	June 2012 August 2014	Ambassador Sylvie Lucas (Luxembourg), February 2013 to present.

*Burundi=Strategic Framework was superseded by Final Outcome Document of the 5th Review adopted on 21 April 2011 and new areas of focus agreed upon.

*Sierra Leone = Peacebuilding Cooperation Framework was superseded by Outcome Document adopted at High-Level Event of 10 June 2009 and new areas of focus agreed upon.

Source: Compiled from Strategic Frameworks for peacebuilding, the Statements of Mutual Commitments Documents adopted on the dates indicated and from records of the periodic reviews, available in the UN Peacebuilding Support Office, New York.

Table 10. Basic Political, Economic, and Social Facts on PBC Agenda Countries

Country	YoPA	Pop. 2014 (million)	GDP (US$ billion) 2014	Human Dev. Index ranking (out of a Total of 187 countries) 2014	Life Expectancy 2014 (Years)	Mo Ibrahim Index of African Governance (out of 52 countries) 2014	ODA Per Capita (US$) Average of 2010-2014	Corruption Perception Index 2014 (out of 175 countries)
Burundi	August 2000	10.16	2.71	180	54.1	38	53	159
Central African Republic	June 2008	4.61	1.62	185	50.2	51	50	150
Guinea	N/A	11.74	6.14	179	56.1	42	30	145
Guinea-Bissau	November 1998	1.70	0.96	177	54.3	48	47	161
Liberia	August 2003	4.29	1.95	175	60.6	31	136	94
Sierra Leone	July 1999	6.09	4.13	183	45.6	38	74	119

YoPA means Year of Peace Agreement.

SOURCES:
Data on gross domestic product, ODA per capita and population are from World Bank data base.
Data on HDI and life expectancy are from UNDP Human Development Report, 2014.
Data on MO Ibrahim Index are from Ibrahim Index on African Governance Report, 2014.
Data on Corruption Perception Index are from Transparency International Corruption Perception Index 2014

Table 11. List of Conferences on Afghanistan

International Conference on Afghanistan, Bonn (2001)
- 5 December 2001
- Established Interim Authority
- Set out roles for UN-mandated force in Kabul
- Legal framework and judicial system

Afghanistan Recovery and Reconstruction Conference (2002)
- Tokyo, Japan
- Co-chaired by Japan, US, Saudi Arabia, and EU
- 21-22 January 2002
- More than 60 countries and 20 international organisation
- Pledged $1.8 billion for 2002
- Pledged $4.5 billion over five years

Afghanistan Development Forum (2002)
- April, 2002
- Held in Kabul
- Preliminary budget launched
- National programme launched

Oslo Donor Conference (2002)
- 18 December 2002
- Pledged $1.24 billion for 2003

Berlin Donor Conference (2004)
- 31 March -1 April 2004
- 65 nations/international organisations
- Pledged $8.2 billion over four years

London Donor Conference (2006)
- 31 January - 2February 2006
- Marked the launch of the Afghanistan Compact
- US pledged $1.1 billion, UK pledged $800 million

Rome Conference for Donor Countries on Rule of Law (2007)
- 2-3 July 2007
- ISISC appointed a legal advisor to lead the drafting of the National Justice Programme
- 24 donor states
- New pledges of approximately $360 million

Paris Donor Conference (2008)
- 12 June 2008
- Pledged over $21 billion

- More than 80 countries
- Major focus was Afghanistan National Development Strategy

International Conference on Afghanistan, Moscow (2009)
- 27 March 2009
- Convened under SCO
- Chinese disclosed that they had provided $180 million in assistance and written off outstanding debts
- Main focus to strengthen regional and international efforts to counteract issues

International Conference on Afghanistan, The Hague (2009)
- 30 March- 5 April 2009
- Representatives from over 90 countries
- UN declared it would take a more active role in Afghan development and aid elections

International Conference on Afghanistan, London (2010)
- 28 January 2010
- Participants agreed to support growth and expansion of Afghan National Army and Afghan National Police to 171,600 and 134,000
- $1.6 billion in debt relief by major creditors
- $25 million pledged by Australia

International Conference on Afghanistan, Kabul (2010)
- 20 July 2010
- Contemplating progress toward London Conference
- Afghanistan asks to align 80 percent of development assistance to national priority programmes introduced
- Afghanistan pledged to improve financial management system, collection of revenues
- 50% of aid to be channeled through Government of Afghanistan

Lisbon Summit (2010)
- 19-20 November 2010
- Karzai announced desire for NATO to return control of country by end of 2014
- Gradual handover of country's provinces to security forces agreed upon

The International Afghanistan Conference in Bonn (2011)
- 5 December 2011
- Discussed future of Afghanistan after the withdrawal
- Pledged economic support until 2024
- UK pledged to maintain current level of $278 million per year

- US estimated $650 million in support of small community-based development projects

Chicago Summit (2012)
- 20-21 May 2012
- NATO Summit
- Declared conclusion of ISAF mission in 2014
- Declared partnership post 2014, contingent upon reforms
- After 2014, switch from combat missions to training missions

International Conference on Afghanistan, Tokyo (2012)
- 8 July 2012
- Pledged $16 billion through 2015
- Conditional on Afghan government making reforms to fight corruption
- The Tokyo Mutual Accountability Framework lists 15 commitments the Afghan government has to meet in next two years
- Made a commitment to channel at least 50% of development assistance through national budget of Afghan Government

Donor Conference in Kabul (2013)
- 6 July 2013
- 40 donor countries attended
- Reiterated $16 billion commitment
- Addressed progress toward Tokyo reforms
- Establishment of $175 million bilateral incentive programme to encourage progress

SOURCE: Compiled by the Institute of State Effectiveness, 17 December 2013.

Notes to Chapter 6. *Reflections on Three Important Questions Concerning the Performance of the Peacebuilding Commission*

1. The report of the panel was published under the title *A More Secure World: Our Shared Responsibility*, UN Doc. A/59/565 of 2 December 2004, para. 261.
2. Ibid., para 264.
3. In Larger Freedom: Towards Development, Security and Human Rights for All, A/59/2005 of 21 March 2005.
4. 2005 World Summit Outcome document, UN Doc. A/60/1 of 15 September 2005.
5. See UN General Assembly Resolution 60/180 of 20 December 2005, and Security Council Resolutions S/1645 and S/1646 of 20 December 2005.
6. Kofi Annan "Africans Must Walk to Freedom in Mandela's Memory" in *Financial Times*, 7 December 2013, page 9.
7. See UN Security Council Resolution 2048 of 17 May 2012.
8. International Crisis Group [ICG] report: Central African Republic: Anatomy of a Phantom State, 2007.
9. Statement of Mutual Commitments on Peacebuilding between the government of Guinea and the Peacebuilding Commission (PBC/5/GUI/2) 23 September 2011, page 3.
10. See Statement of Mutual Commitments on peacebuilding in Liberia (PBC/4/LBR/2), 16 November, 2010, page 2.
11. GA/Resolution A/60/180 para.2(b).
12. In Larger Freedom, para. 115.
13. The terms *reconstruction, rehabilitation and reconciliation* were used interchangeably to refer what is known today as peacebuilding, before the term peacebuilding was coined by the Norwegian sociologist Johann Galtung in his famous article "Three Approaches to Peace: Peacekeeping, Peacemaking, and Peacebuilding", in *Peace, War and Defence: Essays in Peace Research, Vol II* (Copenhagen: Christian Ejlers, 1976), page 282-304 and was later popularized in the UN Secretary-General's 1992 report, An Agenda for Peace.
14. From Excerpts from the Harvard Speech by George Marshall in Special Commemorative Section on The Marshall Plan and its Legacy on the 50th Anniversary, *Foreign Affairs,* vol. 76 no. 3 May/June 1997, page 160-161
15. See Diane Kunz "The Marshall Plan Reconsidered: A Complex of Motives" in Special Commemorative Section on The Marshall Plan and Its Legacy on the 50th Anniversary, Foreign Affairs May/June 1997 Volume 76 Number 3, page 164-165.
16. See Paul Collier, *Wars, Gun and Vote: Democracy in Dangerous Places* (New York: Harper Collins Publishers), 2009,76; the original study on the incidence of relapse was by Paul Collier et al., *Breaking the Conflict Trap: Civil*

War and Development Policy – A World Bank Policy Research Report, (jointly published by the World Bank and Oxford University Press, 2003), page 83.

17. See Paul Collier, *The Bottom Billion: Why the Poorest Countries Are Failing and What Can Be Done About It* (Oxford: Oxford University Press), page 106 and 152

18. See *Collier, Wars, Gun and Vote: Democracy in Dangerous Places,* page 89.

19. See PCNA Advisory Group: Terms of Reference, dated July 2009.

20. see Ebola Situation Report dated 11 March 2015 Available on http://apps.who.int/ebola/current-situation/ebola-situation-report-11-?March-2015. This report gave the breakdown on the three affected countries as of 8 March 2015 as follows: Number of infected people in Guinea 3,285 of which 2,170 died; in Liberia 9,343 of which 4,162 died; and in Sierra Leone 11,619 of 3,629 died.

21. see Ebola: New World Bank Group Study Forecasts Billions in Economic Loss if Epidemic Lasts Longer, Spreads to West Africa, 2014 Available on http://www.worldbank.org/en/news/press-release/2014/10/08).

22. See Summary of the PBC Joint Session of Guinea, Liberia and Sierra Leone Configurations on 'The Ebola Crisis and Peacebuilding Efforts", 3 November 2014, page 3. This session was one of three meetings held by the PBC in response to the Ebola Crisis in Guinea, Liberia, and Sierra Leone. The other two were held on 18 August and 8 September 2014.

Chapter 7

The Centrality and Challenges of Institution Building in Peacebuilding

---

Introduction

This chapter argues that institution building is the most critical task in peacebuilding. Indeed, effective institutions are the main vehicles for facilitating and sustaining the transition of countries from conflict to durable peace. In fragile countries or countries emerging from conflict, virtually every activity aimed at laying the foundation of, or creating the conditions for, durable peace ineluctably entails institution building. Yet, institution-building efforts are marked by several challenges, some of which are examined in the chapter.

Institution building is a complex and painstaking process which extends beyond (re) establishing and nurturing organisational structures and includes embedding the value systems or rules that underpin such organisations. In the best of circumstances, institution building is a challenging task. In the context of countries emerging from conflict, institution building is particularly arduous; in so far as a conflict not only causes death but also inflicts significant damage on the economic and social infrastructures, destroys institutions, and unravels social trust. Many severe political tensions, crises, or even civil conflicts erupt not because of the lack of organisational structures or institutions but because of disputes over the underlying rules or value systems or the failure to adhere to existing rules.

International partners, including the United Nations and regional organisations, play an important role in supporting peacebuilding efforts around the world, including, in particular, support for institution building. It has been noted, for example, that a major aim of UN peacebuilding is "the construction of strong institutions of national government."[1] But after international partners have departed a country emerging from conflict or discontinued their support for peacebuilding to such a country, it is the institutions established with their help and which the country sustains that would carry on the tasks that they once undertook — whether those tasks were provision of security services, mediating disputes, supporting elections, assisting in negotiating of a new constitution, helping in some core public administration functions or providing basic social services. This is a major reason that institution building is essential to and a cross-cutting theme in peacebuilding.

However, if institution building is so central to peacebuilding, why is it such a difficult task to undertake? In part, this is because postconflict country contexts vary considerably. The main determinants to institution building are the degree of state fragility, the extent of institutional damage suffered during the conflict, the desire to adapt or create the institutions that fit the changed context, and the national development aspirations of the country. In other words, there can be no "one-size-fits-all" approach, when it comes to institution building.

In part, this is attributable to the fact that the importance of institution building in peacebuilding is undercut by erroneous perceptions and approaches. A common misperception or suspicion is that institution-building efforts in the context of peacebuilding tends to focus mainly on the creation or establishment of liberal Western institutions, while in fact traditional institutions might just fulfill the need. This debate creates considerable confusion about the proper scale, scope, and orientation of the work international peacebuilders.[2] A related misperception arises from the fact that institution building is quite often conflated with state-building only, when in reality institution-building processes inevitably have to straddle state-building and nation-building activities.[3] Moreover, many peacebuilding efforts have typically adopted a narrow approach to institution building, viewed mainly as a technical task or as emphasising the importance of one sector over the other(s).

And this is in part because not only is the scale and scope of efforts required for institution building huge but also it entails long-term commitment. A glimpse of the time frame needed for institution building in postconflict contexts can be gleaned from this observation: "restoring confidence and transforming security, justice and economic institutions is possible within a generation, even in countries that have experienced severe conflict."[4] The results of institution-building may sometimes be uncertain, in particular, if there are lingering major political disagreements among key national stakeholders.

Overall, countries emerging from conflict encounter several major challenges in undertaking the task of institution building. These include the challenge of timing the commencement of an institution-building effort; the challenge of setting priorities for institution building; the challenge of linking institution building to nationbuilding and state building; the challenge of promoting partnership in support of institution building; and the challenge of financing institution building.

These are the issues that the chapter will examine and draw some conclusions to inform the efforts in institution building in peacebuilding contexts. But before doing so, the paper will explain the terms institutions and institution building, and examine how some of the various definitions of peacebuilding have either hinted at or explicitly highlighted the critical importance of institution building.

What Are Institutions, and What Constitutes Institution Building?

Institutions may be conceived as "rules, enforcement mechanisms and organisations...distinct from policies, which are goals and desired outcomes; institutions are rules, including behavioural norms, by which agents interact and organisations that implement rules and codes of conduct to achieve desired outcomes."[5] The notion of institutions as "the rules of the game" was first articulated in the context of economic development.[6] Institutions can be formal or informal; in each case, however, they guide, shape, and define the interactions of individuals or organisations in economic, political, and social transactions.[7] "The formal rules and underlying values and belief systems must be well understood, shared and internalised by all stakeholders."[8] Formal institutions include laws and regulations and informal institutions include norms and values.

The rules may revolve around such questions as: How is power distributed or shared among the various constituent ethnic groups or political groups? How should economic resources be shared among the various regions or subnational units? Do all socioeconomic classes have equal access to justice and economic opportunities? Is the system of political representation inclusive or not? The values may be reflected in the adjectives attached to the functioning of the organisational structures, highlighting the values that a society or a country deeply cherishes in the functioning of such organisational structures. Thus, we speak of a free press, an independent judiciary, an impartial civil service, civilian control or oversight of armed forces, community policing, and an effective legislature.

The task of institution building is difficult not least because it is easier to design and establish an organisational structure than to create and sustain the underlying value systems and related institutional processes. For example, it is much easier to establish an army than it is to develop and entrench such institutional processes that will lead to civilian oversight and control and embed the values of professionalism; it is also fairly easy to establish courts but very difficult to create the institutional processes for fair and swift trials, for checking arbitrary government, and for protecting and preserving the integrity of judges; and it is also easy to create a government ministry than to staff it with the right expertise and introduce and maintain effective systems and operational procedures.

Institution building is as much about establishing or reestablishing organisational structures as it is about nurturing the rules and values that sustain the structures and support the foundations for peace and development. Viewed from this perspective, institution building is the ultimate peace dividend in as much as institutions in various sectors are the vehicles for delivery of a range of tangible services to the people, for laying the foundation for peace, and for sustaining development.

Institution building consists of five main elements: creating a new organisational structure; rehabilitating an existing organisation; developing the capacity or expertise to undertake the tasks of organisational structure; establishing the rules or embedding the values system; and developing the processes and systems for the effective functioning of the organisations. These five elements should be borne in mind as we examine how various definitions of peacebuilding have highlighted institution building.

The Critical Importance of Institution Building in Peacebuilding

In spite of the lack of conceptual consensus on peacebuilding, reflected in the multiplicity of its definitions,[9] institution building is a common thread that runs through the various definitions of peacebuilding in as much as it is explicitly reflected in several definitions of peacebuilding. To appreciate the implications of this observation, it helps to examine how the definitions or statements on peacebuilding have underlined or reflected the importance of institution building. This chapter's focus on United Nations-centred definitions and statements reflects the reality that the UN has done more than any organisation to advance the conceptual and practical issues relating to peacebuilding.

An Agenda for Peace defined peacebuilding as "actions to identify and support structures which will tend to strengthen and solidify peace in order to avoid relapse into conflict."[10] The phrase "support structure" in that definition refers to institutions.

The Report of the Panel on Peace Operations (also called the Brahimi report) defined peacebuilding as "activities undertaken on the far side of conflict to reassemble the foundations of peace and provide the tools for building on those foundations something that is more than just absence of war."[11] The reference to "reassemble the foundations of peace and provide the tools for building on those foundations" clearly embeds the notion of institution building.

In "No Exit Without Strategy", the UN Secretary-General noted that "the aim of peacebuilding is to build the social, economic and political institutions and attitudes that will prevent the inevitable conflicts that every society generates from turning into violent conflicts."[12] The report added that "the UN system has recently identified three key objectives whose fulfillment has often brought about successful, comprehensive peacebuilding, as including consolidating internal and security; strengthening political institutions and good governance and promoting economic and social rehabilitation and transformation."[13]

The founding resolution establishing the Peacebuilding Commission (PBC) more explicitly recognised the importance of institution building when it stated that one of the main purposes of the Commission is "to focus attention on the reconstruction and institution-building efforts necessary for recovery from conflict and to support the development of integrated strategies in order to lay the foundation for sustainable development."[14]

The UN Secretary-General's Policy Committee defined peacebuilding as "involving a range of measures targeted to reduce the risk of lapsing or relapsing into conflict by strengthening national capacities at all levels for conflict management, and to lay the foundations for sustainable peace development."[15] The notion of "strengthening national capacities" refers to institution building.

The Security Council's discussion on the theme of "post-conflict peacebuilding: institution building" held on 21 January 2011 underlined the centrality of institution building as an integral part of peacebuilding when it acknowledged "the importance

THE CENTRALITY AND CHALLENGES OF INSTITUTION BUILDING   165

of institution building as a critical component of peacebuilding and emphasised the importance of a more effective and coherent national and international response it, so that countries emerging from conflict can deliver core government functions."[16]

In his report on "Peacebuilding in the Aftermath of Conflict", the Secretary-General noted that "functioning government, political, market and social institutions have long been recognised as prerequisites for establishing popular confidence in the state and preventing conflict."[17]

Institution building has manifested itself in various forms in the peacebuilding priorities agreed to in the instruments of engagement between the UN Peacebuilding Commission and all the six countries on its agenda (Burundi, the Central African Republic, Guinea, Guinea-Bissau, Liberia, and Sierra Leone). Thus, in their joint statement at the Security Council debate on the theme of "postconflict peace building: institution building", the Chairs of the five[18] PBC country configurations for Burundi, the Central African Republic, Guinea-Bissau, Liberia and Sierra Leone said that:

> "in our experience, the process of institution building is a critical component of peace building. Where state institutions are missing or fragile, violence more easily spreads through vulnerable societies, organised crime finds easy purchase for illegal activities, and reconciliation and recovery is delayed. The building, rebuilding, and strengthening of core state function is sine qua non condition for overcoming conflict. In such context, local capacity is too often overwhelmed by insurmountable challenges. This is evident in all five post-conflict countries on the agenda of the Peacebuilding Commission despite the best efforts and the commitment of the authorities concerned.[19]

This excerpt from the statement of the Chairs of the PBC country-specific configurations hints at the nature, scope, and complexity of the tasks of institution building in the countries on the agenda of the PBC and mirrors the experiences in other postconflict peacebuilding contexts.

While the various definitions of peacebuilding underline the importance of institution building in one way or the other, there are specific arguments in support of institution building as an integral part of peacebuilding. The most popular argument, which inspires and infuses UN peacebuilding work, is that effective governmental institutions, or in some cases informal institutions, are required to mediate and manage political tensions or crises from spiraling out of control and from avoiding relapse into conflict. Another argument is that the political and economic liberalisation insisted upon mainly by many international partners will not take hold without effective and legitimate governmental institutions.[20] Still another argument is that enhancing the capacity of government of postconflict country to perform the core functions of state is an essential requirement "to wean itself from outside assistance."[21] This view is echoed in the observation that "No state can be sovereign while it relies on an external source to fund its ongoing operations.[22]

And yet another argument is that while some analysts have argued that dysfunctional states should be allowed to wither away and be reconstructed by redrawing national boundaries,[23] there is recognition that lack of institutional capacity reflected in "state weakness and state failure are global concerns because of their spillovers, contagions, instabilities and vitiation of international norms that occur when authority and order disappear."[24] The spread of a health contagion of the Ebola Virus Disease from Guinea, where its first outbreak occurred in December 2013, to Liberia and Sierra Leone, graphically illustrates the need for strong institutions to enable governments to rapidly respond to and cope with contagious diseases which do not respect national borders. Thus, it has been noted that these three countries "confront Ebola with fragile governance structure [even though] their presidents have shown strong leadership in tacking the virus."[25] The case for institution building in peacebuilding rests not only on ensuring national political stability but also on maintaining regional and international peace and security.

The Challenge of Timing the Start of Institution Building Efforts

The rehabilitation of prewar institutions or the creation of new ones is vital to any postconflict peacebuilding process. However, some difficulties usually arise from fierce debates among various stakeholders about whether the preconflict institutional arrangements or organisations should be preserved or whether a new institutional order should be established: those who advocate the latter approach tend to embrace the slogan of "build back better". Yet, it would be wrong to assume that all preconflict institutions — whether defined as rules, values, organisational structures or processes — were dysfunctional and hence in need of replacement. In fact, in some instances, the dysfunctions might arise not from the rules or organisational structures, but from the motivations or competences of the actors working in particular organisations.

Thus, in deciding whether to rehabilitate or to "build back better", it is important that there is an accurate assessment of the causes and consequences of the preconflict institutional dysfunctions. Indeed, so significant is the role of rehabilitation in postconflict work that, before the term peacebuilding[26] was coined in 1976 by Johan Galtung, it featured prominently in the so-called 3Rs framework — Rehabilitation, Reconciliation, and Reconstruction — that was used to describe what now passes for postconflict peacebuilding. The concept of rehabilitation was mainly applied to reviving institutions, restoring social capital, and reinvigorating political cohesion. In retrospect, it seems obvious that the 3Rs framework did not fully capture the complexity of current peacebuilding efforts, but the strands of that framework still permeate much of postconflict work with varying degrees of emphasis.

This notwithstanding, the question is when should an institution building effort begin? The common refrain that postconflict peacebuilding starts as soon as the guns fall silent does not fully take into consideration the complexities of institution building. Precisely because the dysfunctions of the old institutions might have triggered or exacerbated the civil conflict, and because institutional rehabilitation entails recreating trust, considerable care and caution has to be exercised in initiating the process of institution building. Institution building, as the preceding sections have shown, extends beyond re-establishing or creating organistaional structures and includes regenerating trust and value systems. Each of these takes time and requires careful sequencing.

There is no perfect timing to initiate an institution building effort. But prudence would suggest that the period between the "first" peace agreements — that usually involves the major combatants — and the "second" peace agreements provides a good window of opportunity to launch the effort. While the "first" peace agreements are typically mediated by external partners, including the UN and regional organisations, and set out the conditions of ending the conflict, the "second" peace agreements involve the greater participation of citizens, especially through the inclusive political dialogues and constitutional-consultation processes.

Both sets of agreements usually highlight or refer to some types of institutions that should be established to underpin the peace process. Hence, "peace agreements present the most critical opportunity to agree on the key principles on which institution building should rest"[27]. Starting the institution building efforts with the institutions reflected in peace agreements — whether defined as organisational structures or new "rules of the game" — represents a sensible way to commence the efforts at institution building in a postconflict context.

Yet, it would be wrong to conclude that all civil conflicts are brought to an end by peace agreements, mediated or not mediated. There have been instances where conflicts were ended not by peace agreements but rather when the victorious party has inflicted military defeat on the opponents. This was the case in Uganda in 1986, in Ethiopia in 1991, and in Rwanda in 1994. But even in these cases, the question of reestablishing or creating institutions remains. Here, the prudential approach will be to focus the efforts of "victorious party" on building those institutions that help the newly installed government to immediately consolidate its power and authority. Whether a postconflict regime comes to power by peace agreement (negotiated settlement) or victory over armed antagonists (military defeat), or foreign intervention (post invasion), a newly installed government has a strong desire to acquire legitimacy, enhance its authority and strengthen its capacity; all of which helps the regime deliver on the core functions of the state.

Just as there is no perfect timing to initiating institution building, there is no perfect way to institution building. Experimentation and innovation are particularly important in postconflict institution building. This also means that institution building efforts should necessarily be organised in incremental steps: tackling one set of institutional problem at a time, in any given sector; and building on success and recalibrating in case of failures.

The Challenge of Prioritisation of Institution Building in Fragile and Postconflict Contexts

It is one thing to agree on the importance of institution building in the context of peacebuilding; it is quite another to decide on the priorities for institution building. Institution building occurs in a variety of national contexts. As in many other areas of public policy, context matters greatly in institution building. Yet it is often the case that priorities for peacebuilding, in general, and in institution building, in particular, are driven, at least initially by external actors, each of whom has its list of priorities and some hierarchy within such a list. This tendency leads to the violation of the principle of national ownership central to the success and sustenance of institution building efforts.

The tendency for international partners to foist their peacebuilding priorities has led to the acknowledgement that "peacebuilding missions are not merely exercises in conflict management, but instances of much larger phenomenon: the globalisation of a particular model of domestic governance — a liberal market economy — from the core to the periphery. Most international organisations engaged in peacebuilding have internalised the broadly liberal political and economic values of the wealthy powerful industrialised democracies."[28] At the heart of the liberal peacebuilding model are three key institutions: a representative government, market economy, and an effective state that can ensure a high degree of political and social stability for without order and stability there is scant possibility that representative government or a market economy will function.

Most, if not all, international peacebuilding supports are wrapped with a package marked "helping to restore political stability" in the countries emerging from conflict. The focus on order and stability is reflected in the emphasis placed on safety and security in the peacebuilding priorities articulated by UN bodies and other organisations. For instance, a review of the peacebuilding priorities agreed upon between the Peacebuilding Commission and the countries on its agenda shows that security-sector reform features in all the instruments of engagement (the compacts between the PBC and the countries on the agenda).[29]

Security sector also ranks high in what the Secretary-General[30] called "recurring priorities wherein international assistance is frequently requested as a priority in the immediate after conflict. These include:

• "Support to basic safety and security, including mine action, protection of civilians, disarmament, demobilsation and reintegration, strengthening the rule of law and initiation of security sector reform;

• Support to political processes, including electoral processes, promoting inclusive dialogue and reconciliation, and developing conflict-management capacity at national and subnational levels;

• Support to the provision of basic services, such as water and sanitation, health and primary education, and support to the safe and sustainable return and reintegration of internally displaced persons and refugees;

• Support to restoring core government functions, in particular basic public administration and public finance, at the national and subnational levels;

• Support to economic revitalization, including employment generation and livelihoods (in agriculture and public works) particularly for youth and demobilised former combatants, as well as rehabilitation of basic infrastructure."

The World Bank articulates its priority for institution building in peacebuilding by arguing that "strengthening legitimate institutions and governance to provide citizens security, justice and jobs is crucial to break cycles of violence."[31] The United Nations and the World Bank are not alone giving high priority to security sector in the hierarchy of peacebuilding priorities. The RAND Corporation, which has very close ties to the US military establishment, published in 2007 a document titled *The Beginner's Guide to Nation-Building*.[32] that listed the six priorities for nation-building: security; humanitarian relief, governance, economic stabilisation, democratisation, and development.

If national context determines priorities for institution building in peacebuilding and if the initial conditions in countries emerging from conflict differ, why is it that security and justice rank high on most of the lists of priorities for peacebuilding? The answer is that the safety and security of the individual is a pre-condition for all other tasks that follow. As a recent report has acknowledged, "the ability to live one's life in reasonable safety and fairness are critical to both individual and collective self-development. If one fears for life or arbitrary decisions affecting it on a daily basis, it becomes much more difficult to seize opportunities and to make progress in any human endeavour."[33] But that does not settle the argument.

Hovering around the seeming consensus in reforming or rebuilding the institutions of security as a first order priority is the equally challenging question of the sequencing of reforms in the security sector. Although security-sector reforms have typically or traditionally focused on professionalisation of the military, there is a growing view that embedding the values of civilian control or oversight of the military forces is even more important. Guinea provides a striking illustration of how to navigate this problem.

There, the newly elected civilian government under Alpha Conde[34] wrote to the UN Secretary-General on 5 October 2011, a few months after his country was placed on the agenda of the PBC, requesting financial assistance for paying retirement benefits (mainly in the form of a lump sum) for 3,928 soldiers and for recruiting of a high level adviser on SSR to advise the government on the reform of the defence and security sector. Financial support for that programme was met by the Secretary-General's Peacebuilding Fund. The Government's request was preceded by a major study which evaluated the security sector reforms needs of Guinea.[35] The government realised that both the institution building goals of professionalisation and civilian control of the armed forces can only succeed, if the old soldiers and many of the senior ranks of the army were retired. Guinea's approach underlined the fact that security-sector reform is not only training and equipping security institutions. Equally important is civilian oversight over and accountability of the armed forces.

The experience of Guinea-Bissau provides a validation for the Guinea approach. Guinea-Bissau has historically had difficulties in undertaking sustained security sector reforms, in particular civilian control of the armed forces, mainly because members of the "old brigade" have remained in their positions; and in part because of inadequate resources to pay them. As in the case of Guinea, efforts have also been made, although unsuccessfully, to retire the old and senior officers of the armed forces of Guinea-Bissau who have been in the military since the war of liberation. This group sees any attempt at security sector reforms as aimed at removing them from the military without adequate retirement benefits, hence international efforts, including by those Peacebuilding Commission, to establish a pension fund, to address these concerns.

But there is another challenge concerning according high priority to reforms of institutions of the security sector in peacebuilding: the view that countries emerging from conflict are better off working on issues of nation building than on issues of state building. From this perspective, security sector reforms would not assure durable peace, whereas enhanced efforts at nation building issues such as national reconciliation and constitution-making hold greater promise for a durable peace. The argument is that security sector reform, with its emphasis on professionalisation of police and armed forces "would not have helped Yugoslavia to stay together and may have made the fighting worse."[36] There may be some merit to this argument that nation building efforts ought to precede state building efforts. In many important respects, however, this argument and the example drawn from Guinea highlight the tension between "organisational structures" and "value systems" in institution building. Yet again, this highlights another of the many challenges in setting priorities for institution building in peacebuilding.

Granted that (re) building the institutions of the security sector should rank high for all the reasons adduced, what area in institution building should come next? Again, there is not much agreement. But I have argued that the process of sequencing priorities should take into account the minimum functions that a state should perform and suggested that in "the order of importance, these [are] (1) protection of life and property (security); (2) delivery of basic services (education, health, water, and sanitation); and (3) macro-economic management (the ability to mobilise resources from direct and indirect taxes)."[37] The logic for this proposal is straightforward: After a modicum of order and stability is restored, people will begin to feel and see peace dividends, when institutions that deliver basic social services are functioning again. But to do so, the government has to manage the economy in ways that enable it to function, in particular collecting taxes, however small, initially to fund its public services.

The Challenge of Institution Building in State building and Nation building

Institution building takes place in various national contexts: the normal, fragile, and postconflict contexts. Institution building is also a key element in peacebuilding, nation building, and state building. In many important respects, the difference between a normal functioning state and a fragile or postconflict state is that whilst the former has resilient institutions, the latter is generally marked by weaknesses in the design of its institutions, contestation of the underlying value systems and significant deficiencies in the operations of its institutional processes and systems. These dysfunctions are usually harbingers of descent into violence or relapse into conflict.

Institution building is the common thread that runs through peacebuilding, nation building, and state building. To see why that is the case, it is important to examine the definitions of the latter two concepts. Nation building is defined as "actions undertaken, usually by national actors, to forge a common sense of nationhood purpose; to overcome ethnic, sectarian or communal differences; to counter alternate sources of identity and loyalty; and to mobilise a population behind a parallel state building project."[38] State building, on the other hand, is an "endogenous process to enhance capacity, institutions and legitimacy of the state driven by state-society relations."[39] This emphasis on state-society relations is reinforced by this clarification: "State building needs to be understood in the context of state-society relations, the evolution of a state's relationship with society is at the heart of state-building."[40]

Another definition of state building specifically emphasises the institution building approach by noting that state building "is premised on the recognition that achieving security and development in societies emerging from civil war partly depends on the existence of capable, autonomous and legitimate governmental institutions."[41] This approach is significant in that it brings to institution building two important elements — legitimacy and capability — of governmental institutions that are oftentimes treated in a mutually exclusive manner. Yet it bears emphasis that if "the state is the body of the country, the nation is its soul!"[42] This chapter takes the view that institution building applies to both the institutions for the body and for the soul of a country.

Enhancing legitimacy and promoting society relations is one of three aspects of state building. The other two components are the scope of state institutions and the strength of state institutions. "The scope of state institutions refers to the range of governance functions taken by the state...and the strength refers to the capacity of the state to effectively create, implement and enforce decisions and policies in the functional areas it enters."[43] The scope of state functions can be separated out into three roles: minimalist, intermediate and maximalist (see table 12 on the functions of the state). From a postconflict institution-building perspective, this approach is more helpful in that it is better able to guide efforts in state building in an ascending order of functions — from the minimalist to the maximalist.

Another approach[44] lists ten functions of the state without, any attempt at rank-ordering or the prioritisation, as consisting of: legitimate monopoly on the means of violence; administrative;

management of public finances; investment in human capital; delineation of citizenship rights and duties; provision of infrastructure services; formation of the market; management of state assets (including the environment, natural resources, and cultural assets); international relations (including entering into international business and public borrowing); and rule of law.

The fact that there are three interrelated components of state building raises the question as to which of the priorities for institution building in postconflict contexts should be accorded high priority: building democratic institutions or building strong state institutions. Scholars are sharply divided on this matter, with some arguing for democratic reforms to be accorded priority, while others take the opposite view that building strong state institutions should be accorded priority in postconflict contexts.[45]

Table 12. Functions of the State

	Addressing market failure			Improving equity
Minimal Functions	*Providing pure public goods* Defence Law and order Property rights Macroeconomic management Pubic health			*Protecting the poor* Antipoverty programmes Disaster relief
	1	2	3	4
Intermediate Functions	*Addressing externalities* Basic education Environmental protection	*Regulating Monopoly* Utility Regulation Antitrust policy	*Overcoming Imperfect information* Insurance (health, life, pensions) Financial regulation Consumer protection	*Providing social insurance* Redistributing pensions Family allowances Unemployment insurance
Activist Functions	*Coordinating private activity* Fostering markets Cluster initiatives			*Redistribution* Asset redistribution

Source: World Bank: World Development Report, 1997 — The State in a Changing World, page 27

Although the agenda for building state institutions in countries emerging from conflict often, at donors' insistence, default into building democratic institutions: a prudential approach would suggest helping such countries to create or rebuild those institutions that enable them to perform the minimum functions of state. This is because the typical fragile state is characterised by its weak capacity or inability to "deliver core functions to the majority of its people, including the poor. The most important functions of state are territorial control, safety and security, capacity to manage public resources, delivery of basic services and the ability to protect and support the ways in which the poorest people sustain themselves."[46] As such, "the development of robust state institutions may also be an important precondition for stable democratization."[47]

A closely related question is: Where do informal institutions fit into the institution building agenda for postconflict peacebuilding? Like most issues concerning peacebuilding, there is no consensus either among policy makers or academic researchers on this matter. Nonetheless, there is a growing realisation that informal (or what is sometimes referred to as traditional or indigenous) institutions play an important role in various aspects of peacebuilding.

The United Nations, for example, acknowledges the importance of "investing in informal institutions such as local peace councils, traditional dispute resolution and social protection mechanisms and non-formal education networks, alongside formal institutions such as public administrations, parliaments and schools…and strengthening the interface between formal and informal institutions, particularly in rural areas or areas that have been isolated by prolonged conflict."[48]

However, not only is interface between informal or traditional institutions and formal institutions sometimes difficult, there is evidence that some of the processes can work at cross purposes. For example, while local peace initiatives in the arid lands of Kenya have been found useful in resolving conflicts at the local level, they undermine state authority and hence state building in three ways: by undercutting the official laws of Kenya; by working at cross-purposes with democratic decision-making and inclusiveness; and by providing an informal tool for abuse of power by politicians.[49] This case exemplifies the tensions in the use of informal institutions in peacebuilding and the dilemmas between state building and peacebuilding.

These tensions should, however, serve as a cautionary tale rather than as a reason to avoid or neglect promoting interface between formal-informal institutions. Thus, the real challenge then is not abandoning informal institutions but striking the right balance. Increasingly, that balance points to using informal institutions on a transitional (short-term) basis for carefully selected issues; while leaving the formal institutions to grow, develop, and function on a long term basis. More importantly, the decision on the nature and scope of interface and the type of institutions needed have to be country-specific. It has been argued, for example, that "national-level decision makers, be they elites or the masses, state or nonstate actors, must ascertain which institutions will be the most effective in preventing and resolving conflicts in their own society before they become violent."[50]

However one views the role of formal and informal institutions in postconflict peacebuilding, there are pragmatic reasons for using them as appropriate. Informal institutions have the advantage of being closer to and viewed by people as mechanisms that they understand and can relate with, especially in the rural areas. On the other hand, formal institutions are better able to cope with complexity. As postconflict countries begin the process of laying the foundation for peace and development; the political, economic, and social transactions become more complex, and only formal institutions that operate with a high degree of predictability and efficiency can cope with those complex transactions.

As explained earlier, nation building activities aim to foster common values, attitudes, and national identity, even though state-building activities are often times mislabeled as nation building. It is difficult to exaggerate the unifying force of a shared culture — represented in a common language, religion, and regional affinity — in nation building. In multinational states, however, there are three generally agreed peacebuilding activities that offer opportunities for nation building: national reconciliation, constitution-making, and electoral processes. In so far as these processes offer an opportunity for inclusiveness and participation, they can enhance that sense of national identity. Indeed, constitution-making can have a "reconciliation and healing role" and lead to the "creation of a social contract" for citizens of a country.[51] Yet, both constitution-making and elections can oftentimes exacerbate rather calm political tensions and social cleavages, as several studies have shown.[52] It has also been noted that "a post-conflict election is inappropriate as a milestone: it is more like a tombstone,"[53] in as much as deaths often occur as a result of disputes and crises that erupt in the aftermath of many highly contested postconflict elections.

Using the institutional vehicles of reconciliation, constitution-making, and electoral processes for nation building is difficult enough in normal circumstances; in post-conflict settings, the task is nothing but arduous. The challenges in countries emerging from conflict are underlined by the need to rebuild social trust; to promote inclusivity; to strengthen national identity; and to create the spirit of a shared destiny. It is worth noting that the lack of these attributes may have been the root cause(s) of the conflict but also that developing these attributes took many of today's advanced industrialised countries centuries to achieve.

A frequently encountered observation is that two of the three institutional vehicles, constitution-making and elections, are part of the "liberal peacebuilding" agenda. That may well be the case. But as a practical matter, these two institutional vehicles can be designed and adapted in ways that are responsive to nation-building efforts. For example, postconflict constitution-making can help to serve as a compact to generate a new sense of identity by providing clauses that guarantee equal rights for all citizens; to protect minorities; to explicitly prohibit and punish religious or ethnic or gender discrimination; and to promote equality of opportunities. Equally, electoral laws and processes can also contribute to nation building in so far as they affirm the right for all citizens to vote and be voted for as well as by devising the appropriate representational arrangements for the historically marginalised groups in society.

National reconciliation processes occupies a special place in terms of efforts at promoting postconflict political and social cohesion of countries. There are a range of practices that easily commend themselves for consideration and adoption. These include establishing truth and reconciliation commissions; addressing issues of national symbols that particular groups of the society believe are offensive or carry connotations of their "historical victimhood"; apologies or even restitution for some particular egregious political or economic actions of the past; and redressing acts of human rights violations. One particularly fraught issue is how to strike a balance between processes of national reconciliation and the need for justice. This brings into perspective the view that while justice is backward looking; national reconciliation and healing are forward looking. There is "no-one-size-fits-all" in these issues and addressing them will ineluctably have to be the country-specific.

The Challenge of Promoting Partnership in Support of Institution Building

The importance of promoting partnership in support of institution building is widely acknowledged. The partners and stakeholders in institution building are many and diverse. These include the national government of the country emerging from conflict; the citizens and civil society organisations in the country; regional organisations; international nongovernmental organisations; the United Nations; bilateral and multilateral development agencies. The existence of such large numbers of interested and active actors in institution building underline the need for strengthened partnership both between the government and other actors, on one hand, and among the other stakeholders, usually referred to as international partners, on the other hand.

The term partnership can be broad: It entails issues of coordination among various key actors in peacebuilding; promoting a cooperative relationship among local stakeholders; and international financial support for peacebuilding. Since the last of these three issues is discussed in the next section, the focus here is mainly on the first two.

There are several advantages in effective coordination among key stakeholders in countries emerging from conflict: It reduces the strain on the limited administrative capacity of the nascent post-conflict governments; it imposes order and coherence on the work of the diverse international partners working in the country; it avoids fragmentation of programming and financial efforts among international actors; and it potentially contributes to better peacebuilding outcomes. These advantages can lead to the assumption that peacebuilding actors "are unitary and goal-oriented. Although there is probably little controversy regarding the claim that actors are goal-oriented, potentially problematic is the notion that these actors are unitary.[54] More often than not, international peacebuilding "actors are organised in stovepipes, each focused on distinctive priorities, they have a tendency to act in parallel rather than in tandem."[55]

These observations reveal many of the problems associated with coordination in the countries emerging from conflict. There are increasingly many peacebuilding actors working in countries emerging from conflict; the activities of those actors are marked by growing complexity; these actors pursue competing or conflicting priorities; and within the UN system, coordination is difficult because of the different mandates of UN entities. For example, humanitarian agencies have not been much engaged in peacebuilding because they view peacebuilding as political and are generally weary that their active involvement in peacebuilding could potentially compromise their principles of neutrality and impartiality.

Tackling these challenges has led to "calls for improved coordination [which] have become something of a mantra among scholars and practitioners in recent years,"[56] The coordination problems in peacebuilding extend beyond these issues, in particular, many "agencies have different approaches to postwar state building and different philosophies, objectives and conceptions of how to create the conditions for stable and lasting peace in war-torn societies."[57] This is not an obstacle that can easily be overcome with improvement in procedures but at least improved coordination may help attenuate it.

Given these contexts, how can partnership for peacebuilding be enhanced through improved coordination? There are three issues to address in reflecting on these issues: the types of coordination; approaches to coordination; and the role of the UN Peacebuilding Commission as an institutional vehicle for coordinating the sprawling peacebuilding activities. Concerning the first issue, there are three types of coordination. These are "policy, institutional and operational coordination. Policy coordination refers to developing or using a common framework as a guide for collective action. Institutional coordination implies the creation or use of an existing organisational structure for consultation and dialogue. Operational coordination refers to cooperating in the implementation of agreed tasks, based on division of labour to achieve common or shared objectives."[58]

Ideally, improved coordination in support of peacebuilding should entail all three types of coordination. As a practical matter and based on current experiences, it will be difficult to achieve policy coordination, and the current efforts at institutional and operational coordination have produced limited results. The difficulty in making progress in the last two areas is highlighted by the existence of the multiplicity of departments within international agencies and in donor governments handling peacebuilding issues — a development that has generated the impetus for intragovernmental coordination through the so-called Whole-of-Government approach that brings the diplomatic, defence and development departments to act in greater concert and coherence.

This raises the question of the approach for coordination. The current international machinery for state building operates more like "a loosely structured networks of governments and inter-governmental and non-governmental agencies". It is a "network" in the sense that state building actors constitute a system that is neither purely a "market" in which individual actors pursue their individual goals ….nor purely a "hierarchy" or a system of top-down or command structure.[59] Yet, there is a growing recognition that the "network" approach is not able to effectively address the myriad of the coordination problems involved in institution building. Hence, the proposal to combine "the flexibility of the existing networked structure of the international peacebuilding system" [with] some measure of hierarchy."[60]

The creation of the UN Peacebuilding Commission reflected the recognition by the international community of the need to improve UN response to peacebuilding. The essential role assigned to the PBC can be described as political accompaniment of the countries on its agenda. In its original intent and practice, that role can be disaggregated into three main tasks: political advocacy, resource mobilisation, and improved coordination or coherence. The focus here will be on its role in improving coordination. In doing so, it helps to recall the original wording in the founding resolution that assigned that task: "to provide recommendations and information and to improve coordination of all relevant actors within and outside the United Nations."[61] The wording of this resolution is significant in that it envisaged a full spectrum coordination role for the PBC: within the UN and outside the UN, implying an awareness that its remit should extend beyond the UN since the peacebuilding work in postconflict countries will include non-UN actors as well.

After nine years of existence, it is now possible to examine the performance of the PBC on its coordination role. The following five considerations will be paramount: authority, impact on countries on the agenda, support by member states, scope of remit, and relations with IFIs. A close reading of the resolution reveals that although PBC was assigned the task of improving coordination of all relevant actors within and outside the UN, it was not invested with sufficient authority to carry out this task. First, the PBC remains an advisory body to the Security Council and the General Assembly. Though coordination can either be horizontal or vertical: the former is essentially among equals, while the latter entails some degree of "hierarchy" or top-down command. Any effective coordination, as was noted earlier, should involve both network and hierarchy. The fact is that PBC has not been invested with authority for vertical co-ordination. It was dealt a weak hand from the beginning.[62] To explain why that is the case, we examine how it has performed coordinating role in the countries on its agenda.

In doing so, it is useful to imagine how the PBC would have played this role, if it did not have what I call an "authority deficit".

The PBC's instrument of engagement with the countries on the agenda that are variously referred to as strategic framework for peacebuilding or statements of mutual commitments would have been the framework for policy coordination. Instead, there are typically many strategies developed by the various actors working in each of the countries on its agenda. The efforts of the PBC in convening or interfacing with steering groups in the countries on its agenda have produced limited desire to converge around a few, selected priorities.

There are many striking illustrations of the lack of significant support by member states of the Commission for the PBC to play an active coordination role. This has manifested itself in the disinclination of many PBC member states to cohere their bilateral activities with the PBC's activities. And it shows in the lack of coherence between what the Commission members do in the PBC and advocate in other inter-governmental forums. The operative word is limited because in a few country contexts, there have been notable efforts to intensify the synergy on specific priorities between the PBC and some international donors.

The composition of the PBC — with members drawn from UN member states as well as from regional and subregional organisations and international financial institutions — offered much hope that it could potentially bring all the key actors around the table for substantive policy and operational issues in peacebuilding in general and institution building in particular the. PBC, therefore, offers an important forum for promoting policy, institutional and operational coordination. However, the hope that has not matched the performance; and the performance, in turn, has not fulfilled the expectations. In that sense, the scope of the remit of the PBC was set up for failure in so far as the authority vested in the Commission could not enable it make much progress within the UN much less outside it.

One bright spot has been the efforts the PBC has made to strengthen its relations with international financial institutions. That has centered on identifying possible areas of cooperation with these institutions in the countries of the agenda. These efforts potentially offer opportunities for operational coordination in that the international financial institutions can direct financial resources to the institution building priorities that the PBC is working on. A good example has been the Commission's call on the African Development Bank to provide infrastructure support for regional justice and security hubs that the PBC is sponsoring in Liberia.

The World Bank and the PBC have worked in close synergy also in the security and justice sector in Liberia. As detailed in chapter 6, in the "Statement of Mutual Commitments for Peacebuilding in Liberia," the government made a commitment to "increase budgetary allocations for institutions central to security and the rule of law, including the Armed Forces of Liberia, Liberia National Police, Bureau of Immigration and Naturalization and Corrections. Subsequently, a report on public expenditure review jointly financed by the World Bank and the UN Fragility and Conflict Partnership Trust Fund recommended that the government of Liberia increase its budgetary allocations to the security sector to 6 percent of the gross domestic product from the level of 4.9 percent. This recommendation has provided encouragement for the government to increase allocations to the security sector, even if the proposed target is reached gradually. And yet another example of collaboration involved the World Bank and the PBF agreeing to pay the salaries of the public servants in the Central African Republic for four months (May to August 2014). This collaborative effort supported the newly installed government's efforts at institutional rehabilitation, performing core functions of the state, and asserting its authority over its public servants.

The Challenge of Financing Institution Building

Institution building is as much an economic endeavour as it is a political undertaking. This is because every institution building effort requires significant financial commitment alongside political support. Indeed, it is generally acknowledged that "early availability of funding for institution-building and rapid restoration of basic state administrative ...is critical."[63] Yet "domestic resource mobilisation in post-conflict economies is more difficult than economies with no history of recent conflict"...[and]..."hence the importance of external assistance for institutional capacity development, whether provided bilaterally or multilaterally cannot be overemphasized."[64]

Lack of adequate domestic financial resources is but one of the major challenges that countries emerging from conflict confront in their institution-building efforts. This is typically reflected in the "mismatch between fiscal capacities and needs"..[and]..."there is also a great deal of diversity in post war environments."[65] One major source of diversity among postconflict countries is in their initial financial conditions at the end of war. As I have explained in chapter 3:

> Countries emerging from conflict can be classified into three categories on the basis of their initial fiscal conditions and extent of external support when conflict ends. The first category of countries includes those that draw on their own financial resources to meet their postconflict peacebuilding needs. This has been the case with a number of oil producing countries that have emerged from conflict in the past four decades (Nigeria in 1970; Kuwait in 1991; and Angola in 2002). The second category of countries includes those where many donors are ready and willing to help. These are the postconflict countries referred to as "donor darlings". The third category is the postconflict countries referred to as "donor orphans", which often receive very limited external financial support.[66]

This divergence in initial financial situations not only has an influence on the ability of postconflict countries to fund their peacebuilding efforts, in general, and institution building efforts, in particular; but also to decide on the scope and sequencing of those efforts. While the countries in category one, in the excerpt above, may have greater flexibility in asserting national ownership and leadership over their institution building efforts, most postconflict countries face some of the broader challenges in prioritisation and pace as well as scope and sequencing of institution building process.

Deciding on priority between institution building and other aspects of postconflict peacebuilding. Institution building, important though it might be, is but one facet of peacebuilding. When conflict ends, postconflict countries have to decide on the priority they will assign to a range of activities: reconstruction of physical infrastructure (roads, rails, bridges, electrical grid, water systems, and dams); humanitarian assistance (relief to the internally displaced persons and returnees) and institutional rehabilitation (restoration of the public service, including institutions that maintain law and order and ensure basic safety and security). Although effective institutional capacity holds the key to progress on all three priority areas, political and popular pressure and available financial resources as well as the terms of peace agreements (where a conflict was brought to an end by such an agreement) are key determinants in compelling governments to decide the sequence and scope of one priority over the other.

Prioritisation within security sector – donors' preference vs. national preference. That reform of the institutions of security sector should be accorded high priority in post-conflict contexts is generally acknowledged. As was explained earlier in this chapter, however, there is much debate about which of the constituent components of security-sector reforms should command higher priority in funding. In making decisions on this issue, national contexts matter considerably. For example, it has been noted that in Timor-Leste donors preference to offer more financial assistance to the police instead of the popular army – drawn from the guerrilla movement that fought for the country's independence – led to eruption of a fight between the armed forces and the police in May 2006.[67] This reflects the tension between national preference and donor preference because of the financial support by the latter.

Political disagreement among national stakeholders on funding priority for institution-building. The disagreement between donors and national stakeholders over funding for sectoral priorities, as indicated in the previous example, has a national counterpart: disagreement among the national stakeholders themselves. The sources of such disagreements are many and varied. They could stem from insistence by one of the national stakeholders (government, opposition party, leader of former rebel groups, or civil society organisations) that one group of stakeholders is not attaching high priority to a particular institution provided in a peace agreement. It could be the result of the desire for a political leader to ensure that a particular institution is located in his or her geopolitical zone. The disagreement could also be driven by the pressure of a particular group of political leaders to address the special needs of that group. This is usually the case, for example, when soldiers or even ex-combatants threaten that continued peace will be at grave risk if their "special needs" are not given priority funding. Disagreement might also stem from a deeply felt concern that funding sources are not or will not be adequate to reestablish a particular institution at that point in time.

Dependence on financial support on international partners. While the experience of Timor-Leste provides a striking illustration of assertion of donors' preference, there are other important challenges in relying on donors' financial assistance in institution building. These include the fact that "aid flows can be highly volatile;"[68] donors funding practice that allocates a significant share of their resources to an external or parallel sector to the official public sector creates a "dual public sector", as in Afghanistan in 2001-2004 period[69] and the donors' tendency to privilege the foreign supplier over the local supplier creates a "pervasive bias against the local suppliers"[70], reducing the opportunity for the local suppliers to enhance their productive and institutional capacity. An additional issue that relates to the timing of the donor-funded institution building project: their duration often times tends to determined not on how long it takes to complete the institution-building effort but how long the donor is willing to fund it. This introduces a high degree of unpredictability to institution building efforts. The experience of Guinea-Bissau referred to earlier concerning the funding pension to the armed forces highlights another problem: the many pledges of support by international partners are not honoured on a timely basis.

Capacity to collect revenue, allocate, and spend resources on institution building. Most postconflict countries lack the financial resources for initiating and sustaining their institution-building efforts. At the same time, dependence in the long term on foreign financial support is neither realistic nor desirable. This argues for countries emerging from conflict to strengthen their institutional capacity to collect revenue, allocate, and spend their financial resources efficiently. There is a "circular challenge" here: on one hand, countries emerging from conflict typically lack the capacity for fiscal management and, on the other hand, without such an effective capacity to collect revenue, albeit from a very thin economic base, it is not possible to restore or rebuild the capacity for fiscal management. Addressing this challenge will require that some of the initial technical and financial support by donors should be directed at reestablishing the institutional capacity for fiscal and broader macroeconomic management. Indeed, such an approach has been practiced in Rwanda and Burundi, where initial investments by some bilateral donors in reforming tax administration, including training of staff, at the end of civil conflicts in those countries, have yielded significant tax revenue, enabling the governments to meet its wage bills.[71]

Conclusions

In spite of the lack of conceptual consensus on peace building, reflected in the multiplicity of its definitions, the critical importance of institution building is one area where there is a high degree of convergence.

There are many arguments in support of institution building as an integral part of peacebuilding. The most popular argument, which inspires and infuses UN peacebuilding work, is that effective governmental institutions, or in some cases informal institutions, are required to mediate and manage political tensions or crisis from spiraling out of control and from avoiding relapse into conflict. Another argument is that political and economic liberalisation insisted upon mainly by many international partners will not take hold without effective and legitimate governmental institutions. Still another argument is that enhancing the capacity of the government of the postconflict country to perform the core functions of state is an essential requirement to reduce its reliance on external support.

And yet another argument is that while some analysts have suggested that dysfunctional states should be allowed to wither away and be reconstructed by redrawing national boundaries, there is recognition that lack of institutional capacity reflected in state weakness and state failure can lead a diminution of international cooperation in as much as weak or fragile states will not be able to effectively engage in international efforts to tackle a range of important issues on the international agenda. Thus, the case for institution building in peacebuilding rests not only on ensuring national political stability but also on maintaining regional and international peace and security.

Countries emerging from conflict encounter several major challenges in undertaking the task of institution building. This chapter has examined five of such challenges, including the challenge of timing the commencement of institution building efforts; the challenge of prioritisation of institution building efforts; the challenge of linking institution building to nation-building and state building; the challenge of promoting partnership in support of institution building; and the challenge of financing institution building.

Tackling each of these challenges will require a combination of factors, notably national ownership and leadership; political commitment; strengthened partnership–reflected mostly in improved coordination among all key international partners; careful and proper sequencing of priorities; and long-term financial commitment. The progress in institution building will critically depend on how postconflict countries are able to marshal all these elements to bear on that effort.

NOTES to Chapter 7. *The Centrality and Challenges of Institution Building in Peacebuilding*

1. See Geoff Burt and Timothy Donais, "Rethinking Peacebuilding: Two Modes of UN Peacebuilding", 2013 available on www.cigionline.org
2. For a flavour of this debate, see Roland Paris "Saving Liberal Peacebuilding, Review of International Studies, 36, no. 2 (April 2010) page 337-365, in particular the subsection of the paper titled "Is there an alternative to Liberal Peacebuilding" which examines the three alternatives to the liberal approach; trusteeship model, strong man model, and traditional or indigenous model of governance.
3. Schulenburg has argued, for example, that peacebuilding has largely ignored the interconnection between nation-and state-building with adverse effects on the overall peacebuilding process. See Michael v.d. Schulenburg "Is Peacebuilding Trying to Cheat History? From State-building to Nation-building" in *Rethinking Peacebuilding*, (Forthcoming, 2015)
4. World Bank, World Development Report – Conflict, Security and Development (New York: Oxford University Press) 2011, page 2.
5. World Bank, World Development Report – Building Institutions for Markets (New York: Oxford University Press), 2002, page 6.
6. See Douglas C. North, Institutions, Institutional Change and Economic Performance (Cambridge: Cambridge University Press) 1990.
7. Ejeviome Eloho Otobo, "Institutions and Economic Governance for a Market Economy: Pathways for Africa" in Development Policy Management Forum Bulletin, 6, no. 1, 1999, page 9.
8. United Nations Department of Economic and Social Affairs, World Public Sector Report – Reconstructing Public Administration after Conflict: Challenges, Practices and Lessons Learnt (New York: United Nations 2010), page xi.
9. One recent effort to assemble the various definitions of peacebuilding from individual experts and institutional sources is contained in: Alliance for Peacebuilding, (2012) *Peacebuilding 2.0 – Mapping the Boundaries of an Expanding Field*. The report, however, incorrectly attributed the UNDP's definition to UN Peacebuilding Support Office and the UN Peacebuilding Support Office's definition to UNDP.
10. See para. 21 of the Report of the Secretary-General on An Agenda for Peace: Preventive Diplomacy, Peacemaking and Peacebuilding, (UN Doc. A/47/277-S/2411) 17 June 1992.
11. See para. 13 of the Report of the Panel on Peace Operations, UN Doc. A/55/305-S/2000/809), 21 August 2000.
12. See para. 11 of Report of the Secretary-General on No Exit Without Strategy: Security Council Decision-making and the Closure or Transition

of United Nations Peacekeeping Operations, UN Document S/2001/394 of 20 April 200,1 page 2.

13. Ibid, page 4.

14. See para 2(b) of UN Security Council Resolution S/1645 of 20 December 2005 and UN General Assembly resolution 60/180 of 20 December 2005.

15. Secretary-General Policy Committee decision of May 2007 titled "Conceptual Basis for Peacebuilding for the UN System."

16. See para 1 of UN Security Council Presidential Statement, S/PRST/2011/2 of 21 January 2011.

17. Report of the Secretary-General on Peacebuilding in the Aftermath of Conflict, UN document A/67/499-S/2012/746 of 8 October 2012, page 13.

18. Guinea had not come on the agenda of the Peacebuilding Commission at this time. It was placed on the agenda of the PBC on 23 February 2011.

19. See statement by H.E. Ambassador Jan Grauls, Permanent Representative of Belgium to the United Nations on behalf of Brazil, Canada, Jordan, and Switzerland in their respective capacities as Chairs of the country-specific configurations of the Peacebuilding Commission for the Central African Republic, Guinea-Bissau, Sierra Leone, Liberia and Burundi at the Open Debate of the Security Council on Post-Conflict Peacebuilding: Institution Building" on 21 January 2011, page 1.

20. See argument in Roland Paris, *At War's End: Building Peace after Civil Conflict* (Cambridge: Cambridge University Press) 2004.

21. See Francis Fukuyama, *State-Building: Governance and world Order in the 21st Century* (Ithaca, New York: Cornell University Press 2004), page 100-102.

22. See Ashraf Ghani, Clare Lockhart, and Michael Carnahan, "An agenda for State-Building in the Twenty First Century", The Fletcher Forum of World Affairs Volume 30: 1 (WINTER 2006), page 112.

23. This argument is articulated in Jeffrey Herbst, "Let them Fail: State Failure in Theory and Practice: Implications for Policy" in Robert I. Rotberg, ed, *When States Fail: Causes and Consequences* (Princeton: Princeton University Press), 2003.

24. Roland Paris and Timothy D. Sisk, "Introduction: Understanding the Contradictions of Postwar Statebuilding" in Roland Paris and Timothy D. Sisk (ed) *The Dilemmas of StateBuilding: Confronting the Contradictions of Postwar Peace Operations* (London: Routledge) 2009, page 14.

25. Mo Ibrahim, "Building Governance is the Only Sustainable Solution", *Financial Times*, special report on the New Africa, 6 October 2014, page 7.

26. Johan Galtung "Three Approaches to Peace: Peacekeeping, Peacemaking and Peacebuilding" in *Peace, War and Defense: Essays in Peace Research*, vol 2, ed. Johan Galtung (Copenhagen: Christian Ejlers, 1976), page 282-304.

27. See para. 5 of 2014 Report of the Secretary-General on Peacebuilding

in the Aftermath of Conflict, UN Document A/69/399-S/2014/694 of 23 September 2014.

28. Roland Paris, International Peacebuilding and the 'Mission Civilisatrice', Review of International Studies, 28, (2002), page 638.

29. See table 9 in chapter 5 of this book.

30. See the Secretary-General's Report on Peacebuilding in the Immediate Aftermath of Conflict, UN Doc. A/63/881-S/2009/304 of 11 June 2009, page 6.

31. World Bank, World Development Report – "Conflict, Security and Development" (New York: Oxford University Press) 2011, page 2.

32. The document was aimed at influencing the postconflict reconstruction work by US forces in Iraq and Afghanistan.

33. OECD - INCAF: Draft Synthesis Report of the Security and Justice Project – "More Politics, Better Change Management: Improving International Support for Security and Justice Development Programming in Fragile Situations", 2013, page 15.

34. Alpha Conde was elected President in December 2010 and Guinea was placed on the agenda of the PBC on 23 February 2011.

35. See ECOWAS, African Union and United Nations; Report on the Evaluation of Security Sector Reforms in Guinea, May 2010.

36. See Schulenburg, *Rethinking Peacebuilding* (Forthcoming, 2015).

37. See my remarks in *Governance Out of a Box: Priorities and Sequencing in Rebuilding Civil Administration in Post-Conflict Countries* – Report of the Workshop organised in New York by the Crisis Management Initiative of Helsinki, Finland, on 17 September, 2007, page 13.

38. This definition is drawn from Charles T. Call and Elizabeth Coussens, "Ending Wars and Building Peace", *Coping with Crisis Working Papers Series*. New York: International Peace Academy (now Institute) March 2007, 4 and quoted in Charles T. Call with Vanessa H. Wyeth (eds) *Building States to Build Peace* (Boulder, Colorado: Lynne Rienner) 2007, page 5.

39. OECD-DAC, "Statebuilding in Situations of Fragility: Initial Findings", August 2008, page 1.

40. OECD, "Supporting Statebuilding in Situations of Conflict and Fragility: Policy Guidance", *DAC Guidelines and Reference Series*, 2011, page 11.

41. Paris and Sisk "Introduction", page 1-2.

42. See Schulenburg, "Rethinking Peacebuilding" (Forthcoming, 2015)

43. See Jonathan Monten (2013) "Intervention, Aid and Institution-building in Iraq and Afghanistan: A Review and Critique of Comparative Lessons", WIDER Working Paper no. 2013/108, page 3.

44. Such approach can be found in Ghani, Lockhart and Carnahan (2006) "An agenda for State-Building in the Twenty First Century", page 111.

45. For a flavour of this debate, see Jonathan Monten, "Intervention, Aid and Institution-building in Iraq and Afghanistan", page 4.
46. See UK – Department for International Development, "Why We Need to Work More Effectively in Fragile States". 2005, page 7.
47. See Monten, *Intervention, Aid and Institution-building in Iraq and Afghanistan*, page 2.
48. See para. 50 of the Report of the Secretary-General on Peacebuilding in the Aftermath of Conflict, UN Doc. A/67/499-S/2012/746 of 8th October 2012.
49. For evidence, see Tanja Chopra, "When Peacebuilding Contradicts State-building: Note from the Arid Lands of Kenya", International Peacekeeping, 16, no. 4 August 2009, page 531-545.
50. See Charles T. Call, "Knowing Peace When You See it: Setting Standards for Peacebuilding Success", Civil Wars , 10, no. 2 (2008), page 191.
51. Kirsti Samuels, "Postwar Constitution Making: Opportunities and Challenges" in Paris and Sisk, eds, *The Dilemmas of State-Building: Confronting the Contradictions of Postwar Peace Operations* (London: Routledge) 2009, page 178 – 180.
52. See. Schulenburg "Does Peacebuilding Need Two Peace Agreements?: Constitutions, Self-determination and National Unity" in *Rethinking Peacebuilding* (Forthcoming, 2015) as well as Kirsti Samuels Chapter 8 (on Constitution Making) and Timothy D. Sisk, chapter 9 (on Elections processes after civil war) in Roland Paris and Timothy D. Sisk (eds) *The Dilemmas of State-Building: Confronting the Contradictions of Postwar Peace Operations* (London: Routledge 2009).
53. Paul Collier, *Wars, Guns and Votes: Democracy in Dangerous Places* (London: Harper 2009), page 83.
54. Michael Barnett and Christoph Zurcher "The Peacebuilder's Contract: How external statebuilding reinforces weak statehood" in Roland Paris and Timothy D. Sisk eds, *The Dilemmas of State-Building: Confronting The Contradictions of Postwar Peace Operations* (London: Routledge) 2009, page 29
55. Ghani, Lockhart and Carnahan, "An agenda for State-Building in the Twenty First Century", page 118.
56. Paris, "Understanding the 'Coordination Problem' in PostWar Statebuilding, in Roland Paris and Timothy D. Sisk, eds. *The Dilemmas of State-Building: Confronting the Contradictions of Postwar Peace Operations* (London: Routledge, 2009), page 52 and 75.
57. Ibid., page 59.
58. Ejeviome Eloho Otobo, "Coordinating for Meeting the MDGS: Meeting the International Development Goals in Africa", in United Nations Department of Economic and Social Affairs: Supporting Africa's Efforts to Achieve Sustainable Development – Dialogues at the Economic and Social Council (New York –UN-DESA, 2003) 98-99.

59. Paris "Understanding the 'Coordination Problem" in PostWar Statebuilding in Roland Paris and Timothy D. Sisk, eds. 2009, *The Dilemmas of State-Building: Confronting the Contradictions of Post-war Peace Operations* (London: Routledge, 2009), page 57.
60. Ibid., page 75.
61. See para. 2(c) of UN General Assembly Resolution A/60/180 of 20 December 2005 and of Security Council Resolution S/1645/2005 of 20 December 2005.
62. See chapter 6 of this book.
63. See para. 47 of Secretary-General Report on Peacebuilding in the Aftermath of Conflict, UN Document A/69/399-S/2014/694 of 23 September 2014.
64. See Concept Note prepared for the 2014 Annual Session of the Peacebuilding Commission, "Sustainable Support for Peacebuilding: The Domestic and International Aspects" (New York: UN Peacebuilding Support Office 2014), page 2.
65. James K. Boyce and Madalene O'Donnell "Peace and the Purse: An Introduction" in James K. Boyce and Madalene O'Donnell, *Peace and the Purse: Economic Policies for Postwar State building* (Boulder, Colorado: Lynne Rienner Publishers, 2007), page 2.
66. See chapter 3 of this book.
67. Emilia Pires and Michael Francino "National ownership and International Trusteeship: The Case of Timor-Leste, in James K. Boyce and Madalene O'Donnell, *Peace and the Purse: Economic Policies for Postwar Statebuilding* (Boulder, Colorado: Lynne Rienner, 2007), page 142-144.
68. James K. Boyce and Madalene O'Donnell "Policy Implications: The Economics of Postwar Statebuilding Peace" and *The Purse: Economic Policies for Postwar State building*, 2007, page 273.
69. Ashraf Ghani, Clare Lockhart Nurgis Nehan and Baqer Massoud "The Budget as the Linchpin of the State: Lesson from Afganhisatn", in James K. Boyce and Madalene O'Donnell, *Peace and the Purse: Economic Policies for Postwar State building* (Boulder, Colorado: Lynne Rienner, 2007), page 156-162.
70. Boyce and O'Donnell, "Policy Implications", page 291.
71. See Kieran Holmes, Speech on the theme "Domestic Revenue Mobilisation in Countries Emerging from Conflict", at the International Peace Institute, New York, 10 July 2013.

Epilogue

2015 marks the tenth anniversary of the decision to create the peacebuilding architecture and the ninth anniversary of its inception. Nine years is a short time in the life of any institution. However, it is enough time to make an informed assessment of the progress made and challenges encountered by any institution. The various chapters in this book, in particular in chapters 3, 4, 5, and 6, have highlighted many of the challenges to, shortcomings of, and constraints on the performance of PBC. The 2015 Review provides an important opportunity for member states of the United Nations to grapple with the task of enhancing the performance of the PBC. The process for the ten year review of the peacebuilding architecture was set in motion on 15 December 2014, when the Presidents of the UN General Assembly and Security Council requested the Secretary-General to establish an Advisory Group on the review of the peacebuilding architecture. On 22 January 2015 the Secretary-General announced the nomination of seven experts to constitute the Advisory Group.[1]

The 2015 Review will take place against the backdrop of the PBC having acquired something of a full spectrum experience in peacebuilding. Several of the countries on its agenda are making steady progress. One of the countries has relapsed into conflict. And three countries on its agenda were hit by the Ebola Virus Disease epidemic, from which they are still struggling to recover. Those experiences provide a treasure trove of lessons on the role that the PBC can play in helping countries manage their postconflict transitions as it marches into the second decade of its existence. Those lessons can be thought of in terms of what has worked and what could have been done to make the PBC work even much better. The Review should place as much emphasis on the latter as on the former. This is because the ten-year review should be conceived and perceived as an opportunity for redesigning the peacebuilding architecture to better serve countries emerging from conflict.

Thus, an important anticipated outcome of the studies that the Advisory Group would conduct in the five selected postconflict countries will not be so much the specific experiences of those countries in peacebuilding priority setting and implementation, important though they might be. Instead, a highly anticipated outcome would be whether the PBC fulfilled the expectations of the governments of countries currently on the agenda and what the governments of the countries not the agenda of the Commission would have expected the PBC to do to support them. It is the ability of the PBC to fulfill the expectations of the present countries on its agenda, that will attract new countries to come on its agenda and thus confirm its institutional effectiveness.

Institutional effectiveness is often directly correlated with efficient operational modalities or working methods, robust institutional design, and successful policy implementation. The "working method" questions that have hindered the functioning of the PBC are well rehearsed: Does the PBC hold too many meetings? Are the country-specific configurations in their present form sufficiently agile? At what stage of its engagement with a country should the PBC make the transition to a "light engagement" – entailing fewer field visits to countries on the agenda and focusing on a few peacebuilding priorities? Should Vice-chairs be elected for the country-specific configurations? Should the Chairs of the country configurations report directly to the Organisational Committee and thus eliminate country-specific meetings? These issues are important but they pale in comparison to a range of structural issues, some of which have been raised in chapter 6, that have impeded the functioning and effectiveness of the PBC. While the working method issues need to be addressed, significantly enhancing the PBC's performance will critically depend on progress in tackling the "structural policy and institutional" issues. Seven of such issues have been identified here.

1. *Authority of the PBC.* The founding resolution that created the PBC did not confer on it an operational mandate, as generally understood in the United Nations. Rather, being an advisory body to the UN General Assembly and the Security Council, it was envisaged as a forum, among other things, "to bring together various relevant actors" and "to provide recommendations to improve the coordination of relevant actors within and outside the United Nations" so as to ensure sustained international attention to postconflict peacebuilding in the countries on its agenda. While the PBC has made impressive strides in serving as a forum for bringing relevant actors from within and outside the United Nations for discussion on peacebuilding, much remains to be done in strengthening its role in improving coordination in peacebuilding. Effective coordination is usually viewed as essential in many aspects of UN work and even more so with peacebuilding. Enhanced coordination has the advantages of reducing transaction costs on the collaborating partners; reducing the burden on the weak administrative capacities of the countries emerging from conflict; and, more importantly, increasing the impact of the work of the collaborating partners, in so far as it allows each partner to focus its resources on a few priorities.

Improved coordination for peacebuilding by the PBC should be viewed not in "command and control" terms but in "horizontal"[1] terms, where the PBC brings together all relevant actors, on an equal basis, to have in-depth policy discussion on peacebuilding either on thematic or country-specific basis. To the extent that such discussions have been held in or convened by the PBC, they have been mostly for information-sharing. Improved coordination must achieve better outcomes than information sharing and encompass detailed discussion on the timing, sequencing, and contributions by the collaborating partners involved in a particular country or peacebuilding thematic area. Viewed from this perspective, the PBC currently has an "authority deficit" in its convening role for improved coordination of peacebuilding. This authority deficit can only be redressed by reinforcing the existing mandate through clear legislative guidance.

2. *Relations with the Security Council.* Redressing the authority deficit of the PBC can only be undertaken by the two principal organs that established the PBC. But each of these bodies will play a different role to strengthen the PBC's mandate and performance. The Security Council's role in strengthening the authority of the PBC for improved coordination for peacebuilding can manifest in diverse ways: by explicitly legislative directive instructing that peacebuilding components of peacekeeping missions and the peacebuilding work of the special political missions should be reviewed by the PBC before being passed to the Security Council for approval; by seeking the Commission's advice at an early stage in framing of peacekeeping mandates, in line with paragraph 16 of the founding resolution establishing the PBC; and by seeking the Commission's recommendations on how to implement outstanding peacebuilding activities, after peacekeeping missions withdraw.

3. *Assessing the performance of the PBC.* One of the important and most pressing issues for the PBC is how to assess its performance in regards to progress in peacebuilding in the countries on its agenda. It bears special emphasis that one of the criteria of success for the PBC is not just that a country on its agenda has not relapsed into conflict rather it is the specific contributions the PBC has made to laying the foundation for durable peace. Assessing the ability of the PBC to meet the expectations of key national stakeholders, in particular the government is an integral part of that process. At present, various stakeholders make judgments on the PBC's performance not on the basis of objective criteria but perceptions of what they believe PBC should do. The work of PBC is too important to be left to inferences and perceptions. The main challenge is to develop a set of specific criteria to assess the performance of the PBC at every stage of its engagement in a country. The application of such criteria would have to be sensitive to and recognise that political decisions will affect the performance assessment.

4. *Partnership with regional actors.* Strengthened partnership between the PBC and regional institutional actors holds the key to promoting broader and more effective support for countries emerging from conflict. The PBC has intensified its efforts to build partnership with the African Union and the African Development Bank — the two important regional actors in Africa. Despite the progress made by the three institutional actors (AU, AfDB, and PBC), there are several shortcomings that continue to impede their efforts in providing enhanced support to African countries emerging from conflict.

The first of these shortcomings is that most interactions among three institutions remain headquarters-centred with very limited policy and operational interface at the country level.

The second is the lack of an agreement on the division of responsibilities on peacebuilding priorities among the three key institutional actors. The African Development Bank has raised the possibility of addressing this problem by stating that its postconflict work will be "undertaken in close concert with the other relevant parties, including UN agencies, the African Union, and multilateral and bilateral agencies, with clear division of roles and responsibilities"[2] ...[and]... "Leadership in other critical areas, such as peace and security and justice, will be left to other partners.[3] This approach of spelling out the thematic areas, where other partners should take the lead, needs to be embraced, discussed, and agreed upon by the three institutional actors, so that the thematic areas of focus by each institutional actor is clear to all.

The third shortcoming is the absence of joint missions by the three institutions to African countries emerging from conflict. It will be desirable for the three institutions to undertake joint missions to a selected number of countries every year with the aim of both deepening their policy interface at the country level and clarifying areas where each support should provide support within existing priorities.

5. *Resource mobilisation.* One of the most difficult responsibilities entrusted to the PBC is mobilising resources to support postconflict peacebuilding. In the founding resolution that responsibility

was stated in these terms: "to bring together all relevant actors to marshal resources and to advise on and propose in integrated strategies for post- conflict peacebuilding and recovery....and to help to ensure predictable financing for early recovery activities." Here again, partnership with regional actors and IFIs will help PBC's efforts. In the African context, in particular, with AfDB taking the lead on this thematic area of financial resources mobilisation, collaboration among the three institutional actors (AU, AfDB and PBC) should aim at providing adequate support to African countries emerging from conflict to build their capacity to improve domestic revenue, develop their frameworks for financial accountability, and curb illicit financial flows.

Mobilising financial resources for the countries on the PBC agenda represents one facet of its financing needs. The other facet pertains to the PBC obtaining enough financial resources to meet the demand of its own work. The portfolio of the PBC 's activities is growing, involving periodic field visits to countries on the agenda, traveling for consultations with regional and other institutional actors, and participating in donor roundtables. If the PBC is financially constrained in undertaking these crucial tasks, it will not only hinder its effectiveness but call into question its seriousness of purpose. Indeed, the PBC's performance will be gravely impaired, if its authority deficit is combined with a "financial resources deficit." This calls for adequate funding from the regular budget. This is where the support of the UN General Assembly — its second "parent" body — will become vital.

6. *Bringing more countries on the agenda.* As indicated earlier, the viability of the PBC will depend critically on its ability both to attract more countries to its agenda and to offer a robust accompaniment to them up to the point of their exit. Soon after the inception of the PBC in June 2006, the first two countries — Burundi and Sierra Leone — were placed on its agenda. By 2008, two more countries — Guinea-Bissau and the Central African Republic — were placed on the agenda. This meant that on average a country was placed on the PBC agenda every 6 months in its first two years. Liberia and Guinea, the two most recent countries to come on the agenda, did so in 2010 and 2011, respectively. Overall, in the PBC's first

five years, 2006-2011, a country came on its agenda at the average of every fifteen months. No country has come on the agenda in the past four years. This should be cause for serious reflection.

The PBC will need to grapple with three issues as part of that reflection and the 2015 Review provides such an opportunity. The first issue is for the PBC to create a niche in peacebuilding where it intends to support countries emerging from conflict, in general, and those on its agenda, in particular. The more the PBC is seen as being able to accompany countries on specific issues, the more attractive the PBC would become to many postconflict countries. The excerpts from the African Development Bank in the subsection on *Partnership with Regional Actors* show the determined effort of an organisation not only to engage in discussion on division of labour in peacebuilding among various partners but also show a willingness to have other organisations take the lead in certain areas.

The second issue is to examine whether the present operational modalities of the PBC impose high-transaction costs on the governments of the countries that come on the agenda. This turns critically on the PBC considering "the possibilities of multitiered engagement", a proposal made in the report of the co-facilitators of the 2010 Review.[4] The elements of a multitier engagement have been obvious for sometimes. Four-tiers could be considered, consisting of a subregional approach in which the PBC addresses one major peacebuilding issue with a subregional dimension involving a group of countries; an engagement with a country by focusing on one or two main peacebuilding issues; engagement with a country to allow the interested country to draw on the accumulated lessons of experiences by the PBC in managing postconflict transitions; and a modified form of the country-specific configuration, using a steering group format.

The third issue to consider is how PBC can join the efforts of regional organisations around the world which are supporting countries emerging from conflict in the respective regions. Working with regional organisations will increase the possibility of the PBC supporting more countries, provided the PBC can define a niche area in peacebuilding for itself.

7. *Responding to crises.* In the period from 2012-2014, the PBC has been confronted with two major crises in the countries on its agenda: the violent relapse into conflict in the Central African Republic, and the Ebola Virus epidemic in Guinea, Liberia, and Sierra Leone. Both crises were rude reminders that countries emerging from conflict can suddenly be hit by political or epidemiological crisis with devastating consequences for their ongoing peacebuilding processes. Both crises should stir the PBC, first, to review how it performed in these crises that unfolded under its watch; and second, to contemplate how it might address analogous crises in the future. In pondering over the two issues, consideration should be given to such questions as: What tools does the PBC have to respond to the types of crises that have confronted the countries on its agenda? Are the tools adequate? And if not, how should its tools of intervention and support be redesigned and strengthened? Such an effort at introspection will bolster the reputation of the PBC, in addition to better preparing it for future crises.

The future performance of the PBC will ride on its ability to address the policy and institutional challenges outlined above and to tackle a range of working methods issues. Some of the major working methods issues that would have to be addressed include expanding the membership of the country configurations, if not the organisational committee, by incorporating a number of UN entities, such as DPA, DPKO, and UNDP as members, given the field presence of these entities; transmuting the organisational committee into the forum for the first of the three-tiers engagement suggested above; designating or electing Vice-chairs to support the Chairs of the country configurations or Coordinators of the steering groups or whatever name is assigned after the review; and holding policy dialogue with the regional organisations on regular rather than at spasmodic intervals.

Smart reforms are needed to strengthen the PBC. These should combine serious improvements in operational or working methods with major policy and institutional changes. The 2015 Review is an opportunity to make strategic choices about the PBC.

Notes for Epilogue

1. The names and nationality of the members of the Advisory Group are: Mr. Anis Bajwa(Pakistan), Ms.Saraswathi Menon (India), Ms. Funmi Olonisakin(Nigeria), Mr. Ahmedou Ould-Abdallah (Mauritania), Mr. Charles Petrie(France), Mr. Gert Rosenthal (Guatemala), and Ms. Edith Grace Ssempala(Uganda).
2. See paragraph 27 of "The Strategy for Enhanced Engagement in Fragile States", Tunis, Tunisia, January, 2008.
3. See paragraph 3.20 of The Strategy for Enhanced Engagement in Fragile States, Tunis, Tunisia, January, 2008 and page 2 of "Executive Summary of the Strategy on Addressing Fragility and Building Resilience in Africa", June 2014.
4. See paragraph 25 and 95 of the Review of UN Peacebuilding Architecture, UN Doc.A/64/868-S/2010/393, 21 July 2010.

Bibliography

Abdul-Momen, Abulkalam. Speech given by the newly elected Chairman to the Organisational Committee of the PBC, 25 January 2012 at the United nations, New York.

Action Aid, CAFOD, Care International, 2007. "Consolidating the Peace?: Views from Sierra Leone and Burundi on the United Nations Peacebuilding Commission", June 2007. Available at: <http://www.actionaid.org/assets/pdf/peace_consolidating_the_final.pdf>

African Development Bank. *The Strategy for Enhanced Engagement in Fragile States*, Tunis, Tunisia, January 2008.

-------. *The Strategy on Addressing Fragility and Building Resilience in Africa*, Tunis, Tunisia, June 2014.

African Union. *The AU Policy Framework on Postconflict Reconstruction and Development*, July 2006.

-------. PSC Press Statement (PSC/PR/BR/CCVIII) issued at the end of its 208th Meeting, 9 November 2009.

Ahmed, Salman, Paul Keating, and Ugo Salinas. "Shaping the Future of UN Peace Operations: Is there a Doctrine in this house?" *Cambridge Review of International Affairs*, 20, no. 1 (March 2007), page 11-28.

Alliance for Peacebuilding. Peacebuilding 2.0: *Mapping Boundaries of an Expanding Field*, 2012.

Annan, Kofi. "Africans Must Walk to Freedom in Mandela's Memory", *Financial Times*, 7 December 2013, page 9.

Atwood, David, and Fred Tanner. "The UN Peacebuilding Commission and International Geneva", *Disarmament Forum (UNIDIR) 2* (2007), page: 29.

Barnett, Michael, and Christoph Zurcher.2009, "The Peacebuilder's Contract: How External Statebuilding Reinforces Weak Statehood", in *The Dilemmas of State-Building: Confronting the Contradictions of Postwar Peace Operations*, Roland Paris and Timothy D. Sisk (eds) (London: Routledge), page 29.

Burt, Geoff, and Timothy Donais."Rethinking Peacebuilding: Two Modes of UN Peacebuilding", 2013. Available at www.cigionline.org.

Boyce, James K., and Madalene O'Donnell (2007). "An Introduction" in *Peace and the Purse: Economic Policies for Postwar State-building*, James K. Boyce and Madalene O'Donnell (Boulder, Colorado: Lynne Rienner).

-------. "Policy Implications: The Economics of Postwar Statebuilding", in

Peace and the Purse: Economic Policies for Postwar State building, James K. Boyce and Madalene O'Donnell ed. (Boulder, Colorado: Lynne Rienner).

Call, Charles T., and Elizabeth M. Coussens. 2007. "Ending Wars and Building Peace", Coping with Crisis Working Paper Series. New York: International Peace Academy (now International Peace Institute).

Call,Charles T., with Vanessa H. Wyeth, eds. 2007. *Building States to Build Peace* (Boulder, Colorado: Lynne Rienner).

Call, Charles T. "Knowing Peace When You See it: Setting Standards for Peacebuilding Success", *Civil Wars*, 10, no. 2 (2008), page 191.

Chopra, Tanja.) "When Peacebuilding Contradicts State-building: Note from the Arid Lands of Kenya", in *International Peacekeeping*, 16, no. 4 (August 2009), page 531-545.

Collier, Paul et al. *Breaking the Conflict Trap: Civil War and Development Policy – A World Bank Policy Research Report* (jointly published by the World Bank, and Oxford University Press, 2003).

Collier, Paul. *The Bottom Billion: Why the Poorest Countries are Failing and What Can Be Done About it* (New York: Oxford University Press, 2007).

_____. *Wars, Guns and Vote: Democracy in Dangerous Places* (New York: Harper Collins Publishers, 2009).

Cookson, Clive. "WHO Signals Slowdown in Fresh Cases in West Africa", *Financial Times*, 30 October 2014.

Curtis, Devon and Gwinyayi A. Dzinesa, eds. *Peacebuilding, Power, and Politics in Africa* (Johannesburg: Wits University Press, 2013).

Dobbins, James. *The Beginner's Guide to Nation-Building* (Santa Monica: The RAND Corporation, 2007).

ECOWAS, African Union and United Nations: *Report on the Evaluation of Security Sector Reforms in Guinea*, May 2010.

Financial Times, "UN Peacekeeping in the line of Fire", 17 and 18 May, 2008, page 5.

Fukuyama, Francis, State-Building: *Governance and World Order in the 21st Century* (Ithaca, New York: Cornell University Press, 2004).

Galtung, Johan. "Three Approaches to Peace: Peacekeeping, Peacemaking and Peacebuilding" in *Peace, War and Defense: Essays in Peace Research*, (Copenhagen: Christian Ejlers, 1976) vol. 2.

Geopolicity (2012). "Public Expenditure and Needs Assessment Review of the Security Sector in Liberia: Establishing A Sustainable Security Sector i n View of UNMIL Transition", page 10.

Ghani, Ashraf, Clare Lockhart, and Michael Carnahan, "An agenda for State-Building in the Twenty First Century". *The Fletcher Forum of World Affairs* Volume 30: 1 WINTER 2006.

Ghani, Ashraf, Clare Lockhart Nurgis Nehan and Baqer Massoud, "The Budget as the Linchpin of the State: Lesson from Afganhisatn", in *Peace and the Purse: Economic Policies for Postwar State-building*, James K. Boyce and Madalene O'Donnell, eds. (Boulder, Colorado: Lynne Rienner, 2007).

Goldman Sachs, "Dreaming of the BRICs: The Path to 2050", Global Economic Paper no. 99,2003.

Grauls, Jan. Statement to the United Nations Security Council in his capacity as Chair of the PBC country configuration for the Central African Republic on behalf of Brazil, Canada, Jordan, and Switzerland in their respective capacities as Chairs of the country-specific configurations of the Peacebuilding Commission for Central African Republic. Guinea-Bissau, Sierra Leone, Liberia, and Burundi at the Open debate of the Security Council on Postconflict Peacebuilding: Institution building", 21 January 2011.

Herbst, Jeffrey. "Let them Fail: State Failure in Theory and Practice: Implications for Policy", in *When States Fail: Causes and Consequences*, Robert I. Rotberg, ed. (Princeton: Princeton University Press, 2003).

Holmes, Kieran. Speech on the theme of Domestic Revenue Mobilisation in Countries Emerging from Conflict, at the International Peace Institute, New York, 10 July, 2013.

Ibrahim, Mo. "Building Governance is the Only Sustainable Solution", *Financial Times* Special Report on "The New Africa", 6 October 2014.

International Crisis Group [ICG-2007] Report: *Central African Republic: Anatomy of a Phantom State*.

Koroma, Ernest Bai. Presidential Address on the occasion of the State Opening of the Third Parliament, Freetown, Sierra Leone, 5 October 2007.

Kunz, Diane. "The Marshall Plan Reconsidered: A Complex of Motives" in Special Commemorative Section on The Marshall Plan and its Legacy on the 50th Anniversary, *Foreign Affairs*, 76, no 3. (May/June 1997) page 164-165.

Malloch-Brown, Mark. "Holmes Lecture: Can the UN Be Reformed?" annual meeting of the Academic Council on UN system (ACUNS), 7 June 2007, page 7.

Marshall, George. Excerpt from the Harvard Commencement Address in 1947 in Special Commemorative Section on the Marshall Plan and its Legacy on the 50th Anniversary, *Foreign Affairs,* 76, no. 3 (May/June 1997), page 160-161.

McAskie, Carolyn. 'The International Peacebuilding Challenge: Can New Players and New Approaches Bring New Results", Lecture delivered at the Simon Fraser University School for International Studies, Vancouver, British Columbia, Canada, 19 October 2007.

Monten, Jonathan."Intervention, Aid and Institution-building in Iraq and

Afghanistan: A Review and Critique of Comparative Lessons", WIDER Working Paper No. 2013/108.

NYU Center on International Cooperation and the International Peace Institute, "Taking Stock, Looking Forward: A Strategic Review of the Peacebuilding Commission" — An Independent Analysis, April 2008.

North, Douglas C. *Institutions, Institutional Change and Economic Performance* (Cambridge: Cambridge University Press, 1990).

Ntakirutimana, Joseph. Statement by Ambassador of Burundi to the United Nations General Assembly, 10 October 2007, p. 3. Available at: <http://www.un.org/News/Press/docs/2007/ga10635.doc.htm>. [GA/10635]

OECD-DAC. State building in Situations of Fragility: Initial Findings, August 2008.

OECD Supporting State building in Situations of Conflict and Fragility: Policy Guidance, DAC Guidelines and Reference Series, 2011.

OECD – INCAF. Draft Synthesis Report of the Security and Justice Project – More Politics, Better Change Management: Improving International Support for Security and Justice Development Programming in Fragile Situations, 2013.

Olonisakin, Funmi and Eka Ikpe. "The United Nations Peacebuilding Commission: Problems and Prospects", in *Peacebuilding, Power and Politics in Africa*, Devon Curtis and Gwinyayi A. Dzinesa, eds. (Johannesburg: Wits University Press 2013).

O'Niell, Jim. "Dwindling US Trade Deficit Could Shape World Trade", *Financial Times*, 26 September 2007.

Otobo, Ejeviome Eloho. "Institutions and Economic Governance for a Market Economy: Pathways for Africa" in Development Policy Management Forum Bulletin, 6, No. 1, 1999, pg. 9.

-----------. "Coordinating for Meeting of the MDGS: Meeting The International development Goals in Africa", in *United Nations Department of Economic and Social Affairs: Supporting Africa's Efforts to Achieve Sustainable Development – Dialogues at the Economic and Social Council* (New York – UN-DESA, 2003).

-----------. see Brief Remarks in *Governance Out of a Box: Priorities and Sequencing in Rebuilding Civil Administration in Post-Conflict Countries* – Report of the workshop organised in New York by the Crisis Management Initiative of Helsinki, Finland, 17 September, 2007.

-----------. "A United Nations Architecture to Build Peace in Postconflict Situations", *World Bank Institute: Development Outreach Magazine* devoted to the theme of Fragility and Conflict, October 2009, page 46-49.

----------. "The New Peacebuilding Architecture: An Institutional Innovation of the United Nations", in *United Nations Reform and the New Collective*

Security, Peter Danchin and Horst Fischer, eds. (Cambridge: Cambridge University Press, 2010).

--------. "The UN Peacebuilding Architecture: African Countries as Early Beneficiaries", in *NACHBAR AFRIKA (Neighbour Africa): Dimensionen eines Kontinents (Dimensions of a Continent)*, Irene FREUDENSCHUSS-REICH & Georg LENNKH, eds.(2010), (Vienna Austria: Prassagen Verlag, 2010).

---------. "Leading the Peacebuilding Commission: An Institutional History in the Making", Views from Practice no. 1/2013, March 2013, Brussels: Global Governance Institute.

Paris, Roland. "International Peacebuilding and the 'Mission Civilisatrice'", *Review of International Studies*, 28,2004, page 637-656.

---------. *At War's End: Building Peace after Civil Conflict* (Cambridge: Cambridge University Press, 2004).

-----------. "Saving Liberal Peacebuilding", *Review of International Studies*, 36, no. 2 (April 2010).

-----------. "Understanding the 'Coordination Problem' in Post War Statebuilding", in *The Dilemmas of State-Building: Confronting the Contradictions of Post-war Peace Operations*, Roland Paris and Timothy D. Sisk, eds. (London: Routledge, 2009).

PBC. Chair's of Country Configuration Declaration adopted by the Peacebuilding Commission Country-Specific Meeting on Sierra Leone on the upcoming presidential and parliamentary elections in Sierra Leone, UN Doc. PBC/1/SLE/4, 22 June 2007.

-------. Chairman's (of the Organisational Committee) non-paper entitled "Points to Be Considered for Adding a New Country to the Peacebuilding Commission Agenda", 26 November 2007.

-------. Conclusions and Recommendations of the Peacebuilding Commission following the report of the Chair of the Burundi configuration in identical letters dated 20 September 2007 from the Chairman of the Burundi configuration of the Peacebuilding Commission to the President of the Security Council, the President of the General Assembly, and the President of the Economic and Social Council, UN Doc. PBC/2/BDI/2, 21 September 2007.

-------. Conclusions and Recommendations of the biannual review of the implementation of the Strategic Framework for Peacebuilding in Burundi, UN Doc. PBC/2/BDI/L.2, 19 June 2008.

-------. Conclusions and recommendations of the biannual review of the implementation of the Sierra Leone Peacebuilding Cooperation Framework, UN Doc. PBC/2/SLE/2, 19 June 2008.

-------. "Declaration on Peacebuilding: The Way Towards Sustainable Peace and Security" (PBC/6/OC/6), 25 September 2012.

-------. Letters of solicitation from the Chair of the Guinea-Bissau configuration to the members of the configuration for support for the elections of 2008, 2009, and 2012 are respectively dated 8 May 2008, 3 June 2009, and 14 February 2012.

-------. Letter from the Chair of PBC Organisational Committee to the Secretary-General on Financing Field Missions contained in UN Doc. A/62/493, dated 18 October 2007.

-------. Letter from the Chair of the Sierra Leone configuration to members of the configuration, dated 27 October 2009.

-------. Letter from the Chair of the Guinea-Bissau configuration to the Minister of Foreign Affairs dated 6 May 2010.

-------. Letter of reply from the Minister of Foreign Affairs of Guinea-Bissau to the Chair of the Guinea-Bissau configuration dated 21 May 2010.

-------. Letter (unpublished) from Chair of Guinea-Bissau configuration to the President of the Security Council for the month of April 2012, dated 12 April 2012.

-------. Outcome of the Peacebuilding Commission High-level Special Session on Sierra Leone, UN Doc. PBC/3/SLE/2, 10 June 2009.

--------. Report of the Peacebuilding Commission on its First session, UN Doc. A/62/137-S/2007/458, 25 July 2007.

-------. Report of the Peacebuilding Commission on its Second session, UN Doc. A/63/92-S/2008/417, 24 June 2008.

-------. Report of the Peacebuilding Commission on its Third session, UN Doc. A/64/341-S/2009/444, 8 September 2009.

PBC Report of the Peacebuilding Commission on its Fourth session, UN Doc. A/65/701- S/2011/41, 28 January 2011.

-------. Report of the Peacebuilding Commission on its Sixth session, UN Doc. A/67/715 – S/2013/63, 29 January 2013.

-------. Report of the Peacebuilding Commission on its Eighth session, UN Doc. PBC/8/OC.L.1/17 December, 2014.

-------. Report of Peacebuilding Commission mission to Sierra Leone from 19-25 March 2007, UN Doc. PBC/1/SLE/2, 23 April 2007.

-------. Report of the fact-finding mission of the Chair of the Burundi country – Specific Meeting of the Peacebuilding Commission to Burundi, 5 to 7 September 2007.

-------. Report of the Mission of the Chair of the Sierra Leone Configuration to Sierra Leone, 8-15 October 2007.

-------. Rules of Procedure in UN Doc. PBC/1/OC/3/Rev.1, 5 December, 2012.

-------. Statement issued by the Chair of PBC Guinea configuration, 20 July 2011.

-------. Statement issued by the Chair of PBC Guinea-Bissau configuration, 13 April 2012.

-------. Statement issued y the Sierra Leone configuration of the Peacebuilding Commission, 19 December 2012.

-------. Statement issued by the Chair of PBC Guinea configuration, 6 March 2013.

-------. Statement issued by the Chair of PBC Guinea configuration, 8 July 2013.

-------. Statement issued by the Chair of PBC Guinea configuration, 17 September 2013.

-------. Statement issued by the Chair of PBC Guinea configuration, 24 October 2013.

-------. Statement of the Chair of Burundi configuration to second sectoral conference in Bujumbura devoted to governance, 28 October 2013.

-------. Statement issued by the Central African Republic configuration, 24 December 2012.

-------. Statement issued by Central African Republic configuration, 21 May 2013.

-------. Statement of Mutual Commitments for Peacebuilding to Liberia, UN Doc. A/PBC/4/LBR/1, 16 November, 2010.

--------. Statement of Mutual Commitments on peacebuilding between the government of Guinea and the Peacebuilding Commission, PBC/5/GUI/2, 23 September 2011.

--------. Strategic Framework for Peacebuilding in Burundi, UN Doc. PBC/1/BDI/4, 30 July 2007.

---------. Peacebuilding Cooperation Framework for Sierra Leone, UN Doc. PBC/2/SLE/1, 3 December 2007.

---------. Summary Statement by the Chair of the Sierra Leone configuration on Peacebuilding Commission High-Level Stakeholders Consultation, Sierra Leone, 19 May 2007.

-------. The 2011 Roadmap of Actions, adopted by the Organisational Committee of the PBC, 25 January 2011.

_____. Report on the Working Group on Lessons Learnt of the Peacebuilding Commission, May 2010.

PBSO. "Improving the Country Specific Meetings: A new approach for new countries coming on the agenda of the PBC, 9 October 2009.

-------. "Resource Mobilisation for Peacebuilding Priorities: The Role of the

Peacebuilding Commission", 2012 Available at http://www.un.org/en/peacebuilding/pdf/resource-mobilisation.

-------. Background Note on Synergies between the PBC and the PBF prepared for the PBF Advisory Group Meeting, 7-8 October 2013.

-------. Concept Note prepared for the 2014 Annual Session of the Peacebuilding Commission entitled "Sustainable Support for Peacebuilding: The Domestic and International Aspects" 2014.

Pires, Emilia, and Michael Francino. "National ownership and International Trusteeship: The Case of Timor-Leste, in *Peace and the Purse: Economic Policies for Postwar State-building*, James K. Boyce and Madalene O'Donnell, eds. (Boulder, Colorado: Lynne Rienner, 2007).

Ponzio, Richard, "The United Nations Peacebuilding Commission: Origins and Initial Practice", *Disarmament Forum (UNIDIR)*, 2007. 2, 8. Available at http://www.unidir.org/pdf/articles/pdf-art2627.pdf.

Ramos-Horta, Jose, Address by President of the Democratic Republic of Timor-Leste to the 62nd session of the United Nations General Assembly, 27 September 2007.

Report of the Panel on United Nations Peace Operations (also called Brahimi Report), UN Doc. A/55/305-S/2000/809, 13 November 2000.

Report of High Level on Threats, Challenges and Change — A More Secure World: Our Shared Responsibility, UN Doc. A/59/565, 2 December 2004.

Samuels, Kirsti, "Postwar Constitution Building: Opportunities and Challenges", in *The Dilemmas of State-Building: Confronting the Contradictions of Post-war Peace Operation*, Roland Paris and Timothy D. Sisk, eds. (London: Routledge, 2009).

Schulenburg, Michael, "Is Peacebuilding Trying to Cheat History: From State-building to Nation-building", in *Rethinking Peacebuilding*, Forthcoming, 2015.

-------. "Does Peacebuilding Need Two Peace Agreements?: Constitutions, Self-determination and National Unity", in Rethinking Peacebuilding, Forthcoming, 2015.

Security Council Report (the NGO) "Special Research Report No. 2: Peacebuilding Commission", 5 October 2007. Available at: http://www.securitycouncilreport.org/atf/cf/.

-------. The Security Council and the Peacebuilding Commission, Special Research Report, 2013.

Sisk, Timothy D. "Pathways of the Political: Electoral Processes after Civil War", in *The Dilemmas of State-Building: Confronting the Contradictions of Post-war Peace Operations*, Roland Paris and Timothy D. Sisk, eds. (London: Routledge, 2009).

Surhrke, Astri, and Ingrid Samset, "What's in a figure? Estimating Recurrence of Civil War", *International Peacekeeping* 14, No. 2, (2007) page 195-203.

Tah, Christiana and Judy Cheng-Hopkins, "Rebuilding Liberia, One Hub at a Time", *Mail and Guardian*, South Africa, 10 February 2013.

Takasu, Yukio, Statement by Chairman of the Peacebuilding Commission, at the Debate at Security Council on the First Report of the Peacebuilding Commission,17 October 2007.

UK - Department for International Development, *Why We Need to Work More Effectively in Fragile States*, 2005.

United Nations Department of Economic and Social Affairs, *World Public Sector Report – Reconstructing Public Administration after Conflict: Challenges, Practices and Lessons Learnt* (New York: United Nations, 2010).

UN General Assembly, 2005 World Summit Outcome Document, UN Doc. A/60/1, 15 September 2005.

-------. Review of the United Nations Peacebuilding Architecture, UN Doc. A/64/868-S/2010/393, 21 July 2010.

-------. Document showing Expenditure of PBC Field Visits for 2008-2009,2010-2011 and 2012-2013 (see Supplementary Financial Information for Advisory Committee on Administrative and Budgetary Questions: Proposed Programme Budget for 2012-2013 in A/66/6(section 3), 31 May 2011.

-------. Resolution, UN Doc. A/RES/60/180, 20 December 2005: The Peacebuilding Commission.

UN Security Council l Resolution, UN Doc. S/1645, 20 December 2005: The Peacebuilding Commission.

-------. Presidential Statement, UN Doc. S/PRST/2011/2, 21 January 2011.

-------. Security Council Resolution S/2048, 17 May 2012: The Situation in Guinea-Bissau.

UN Secretary General Report, *An Agenda for Peace: Preventive Diplomacy, Peacemaking and Peacebuilding*, UN Doc. A/47/277-S/2411, 17 June 1992.

-------. *No Exit Without Strategy: Security Council Decision-making and the Closure Transition of United Nations Peacekeeping Operations*, UN Doc. S/2001/394, 20 April 2001.

-------. *In Larger Freedom: Towards Development, Security and Human Rights for all*, UN Doc. A/59/2005, 21 March 2005).

-------. Policy Committee Decision of May 2007 titled "Conceptual Basis for Peacebuilding for the UN system."

-------. *Financing Field Missions of the Peacebuilding Commission: Note by Secretary-General*, UN Doc. A/62/670, 31 January 2008.

-------. *Report of the Secretary General on Peacebuilding in the Aftermath of Conflict*, UN Doc. A/69/399-S/2014/694, 23 September 2014.

-------. Document on The Terms of Reference are Annexed to Arrangements for Establishing the Peacebuilding Fund, report of the Secretary General, UN Doc. A/60/984 22 August 2006.

-------. *Report on Peacebuilding in the Immediate Aftermath of Conflict*, UN Document A/63/881-S/2009/304 of 11 June 2009.

-------. *Report on Arrangements for the Revision of the Terms of Reference of the Peacebuilding Fund*, UN Doc. A/63/818, 13 April 2009.

Wegter, Bartjan, "Emerging from the Crib: The Difficult First Steps of the Newly Born UN Peacebuilding Commission", *International Organisation Law Review*, 12/2008 4(2) 343-355.

World Bank, World Development Report — *The State in a Changing World* (New York: Oxford University Press, 1997).

-------. World Development Report — *Building Institutions for Markets* (New York: Oxford University Press, 2002).

-------. World Development Report — *Conflict, Security and Development* (New York: Oxford University Press, 2011).

About the Book

The decision to create the United Nations Peacebuilding Commission (PBC) was one of the major outcomes of the Summit of World leaders held in 2005 to mark the 60th anniversary of the United Nations. The Commission was inaugurated in June 2006 by Kofi Annan, the then UN Secretary-General. Today, the Commission has six countries on its agenda, all from Africa.

In this book, Ejeviome Eloho Otobo, who was appointed as the first Director and Deputy Head of the UN Peacebuilding Support Office, presents an in-depth and first-hand account of the performance of the Peacebuilding Commission.

The book is at once a historical record and an analytical work. As a historical account, it provides an overview of the evolution of the structure and functioning of the PBC as well as the challenges that it encountered in its formative years. And as an analytical piece, it provides rich insights into the expectations of and frustrations, with the Commission, assesses its performance in fulfilling those expectations and offers proposals on ways the performance of the Commission could be improved.

The author notes that the PBC will sometimes be confronted with, and will be required to respond to, a range of crises — from political crisis to economic crisis and natural or man-made disasters — in the countries on the agenda. Reflecting on the Ebola epidemic that has afflicted three of the countries on the PBC agenda, the author offers suggestions on how the PBC should respond in such country contexts. The book also takes up one of the biggest challenges that confront countries emerging from conflict: how to tackle the challenges of institution building.

This volume is highly recommended for policy makers, scholars, and students interested in postconflict transition, institution building, and the intersecting issues of peacebuilding and development.

Index

3Rs framework — rehabilitation, reconciliation and reconstruction, 138

Abdul Momen, Abulkalam, 75
Abuja Agreement of November 1998, 123
Accra Comprehensive Peace Agreement, 132
Action Aid, 26
Activist Functions *see* functions of the state, 176
Addressing Fragility, 90
Adebajo, Adekeye, 81n
Advisory Group on the review of the peacebuilding architecture, 197
Advisory Group, 142
Advocacy, Resource Mobilisation and (fostering) Coherence (ARC), 89
Afghanistan Development Forum, 153
Afghanistan Recovery and Reconstructions Conference, 153
Afghanistan, 138, 144
Africa Union, 63, 66, 95, 134, 201
Africa, 1, 147
  and the PBC, 63
  decolonization in, 1, 43
  peacebuilding in, 1, 43
African Development Bank (AfDB), 68, 69, 86, 100, 143, 185, 201
African Development Bank's Country Strategy, 91
African Great Lakes region, 17
African Mission in Burundi (AMIB), 14
African Party for the Independence of Guinea and Cape Verde (PAIGC), 124
African Union Africa-led International Support Mission in Central African Republic- MISCA, 127
African Union Mission in Burundi (AMIB), 118
Agenda for Change (Sierra Leone), 92 121
Agenda for Prosperity, 121
Ahmed, Salman, 207
All Peoples Congress, 120
Alliance for Peacebuilding, 133, 191
"An Agenda for Peace: Preventive Diplomacy, Peacemaking and Peacebuilding", 43
"An Agenda for Peace", 10, 163
Angola, 26, 47
Angolan Technical Military Cooperation Mission (MISSANG), 124
Annan, Kofi, 121
"anti-balaka", 126
"anti-machete", 126
Armed Forces of Liberia, 100, 185
Arusha Peace and Reconciliation

Agreement of 2000, 118
Arusha peace negotiations, 118
Asset Redistribution, 176
"At Crossroads of Peacekeeping, Peacemaking, and Peacebuilding", 66
Atwood, David, 32, 207
AU Multidimensional Committee on PRCD, 63
AU Peace and Security Council (AU-PSC), 63
"authority deficit", 183-184

Bajwa, Anis, 205
Barnett, Michael, 194, 207
Basic education, 176
Basic safety security, 129, 170
Basic services, 170
Berlin Donor conference, 153
Biannual reviews, 211
Boyce, James K., 214
Bozizé, François, 125, 129
Brahimi Report, 10, 164
Brazil, 26
Brussels, 131
"Build back better", 167
Building Resilience, 205, 207
Bureau of Immigration and Naturalization and Corrections, 100
Bureau of Immigration, 185
Burkina Faso, 133
Burt, Geoff, 191
Burundi peace negotiations, 14
Burundi Strategic Framework, 18
Burundi, 3, 13, 14, 15, 20, 26, 44, 50, 84
   Civil war in, 118
Business for Peacebuilding: The Role of Private Sector, 86
Buyoya, Pierre, 118

CAFOD, 26
Call, Charles T., 193
Camara, Moussa Dadis, 133
Capacity building, 17, 67
CARE International, 26
Carnahan, Michael, 192
Catholic Aid Agency for England and Wales *see* CAFOD
Central African Armed Forces (FACA), 129
Central African Republic, 15, 28, 44, 50, 87, 103, 117
Chair of the Burundi configuration, 90
Chair of the Central African Republic country configuration, 91
Chair of the Guinea configuration, 90
Chair of the Guinea-Bissau country configuration, 90
Chair of the Liberian configuration, 89
Chair's Group *see* PBC
Cheng-Hopkins, Judy, 112
Chicago summit, 155
"Chief engineer", 89
Chile, 99
China, 26
Chopra, Tanja, 194
Christian, Leslie Kojo, 75
Christoph, Zurcher, 194
Civil society organizations, 15, 18, 22-24
"CNN effect", the, 4, 36
Collier, Paul, 15, 139
Commission for management of strategic resources, 119
Comoros, 50
Comparore, Blaise, 133
Comprehensive Ceasefire

INDEX 221

Agreement, 119
Comprehensive Framework Agreement of 2006, 19
Conceptual consensus, 163
Conde, Alpha, 133, 134, 171
Conflict cycle, 21
Consolation prize, 59
Consolidation of democracy, 148
Conte, Lasana, 133
Convention of Patriots for Justice and Peace (CPJP), 126
Cookson, Clive, 208
Cooperation Framework for Sierra Leone, 18
Coordination, 180-183
   horizontal Coordination
   improved coordination
   institutional coordination
   policy Coordination
   operational coordination
   vertical coordination
Core government functions, 165
COSOC Ad Hoc Advisory Group, 141
Cote d'Ivoire, 28, 50
Countries Emerging from Conflict, 141
Country Assistance Strategy, 91
Country Specific Meeting (CSM), 18, 19
Country-Specific Configurations, 12, 165, 196
   Burundi (see Burundi)
   Central African Republic (see CAR)
   Guinea (see Guinea)
   Guinea-Bissau (see Guinea-Bissau)
   Liberia (see Liberia)
   Sierra Leone (see Sierra Leone)
Country-specific meetings, 12, 15, 16, 88, 198

Country-strategy paper, 69
Coussens, Elizabeth M., 193
Curtis, Devon, 208

Danchin, Peter, 211
decolonization, 1
Demobilisation, 37, 41, 49
Democratic and Popular Forces of the CAR (FDPC), 125
Democratic decision-making, 177
Democratic Republic of Congo, 50
Department of Peacekeeping Operations - DPKO, 204
Department of Political Affairs - DPA, 204
Development Assistance Committee (DAC), 26
Development Trust Fund, 104
Dialogue's Preparatory Committee (CPDPI), 125
Disarmament, Demobilisation and Reintegration, 37, 41
Djotodia, Michel, 126
Dobbins, James, 208
Doe, Samuel, 132
Donais, Timothy, 207
"donor darlings", 47, 138, 186q
"donor orphans", 47, 138, 186q
Donor conference in Kabul, 155
Donors Conference on Burundi, 69
Drug trafficking, 37, 53, 105
Dual public sector, 188
Dysfunctional, 189
Dzinesa, Gwinyayi A, 208

Ebola Virus Disease, 6, 145-147, 166, 197, 204
   effects of, on peacebuilding efforts, 145-146
ECOMOG *see* Economic Community of West African States Ceasefire and Monitoring Group

Economic and Monetary Community of Central Africa (CEMAC), 125
Economic and Social Council, 11, 14
Economic Commission for Africa (ECA), 146
Economic Community of Central African States (ECCAS), 125, 126
Economic Community of West African States see ECOWAS
Economic Community of West African States Ceasefire and Monitoring Group (ECOMOG), 14, 119, 132
Economic revitalization, 170
ECOSOC Ad Hoc Advisory Group on Countries Emerging from Conflict, 141
ECOSOC, 116
ECOWAS Mission in Guinea-Bissau (ECOMIB), 124
ECOWAS Mission in Liberia (ECOMIL), 132
ECOWAS, 123, 128, 134
Electoral processes, 170, 179
Electric power supply; national emergency, 84
"Emerging Lessons and Practices in Peacebuilding, 2007-2009", 59
EMI Music, 64
Employment generation and livelihoods, 170
Energy sector, 19
Enhanced Engagement, 205
Epidemiological crisis, 204
Ethiopia, 168
European Commission, 135, 143
European Union Commission, 63
European Union, 59, 66

Financial Times, 207
financing gap, 51
Fischer, Horst, 211
Forces for Defense of Democracy (FDD), 118
Forms of Engagement, 67, 198, 207
  enhanced engagement
  "light engagement"
  "multitiered engagement"
Formal institutions, 162
Fragile States, 95
Francino, Michael, 195
Freudenschuss-Reich, Irene, 211
Front Nationale du Liberation (FNL), 84
Functions of the State, 176
  minimal functions
  intermediate functions
  activist functions
Fukuyama, Francis, 192, 208
Funding gaps, 24
funding raising, 85

Galtung, Johan, 156
"Gaping hole", 1
Gasana, Eugene- Richard, 75
Gbarnga hub, 89
Gender dimension, 16
Gender discrimination, 179
General Assembly resolution 60/180, 82
General Assembly, 9, 11, 13, 183
General Batista Tagme Na Waie, 127
General Inspection and Local Administration, 24
Ghani, Ashraf, 192
"Give Peace a Chance", 48, 64
Global Compact, 86
global economic and financial crisis, 144
Global Employment Facility, 71
"global good citizenship", 98
Global Governance Institute, 4

Goldman Sachs, 209
Gomes, Carlos Jr., 123, 127
Good governance, 16, 164
Grauls, Jan, 150, 192
Gross Domestic Product, 185
Group of Friends meeting, 131
Grunditz, Marten, 150
Guinea, 50, 117, 132, 145, 166
Guinea-Bissau, 15, 28, 44, 117, 123
Guinea-Conakry, 28, 74

Haiti, 28, 50
Hammarskjöld, Dag, 28
Herbst, Jeffrey, 192
Hernandez, Carmen Gallardo, 75
High Level Panel on Threats, Challenges and Change, 9, 95, 115, 138
High-Level Meeting on Peace and Statebuilding: The Rwandan Experience, 68
High–level Stakeholders Consultation on Sierra Leone, 22, 40
Holmes, Kieran, 195
Human Development Index (HDI), 14
Hussein, Zeid Ra'ad Al, 150
Hutu, 118

Ibrahim, Mo, 152
Ikpe, Ika, 210
IMF Review, 85
Immediate Response Facility of the Peacebuilding Fund - IRF, 109
Inclusive Political Dialogue, 49
India, 26
Indjai, General Antonio, 123, 128
Indonesia, 99
Induta, Admiral Zamora, 123, 127
Informal institutions, 162, 166, 177
In-kind contributions, 48
In-kook, Park, 75
Institutional donors, 4, 42, 59

Institutional architecture, 115
Institutional performance, 5
Institutional Resilience Assessment, 146
Institution building, 6, 159-175, 189
    Challenge of financing, 185
    Elements of, 163
Institutions, 162
    Institutional gap, 115
    Institution building, 137
    Institutional coordination, 182
    Institutional Effectiveness, 198
    Institutional linchpin, 1
Instruments of Engagement of PBC:
    Peacebuilding Cooperation Framework, 17
    Statement of Mutual Commitments for peacebuilding, 64
    Strategic Framework for peacebuilding, 64
Insurance, 176
Integrated Office in Burundi (BINUB), 14, 24
Integrated Peacebuilding Strategy (IPBS), 15-18, 20q, 45
Integrated Peacebuilding Strategy for Sierra Leone, 17
Inter-African Mission to Monitor the Implementation of the Bangui Accords (MISAB), 125
International Afghanistan conference in Bonn, 154
International aid agencies, 140
International community, the, 1
International conference on Afghanistan Kabul, 153
International conference on Afghanistan Moscow, 154
International conference on Afghanistan The Hague, 154
International conference on Afghanistan, Tokyo, 155

International Financial Institutions, 36, 184
International Monetary Fund (IMF), 4, 22, 42, 59, 66, 84, 145
International Network on Conflict and Fragility - INCAF, 193
International Peace Institute, 66
International peacebuilding, 181
International Special Court, 120, 132
International Special Court for Sierra Leone, 120
Ireland, 65
iTunes, 64

Japan, 99
Johnson Sirleaf, Ellen, 132, 134
Joint Declaration of Ouagadougou, 133
Joint Declaration on Post-Crisis Assessments and Recovery Planning, 143
Joint Steering Committee (JSC), 73
Joint Verification and Monitoring Mechanism (JVMM), 19, 22, 84
Joint Vision of the UN Family in Support of Agenda for Change, 91
José Américo Bubo Na Tchuto, 127, 128
JSC mechanisms, 73
Justice sector reforms, 16

Kabbah, Ahmed Tejan, 119
Kasese-Bota, Mwaba Patricia, 75
Keating, Paul, 207
Kenya, 28, 50
Konate, General Sekouba, 133
Koroma, Ernest Bai, 209
Koroma, Major Johnny Paul, 119
Kunz, Diane, 139
Koroma, Ernest Bai, 209
Kunz, Diane, 209
Kuwait, 47, 137

Lack of institutional capacity, 186, 187, 189
Land reforms, 16
"Learning by doing", 27
Lennkh, Georg, 43n
Lennon, John, 64
"liberal peacebuilding" agenda, 179
Liberal peacebuilding, 83
Liberia National Police, 100, 185
Liberia, 28, 50, 117, 119, 131-132, 145, 166
Liberians United for Reconciliation and Democracy (LURD), 132
Libreville Agreement, 126
Liden, Anders, 148
"light PBC engagement", 64
Lisbon summit, 154
Lockhart, Clare, 192
Lome Peace Agreement, 119, 121
London Donor conference, 153
Loulichki, Mohammed, 150
Lovald, John, 22, 91
Lucas, Sylvie, 150

Machado, Luiz Alberto Figueiredo, 149
Majoor, Frank, 149
Malloch-Brown Mark, 12
Mandela, Nelson, 118, 121
Mano River Union, 95
Marshal, 85
Marshall Plan, the, 138, 144
Marshall, George, 138
Marshalling resources, 25
Martins, Ismael A. Gaspar, 75
Massoud, Baqer, 195, 209
Maurer, Peter, 148
McAskie, Carolyn, 29, 209
McNee, John, 149
Menon, Saraswathi, 205
Mexico, 65
Menon, Saraswathi, 205

Microfinance, 61
Military pension fund, 130
Ministry of Good Governance, 24
Mission for the Consolidation of Peace in Central African Republic - MICOPAX, 125, 127
Monitoring and Tracking Mechanism, 17
Monten, Jonathan, 193
"Money on the table", 86
Multidonor Trust Fund, 38
Multinational Force in Central Africa, 125
Munoz, Heraldo, 75
Mutual accountability, 155
Multinational Force in Central Africa (FOMUC), 125

nation building, 6, 173, 178
National Convergence Kwa Na Kwa (KNK) party, 126
National Council for Defense of Democracy (CNDD), 118
National Electoral Commission, 24, 149
National Liberation Forces (FNL), 118
National ownership, 7
National Patriotic Front of Liberia (NPLF), 131
national preference and donor preference, 187
National reconciliation processes, 180
National Steering Committee (Comite de Pilotage), 23
Natural resources management, 69
Naturalization and Corrections, 185
Ndadaye, Melchior, 118
Ndjamena Roadmap, 126
Negotiated settlement, 168

Nehan, Nurgis, 195, 209
Nepal, 28, 50
Netherlands, 22
New Deal Compact, 91
New York, 131
Nguendet, Alexandre Ferdinand, 127
Nhamadjo, Manuel Serifo, 124
Nigeria, 26, 47, 121, 137
Nkurunziza, Pierre, 119
"No Exit Without Strategy", 164
North, Douglas C., 191, 210
Norway, 22
Ntakirutimana, Joseph, 33, 210
Nyerere, Julius, 118
NYU Center on International Cooperation and the International Peace Institute, 33, 210

O'Donnell, Madalene, 214, 207
O'Niell, Jim, 32, 210
OECD-DAC, 193, 210
OECD-INCAF, 210
Official Development Assistance (ODA), 14, 26, 48
Oil-producing countries, 47,
"Old generation of soldiers", 128
Olonisakin, Funmi, 111
Ono, Yoko, 48, 64
Operational coordination, 182
Organisation of American States, 63
Organisation of Islamic Cooperation, 59, 66
Organisational Committee *see* Peacebuilding Commission (PBC)
Oslo Donor conference, 153
Otobo, Ejeviome Eloho, 217
Ould-Abdallah, Ahmedou, 205
Outcome Document, 54, 78, 105, 151, 116, 138, 215

PALIPEHUTU-FNL, 22
Palous, Martin, 75
Panel on United Nations Peace
 Operations (the Brahimi Report),
 10
Paris Declaration, 17
Paris donor conference, 153
Paris, Roland, 191
Parliamentary elections, 17, 19, 23
Partnership, 40, 42, 58
Partnerships for peacebuilding,
 65-66
Partnerships with foundations, 61
Party for the Liberation of the Hutu
 People (Palipehutu), 118
Patasse, Ange-Felix, 124
Patriota, Antonio de Aguiar, 149
PBC Agenda countries, 48
PBC agenda, 47, 64, 138, 144
PBC Chair, 66
PBC configurations, 57
 Country-specific Configurations,
 57
 Organisational Committee, 57,
 105
 Working Group on Lessons
 Learnt (WGLL), 57, 59, 69, 105
PBC country-specific
 configurations, 165
PBC engagement, 49, 130-131, 133,
 135, 140
PBC Guinea configuration, 134
PBC Liberia configuration, 134
PBC Rules of Procedure, 87
PBC *see* Peacebuilding Commission
PBC Strategic Framework for
 Peacebuilding, 93
PBC-PBF synergy, 94
PBC-Peacebuilding Fund (PBF)
 synergy, 70
PBC's Outreach, 62-63
PBF Advisory Group Meeting, 113,
214
peacebuilding architecture, 9-13, 27,
 197
Peacebuilding as social justice, 82
Peacebuilding as stabilization, 83
Peacebuilding Commission (PBC),
 1, 5, 10, 17, 20, 35, 44, 52, 81, 115,
 127, 133-134, 164, 170, 199-204
 an important instrument of the
 United Nations, 116
 and consolidation of peace in
 Africa, 63
 and the AfDB, 69
 "authority deficit, 183, 199, 200,
 202
 Burundi and Sierra Leone, first
 two countries under, 14, 15,
 117, 140
 Chair's Group, 63, 71, 102
 country-specific configurations,
 12
 created to advance the cause of
 peacebuilding, 1
 Creation of the, 183
 Engagement with Burundi and
 Sierra Leone, 15
 facts from the fictions in the
 experience of, 83-102
 "financial resources deficit," 202
 financing of the PBC field
 missions, 61
 first six years, 58-65
 frustrations, 103-106
 functions, 11
 future of the, 107-108
 inaugurated in 2006, 1
 institutional lynchpin of the
 architecture, 36
 instrument of engagement of the,
 184
 Marshalling resources, 25
 Organisational Committee of

the, 64, 67, 87
Organisational Committee, 12
Peacebuilding efforts, 87, 95, 117
pushing of the envelope in the, 60
relations with international financial institutions, 184
Relations with Security Council, 74, 96, 97
response of the, to the Ebola pandemic, 145, 145-147
Roadmap of action, 66, 67
strong partnership between the AU and the, 63
tasks, 2
2015 Review of the, 147, 197
working group on lessons learnt, 12
Peacebuilding Cooperation Framework for Sierra Leone, 93
Peacebuilding Cooperation Framework, 17, 23, 84, 122
Peacebuilding Fund (PBF), 2, 3, 10, 13, 20, 44, 47, 64, 122, 135
and the World Bank the, 100
Immediate Response Facility
Peacebuilding Recovery Facility
Terms of reference 2006, 216
Terms of reference 2009, 70, 92
Window 1, 13
Window II, 13
Window III, 13
peacebuilding priorities, 16
Peacebuilding Support Office (PBSO), 2, 10, 12, 40, 44, 59, 143
"Peacebuilding: The Way Towards Sustainable Peace and Security", 72
Peacebuilding, 1, 82, 159-175, 177
Frameworks for understanding, 82

strategic framework for, 184
institution building in, 159-175, 190
invention of, 167
postconflict peacebuilding, 167
Role of the private sector in, 61
Peacekeeping, 10, 21, 26
Peacemaking, 10, 21, 43, 66
Pereira, Raimundo, 123, 128
Permanent members of security council, 98
Permanent Mission of Denmark to the United Nations, 26
Petrie, Charles, 205
"phantom State" *see* Central African Republic
Philanthropic foundations, 63
Pires, Emilia, 195, 214
Policy coordination, 182, 184
Political advocacy, 90, 183
Political Declaration, 72
Political Transition Pact, 124
Ponzio, Richard, 32, 214
Popular Army for the Restoration of Democracy (APRD), 125
postconflict activities, 2
Postconflict countries, 1, 2, 47, 121, 138, 140, 186
Post-Conflict Needs Assessment (PCNA), 143
postconflict peacebuilding, 2, 4, 10, 41, 43, 44, 115, 120, 178, 199
postconflict peacebuilding, 21
Postconflict Reconstruction and Development (PRCD), 63
Post-conflict recovery, 2, 44, 140
Postconflict regime, 168
post-World War II, 144
Post invasion, 168
Potential added value, 11
Poverty Reduction Strategy 2013-2016 (Burundi), 91

Poverty Reduction Strategy Paper, 25
President Conde, 90
Presidential elections, 41, 87
Pretoria Protocols, 118
Proactive leader, 58
Promoting partnership with the private sector, 86
Public Administration Reform, 149
Public financial management, 69

Ramos-Horta Jose, 33, 214
RAND Corporation, 171
Redistribution, 174
Regional Actors, 40, 121
Regional affinity, 178
Regional Justice and Security Hubs in Liberia, 185
   Buchanan, 135
   Gbarnga, 135
   Harper, 135
   Tubmanburg, 135
   Zwedru, 135
Reintegration, 37, 122, 131, 148, 170
Relapse to conflict, 21
"relief to development gap", 25
Religious groups, 18
Remittances, 61
Report of the Panel on Peace Operations, 164
Resource Mobilization for Peacebuilding Priorities: The Role of the Peacebuilding Commission, 86
"retirement of soldiers with dignity", 130
Revenue generation, 69
Review of Civilian Capacity in the Aftermath of Conflict, 67
Revolutionary United Front (RUF), 119
Rice, Susan, 102
Rishchynski, Guillermo, 149
Roadmap for National Reconciliation, 135
Rome Conference for Donor Countries on Rule of Law, 153
Rosenthal, Gert, 75, 205
Rule of law, 100, 124, 133
Russia, 26
Rwanda, 68, 99, 168

Safety and security, 171
Salinas, Ugo, 32, 207
Samba-Panza, Catherine, 127
Samset, Ingrid, 31, 215
Samuels, Kirsti, 194, 214
Sanha, Malam Bacai 123
Sankoh, Foday, 119, 121
Schulenburg, Michael, 191
Secretary-General's policy committee, 164
Security Council resolution 1645, 82
Security council report (the NGO), 23, 26, 29
Security Council, the, 65, 142
   one of the "joint parents" of the PBC, 142
Security Sector Reforms, 16, 41, 49
Security sector roadmap, 134
Seger, Paul, 148
Seleka Alliance, 126, 129
Seleka Rebellion, the, 129
Senior policy group on peacebuilding, 12
Sergeyev, Yuri, 75
Sierra Leone configuration, 91
Sierra Leone CSM, 23
Sierra Leone National Aid Policy, 17
Sierra Leone peace negotiations, 14
Sierra Leone Peacebuilding Cooperation Framework, 22
Sierra Leone Peoples Party, 120

Sierra Leone, 3, 13, 14, 14, 20, 26, 44, 50, 84
  Civil war in, 119
  Ebola outbreak in, 145, 166, 204
"signaling function", 102
Sisk, Timothy D., 192
Skoog, Olof, 150
Social Renovation Party (PRS), 124
Socio-economic recovery, 16
Somalia, 50
Sony/ATV Music Publishing, 64
South Africa, 65
Special Representative of the Secretary General, 142
"spoilers", 136
Ssempala, Edith Grace, 205
Stabilization, 83
state building, 7, 173, 174
Statement of Mutual Commitments (SMC), 94, 133, 134
Statement of Mutual Commitments for Peacebuilding in Liberia, 100
Statement of Mutual Commitments on Peacebuilding, 91
Strategic Framework for Peacebuilding in Burundi, 16, 18, 23, 93
Strategic Framework for Peacebuilding, 91
Strategic Framework, the, 16
  Articulation of, 16
Sub regional dimensión,16
Surhrke, Astri, 31, 215

Task Force on Private Sector, 99
Taylor, Charles, 119, 121, 132
The Arusha Peace and Reconciliation Agreement of 2000, 14
The Beginner's Guide to Nation-Building, 171
The Hague, 121, 132

The Outcome of the PBC Task Force on Private Sector, 61
The Security Council Report, 26
"the triple obstacles", 84
"the triple threats", 84
Tiangaye, Nicolas, 126, 127
Timor-Leste, 28, 50, 187
Tolbert, William, 132
Toure, General Amadou Toumani, 125
Toure, Sekou, 133
Tah, Christiana, 112, 215
Takasu, Yukio, 33, 215
Tanner, Fred, 32, 207
The "conductor of a symphony orchestra", 57
The international Criminal Court, 132
Tillander, Staffan, 150
Traditional associations, 18
Traditional donor, 144
Traditional or indigenous, 177
Transitional justice, 107
Truth and Reconciliation Commission, 134
Turkey, 66
Tutsi, 118
  2005 World Summit, 1, 35, 44
  2010 Roadmap of Actions, 66-67
  2011 Roadmap for Actions, 69
  2012 Annual Roadmap, 69
  2015 Donor Conference, 128
  2015 Review of the PBC, 2, 147, 197

Uganda, 168
UK, 99
UN Assistance Mission (UNAMSIL), 119
UN Assistance Mission in Sierra Leone (UNAMSIL), 14
UN Development Programme, 24

UN Fragility and Conflict Partnership Trust Fund, 185
UN General Assembly, 65
UN Integrated Office in Sierra Leone (UNIOSIL), 14, 120
UN Integrated Peacebuilding Office in Central African Republic (BINUCA), 125
UN Mission in Central African Republic (MINURCA), 125
UN Mission in Liberia (UNMIL), 132, 134, 135
UN missions, 46, 122
UN Partnership Trust Fund, 100
UN Peacebuilding Architecture (PBA), 3, 9-13, 20q, 44, 48, 65, 92
components of:
    Peacebuilding Commission, 3, 10, 11, 35, 40
    Peacebuilding Fund, 3, 11, 13, 35, 40, 122, 135
    Peacebuilding Support Office, 3, 11, 12, 35, 40
    Peacebuilding Support Office, 2010 Review of the, 65, 66, 81, 85, 203
UN Country Team, 15
UN Peacebuilding Commission, 63, 165, 182, 183
UN Political Office in Central African Republic (BONUCA), 125
UN's postconflict peacebuilding work, 1
UNDP, 204
Unemployment insurance, 176
Union of Democratic and Republican Forces (UFDR), 125, 126
United Nations Assistance Mission in Sierra Leone (UNAMSIL), 120
United Nations Children's Fund (UNICEF), 143, 146
United Nations Department of Economic and Social Affairs, 191, 210
United Nations Development Programme *see* UNDP
United Nations Department of Economic and Social Affairs, 191, 210
United Nations Human Settlements Programme (UN Habitat), 143
United Nations in support of Sierra Leone's Agenda for Change, 123
United Nations institutional machinery, 1
United Nations Integrated Peacebuilding Mission in Sierra Leone, 71
United Nations Integrated Peacebuilding Office in Central African Republic, 125
United Nations Integrated Peacebuilding Support Office (UNIOGBIS), 123
United Nations Mission in Central Africa, 125
United Nations Mission in Liberia, 132
United Nations Mission in Timor-Leste (UNMIT), 28
United Nations Office in Burundi, 119
United Nations Operations in Burundi (ONUB), 14, 118
United Nations Peace Operations, 43
United Nations Peace Operations, Panel, 66
United Nations Peacebuilding Commission, 27
United Nations Peacebuilding Support Office in Guinea-Bissau (UNOGBIS), 123

United Nations peacekeeping
    operations, 14, 117
United Nations Political Office in
    Central African Republic, 125
United Nations (UN), 1, 9, 22, 36,
    52, 115, 134, 135, 160, 199
    and peacebuilding in Africa, 43
    and the PBC, 116, 141
    Involvement in Sierra Leone, 120
UNOMSIL, 120
US Drug Enforcement Agency, 128
US military, 171
USA, 139
Utility Regulation, 176

Vieira, Joao Bernardo, 123, 127
Vilovic, Ranko, 75
Viotti, Maria Luiza Ribeiro, 149

Wa Kodro Salute Patriotic
    Convention (CPSK), 126
"war of greed", 119
Wegter, Bartjan, 112, 216
WHO, 146
World Health Organisation *see*
    WHO
Whole-of-Government approach,
    182
Wittig, Peter, 75
Women's associations, 18
Working Group on Lessons Learnt
    see Peacebuilding Commission
    (PBC)
Working Group on Lessons Learnt,
    creation of, 59, 69
World Bank, 3, 4, 42, 59, 66, 71, 86,
    143, 170, 185
    Executive Directors, 71
    Country Assistance Strategy, 71
    Meeting with PBC, 71

World Bank-UN Partnership
    Framework for Crisis and Post-
    Crisis Situations, 42
World Summit Outcome
    Document, 78, 138
World Summit, 9, 116
Wyeth, Vanessa H., 193

Yala, Kumba, 123
Year of Peace Agreement, 152
Youth employment, 17
Yugoslavia, 172

Zinsou, Jean-Francois, 75
Zurcher, Christoph, 194, 207

www.ingramcontent.com/pod-product-compliance
Lightning Source LLC
Chambersburg PA
CBHW020647300426
44112CB00007B/269